The Art of Rest was inspired by ground-breaking
research Claudia Hammond collaborated on – 'The
Rest Test' – the largest global survey into rest ever
undertaken, which was completed by 18,000 people
across 135 different countries. Much has been
written about sleep, but rest is different: it is how we
unwind, calm our minds and recharge our bodies.
Those who spend the optimal amount of time
resting have higher levels of well-being.

Counting down through the top ten activities which
people find most restful, Hammond explains why
rest matters, examines the science behind each activity
to establish what really works and offers a roadmap
for a new, more restful and balanced life where we
can each discover our own prescription for rest.

The
Art *of* Rest

The
Art *of* Rest

How to Find Respite in
the Modern Age

Claudia Hammond

CANONGATE

First published in Great Britain in 2019
by Canongate Books Ltd,
14 High Street, Edinburgh EH1 1TE

canongate.co.uk

3

British Library Cataloguing-in-Publication Data
A catalogue record for this book is available on
request from the British Library

ISBN 978 1 78689 280 5

Typeset in Garamond MT Std 11.5/15 pt by
Palimpsest Book Production Ltd, Falkirk, Stirlingshire

Printed and bound in Great Britain by Clays Ltd, Elcograf S.p.A.

For Jo and Grant

CONTENTS

A CALL TO REST

The Rest Deficit

Picture a hammock – one of those multicoloured stripy ones. It sways back and forth gently in a light tropical breeze. The air is deliciously warm. Far below the hotel balcony, the sea (turquoise, of course) glints in the sunshine.

For many of us this is the classic image of rest, where no one requires anything from us. But it's not straightforward. Hammocks can be tricky. You have to get in without over-balancing and tipping out of the other side. You need to shuffle up or down the hammock to find a place where you can lie in comfort. You might need to get up to fetch a cushion for your head – and then go through the whole fuss and bother again. Finally, though, you achieve the right balance. A feeling of serenity washes over you. You can relax.

Or can you?

Even once you are comfortable in your hammock it can be hard to sustain the sense of restfulness. This feeling reflects our relationship with rest in general. We have an ambivalence towards it. We yearn for rest, but then feel anxious that perhaps we are being lazy. Perhaps we are not making the most of our lives.

One of the things that distinguishes us human beings from many other animals is our curiosity. Even now that many of us have everything we need to stay alive, we still want to see what is over the next hill or across the ocean or on a distant planet. We have an urge to explore, to discover more, to find meaning. Our curiosity has been key to our survival and our success as a species, but the downside of this curiosity is that it can make us restless. We always feel we must be doing something. And we have come to define 'doing something' very narrowly. It means, for most of us, being busy. And not just some of the time, but all of the time.

Yet Socrates told us to beware the barrenness of a busy life. If we're busy all the time, life lacks essential rhythm. We miss out on the contrasts between doing and not doing. This oscillation is natural and healthy. As if we are back in that hammock, we should swing back and forth between activity and rest, taking the latter as seriously as the former.

We need to rest more. And to rest better. For its own sake, of course, but also for the sake of our wider lives. Resting is good not just for well-being but for productivity. A quick search online reveals that this is the age of self-care. Whatever you think about the term, the concept is a good thing. And the best kind of self-care, I will argue, is rest.

Yet at the moment we suffer from a rest deficit. This was perhaps the most significant finding of the major survey that informs the structure of this book. The survey was called the Rest Test, and 18,000 people living in 135 different countries chose to take part. I will be returning to the Rest Test later in this introductory chapter, but, as I say, among its most important findings was that many of us feel we are not getting enough rest. Two thirds of respondents said this was true of them and that they would like more rest. Women reported getting an average of ten minutes less time to rest each day than men, and people with caring responsibilities also had less rest. But it was younger people, both men and women, working either shifts or traditional full-time hours, who felt they rested the least.

This chimes with a general sense that younger people are stressed out and struggling to cope with life's pressures. In January 2019 a BuzzFeed article called 'How Millennials Became the Burnout Generation' went viral.[1] The journalist Anne Helen Petersen began by explaining how there were so many jobs on her to-do list that she had developed 'errand paralysis', leaving her unable to accomplish any of the tasks. Some older people are dismissive of this angst and label millennials derogatively as 'snowflakes'. But I think Petersen and her generation are on to something. Certainly, I can relate to her naming her backlog of emails her 'inbox of shame', as I currently have 50,449 emails in my inbox. The point is wider than this, though.

There's no doubt that being in your twenties today is challenging, with intense competition for university places and jobs, coupled with an all-too-real prospect, depending on where you live, that property prices might mean you will forever be forced to live the itinerant life of a tenant. On top of that, the prospect of this generation becoming more prosperous than their parents is vanishing and millennials can't expect to benefit from the generous pension schemes that still exist for some of the older generation today. But for every one of these pressures, Generation Xers and Baby Boomers have their own. Millennials might be more open about confessing it, but most, if not all, of us often feel stressed out by a seemingly never-ending stream of tasks. Modern work practices, modern lifestyles and modern technology have combined and conspired to make life in the early twenty-first century ceaselessly demanding. Thanks to our clever phones, we feel forever on call, knowing that even when we do rest, that rest can be interrupted by anyone at any moment.

We want to rest more, we could rest more, we are perhaps resting more than we think we are – but we certainly don't feel rested.

I'm not especially good at resting myself, or I wasn't until I start focusing on the topic. When I told friends that after writing books covering emotions, time perception and the psychology of money I had started writing one on rest, their first reaction was usually, 'But you're always working. You never rest!'

If someone asks me how things are going, I tend to answer, 'Fine, busy, too busy really.' This feels true of my life, but how much is it also a claim to status? If you say you are busy then it implies you are wanted. You are in demand. As the time use researcher Jonathan Gershuny puts it, busyness has become 'a badge of honour'. In contrast to the nineteenth century, in the twenty-first century it is work, and not leisure, that gives us social status. Our busyness illustrates just how important we are, but at the same time we feel exhausted.

And yet, it is not true that I am working all the time, even when I am supposedly working. While I have been researching and writing this book, I have as often as not *not* been researching and writing it. I'm easily and often distracted by Facebook or Twitter. I constantly go downstairs to make a cup of tea. I've positioned my desk in my study upstairs so that I look on to the street, and I'm always pleased to spot other freelance neighbours out in the road chatting. Naturally I can't resist going to join them; I hate to miss out on the news.

How much rest I get from these constant distractions is another matter. There is obviously a large element of displacement activity about them. Restlessly. I yearn to get to a place where I have done everything I need to do, where all the items on my 'to-do' list are neatly ticked off, and at last I can relax. Jobs done. Worries over. The problem is that I fail again and again to attain this blessed state, leaving me feeling unsettled and anxious even when I'm not actually doing any of the many tasks confronting me.

This rest deficit, both perceived and real, is damaging in many ways. Today, in the UK, half a million people are suffering from work-related stress.[2] In the US, 13 per cent of injuries sustained at work can be attributed to fatigue. More than a quarter of people have fallen asleep at work and 16 per cent have fallen asleep recently while driving.[3] When you add on caring responsibilities and housework and the general admin of modern life, it is no surprise perhaps that three quarters of us have been so stressed at some point over the last year that we have felt overwhelmed or unable to cope.[4]

Tiredness can have a serious impact on our cognitive abilities. A task which seems easy when you're fresh is rendered far more difficult when you are fatigued. Tiredness leads to memory lapses, a blunting of emotions, a lack of concentration, more frequent misunderstandings and impaired judgement. Not the state you want your pilot or your doctor to be in.

And the rest deficit is not only a problem for adults. In

the past two decades break times at school have been squeezed in order to accommodate more lessons. For instance, only 1 per cent of British secondary schools now have an afternoon break.[5] Yet there is good evidence showing that breaks aid concentration,[6] so cutting break times is likely to be counter-productive in maximising exam results, as well as depriving children of the opportunity to socialise or exercise.

The effects of a deficit of sleep are now well-understood and the list of problems it causes is long: an increased risk of type 2 diabetes, heart disease, stroke, hypertension, pain, pro-inflammatory responses, mood disorders, memory difficulties, metabolic syndrome, obesity and colorectal cancer, most of which can shorten your life expectancy.[7] Rest has not, so far, received the same amount of attention as sleep, but there is evidence that spending time relaxing helps us to make better decisions, lowers our risk of depression, boosts our memories and means we catch fewer colds.

So I will argue that it is just as important to rest well as it is to sleep well. This book is a call to rest. We need to start valuing it, validating it, vaunting it. Rest is not a luxury, it's a necessity. It's essential.

But what is rest anyway?

The Essence of Rest

Free Fulfilling Warm Restorative Dark Recumbent Dreamy Delicious Cool Clarifying Quiet Necessary Mindless Sublime Safe Serene Healing Precious Private Yearned for Unthinking Uplifting

These are some of the words the 18,000 people who took part in the Rest Test used in answer to the question 'What does rest mean to you?'

But here are some other words they used about rest.

> Feeble Fragile Fidgety Challenging Aching Annoying
> Guilty Unjustified Idle Irritating Indulgent Selfish
> Elusive Worrying Waste of time

Rest clearly means different things to different people. Medical research papers often use the terms sleep and rest interchangeably. But rest is more complex than sleep because there are so many different ways of doing it. To be clear, the rest I'm talking about involves any restful activity that we do while we're awake. The list could, of course, be endless, so this book will only focus on some of the more popular forms of rest. As for sleep, you might drift off to sleep in the middle of resting. You might even fall asleep while reading this book, which is not necessarily a bad thing. But sleep and rest are clearly not the same.

For a start, rest can involve physical exertion, sometimes of a strenuous kind, such as playing football or running. For some people, it is the tiring out of the body through vigorous exercise that allows the mind to rest and it is during physical activity that restfulness is achieved.

That said, for many others the feeling of restfulness tends to come after the physical activity has been completed. We must all have enjoyed the delicious satisfaction that comes from resting after hard work or the achievement of a goal. Just as 'the sleep of the labouring man is sweet', as it says in Ecclesiastes, so, I like to say, is the rest of the energetic woman.

But while rest can be animated, it can also be sedentary. Sitting in a comfy chair or lying in a hot bath are popular ways to rest, as we shall see. And it isn't just the physical relaxation that is so valued; many people feel that it is not until their bodies are fully rested that their minds are able to rest. But here again, views differ. For some people, rest involves expending no mental effort, while other people relax by reading *Finnegans Wake* or doing cryptic crosswords.

For most of us, another thing rest is not, is work. Two thirds of people believe that rest is the opposite of work. But this view might depend on how you define work. It's possible that you would prefer a day in the office or on the shop floor if the alternative were spending the day looking after young children at home or caring for an ill relative. And then there are those people who seem to find weekends and holidays away from the buzz of their jobs anything but restful. Many of us might wonder whether such people need a better work/life balance, but exactly where the right balance lies will always be a subjective matter. Certainly, enforced rest through unemployment or illness, when the balance tips too much into inaction, leaves us not restful but restless. We want to be up and out, but we are trapped by circumstance in miserable inactivity. And think of the pain of depression, which can leave people unable to get out of bed, sunk in a physical lassitude that is both relentless and exhausting. Or consider prisoners, lying on their bunks in their cells for hour after hour. There is no real rest in such a condition.

In getting to the essence of rest it is worth considering its origin as a word. The Old English word ræste is derived from the Old High German word rasta and the Old Norse word rost, which in addition to 'rest', in the sense we understand it, also meant 'league of miles', or 'distance after which one rests'. So the etymology strengthens the notion that rest comes after or through activity. If all you do is rest you will not feel rested, but after a certain point rest is needed and deserved. You are then in a state of proper restfulness.

The research I'm featuring in this book bears this out. People who told us they felt fully rested had well-being scores twice as high as those who say they needed more rest. But there is, it seems, an optimal amount of rest that is good for us. Above this point, well-being levels begin to drop again. And, as I have discussed already, the nourishing effect of rest seems to disappear completely once it's enforced. It's all a matter of achieving the right balance.

It might help if we could all have a personalised prescription for the right dose of rest for our individual needs, but though doctors often do prescribe rest, they are vague about the type and amount. 'Get some rest,' they say. But does that just mean staying in bed? Or should we do our favourite hobby or go out to see our friends, if that's what we consider restful?

The fact is we are all on our own on this one. It is a case of self-diagnosis and self-prescription. But that doesn't mean we can't learn from others. Everybody rests in their own way, but there are many common elements to the different ways we choose to rest.

The Rest Test

I've referred to it already, but underlying some of my thinking in this book are the results of a major survey called the Rest

Test. It stemmed from two years I spent as part of a multi-disciplinary team, many of whose members were from Durham University, studying rest. That'll be easy, friends joked, on hearing that we had been lucky enough to win a grant to become the first residents on the fifth floor of the Wellcome Collection in London. You can just sit around and laze about.

We didn't, of course (although we did obtain a hammock which proved popular with visitors). In our group there were historians, poets, artists, psychologists, neuroscientists, geographers and even a composer – all talented, driven, high-energy people. We threw ourselves into the project and over the two years produced an exhibition, a book, many public events, academic papers, poems and original musical compositions, one of which was premiered on BBC Radio 3. Our home was on the constantly busy Euston Road in the middle of London. We called our team Hubbub.

Our name was carefully chosen. It acknowledged that for many of us the hub and bub of life, the hurly-burly, drowns out peace and quiet and the chance to rest. It also alluded to the fact that in the modern world meaningful rest comes not from abandoning our busy lives but through making adjustments and achieving a better balance between work, rest and play.

It was halfway through our residency, that the Hubbub team launched our online survey called the Rest Test on the two BBC radio shows I present – *All in the Mind* on Radio 4 and *Health Check* on the World Service. In the first part of the survey people answered questions about how much rest they get, how much they would ideally like and which activities they find most restful. In the second they filled in questionnaires measuring personality, well-being and the tendency for the mind to wander.

When we launched the survey, we were taking a gamble. We had no idea how many people would be interested enough in the topic of rest to spend up to forty minutes completing the questionnaire. But it turned out that rest was a pressing issue for a large number of people all around the world. As I've mentioned already, 18,000 people living in 135 different countries took part. We were astonished and delighted by this level of response.

For this book, what I've done since is to investigate in detail each of the top ten activities which people who took part in the survey told us they considered restful. There were some surprises. Spending time with friends and family, for example, didn't make it into the top ten. It came in at number 12. This might seem strange, considering that many people say connecting with others is what human life is all about. Decades of research in positive psychology has shown that it is not success at work, health, money or intelligence that the happiest people have, but enjoyable relationships with other people. William Morris said, 'Fellowship is heaven, and lack of fellowship is hell: fellowship is life, and lack of fellowship is death.' But bear in mind that we were not looking for the activities which people found most enjoyable or that made them happiest or that they most valued, we were after what they found most restful. And it is notable in that context, that the top five most restful activities are all often done alone. It seems when we rest, we very often want to escape from other people.

Another activity that didn't make the Rest Test top ten is my personal favourite, gardening. While not physically restful, gardening allows my mind to switch off like no other activity and it is how I rest best. Through gardening I get to spend time in the open air, and to feel the soil between my fingers, and – sometimes – the sun on my back. I like the fact that while I put a lot of thought and effort into my garden, most of the work is done by nature when I'm not there. And I get to enjoy the beautifully satisfying results. Though not every time. The weather makes gardening ever unpredictable. Experience helps, of course. Over time you gradually learn what works in your soil and what doesn't. Experts can advise you, but a hot spell or a cold spell or a wet spell – or slugs or snails or squirrels or foxes – can mean your effort is wasted. You never quite get your garden to be perfect, but it always feels as though, if everything aligns – and it might – then there is a chance of near perfection. This is what makes it so compelling; like all the best games, it's the exquisite combination of skill (right plant, right place) and luck (right weather, right time).

But, as I say, gardening didn't get into the top ten, and neither did arts and crafts, nor having pets. And there is one other omission which might surprise you. When people were free to put down any activity at all, in their own words, spending time online or on social media didn't come high on the list as restful. We may spend increasing amounts of time browsing the internet, uploading selfies or checking social media. But although we do it a lot, and often enjoy it, we seem to know it doesn't make us feel rested. In the following chapters you will see what did make the cut.

I hope I will provoke you to rethink rest and to consider its place in your own life. By the end of the book, I'd like each individual reader to have taken away a prescription or a fresh way of thinking about how they use their time.

So, in the rundown of our worldwide top ten activities, I'll be looking hard at the evidence. Spending time out in nature among the trees may sound lovely, but can we prove it is restful? And by prove it, I mean somehow measure the positive benefits in a robust scientific way. Along the way, the book will overturn a few contemporary assumptions – that mindfulness can help most people with depression, that watching TV is a waste of time or that daydreaming is something we should always fight.

The same activities won't work for everyone, but this book will, I hope, help you see which might work for you. Not every activity will appeal to all of us, but every one has something to teach us about how to achieve restfulness. And the more you know about how important restful activities are, I find, the easier it is to do them deliberately and without guilt. Like the music charts, the Rest Test top ten is counted down in reverse order, starting with the tenth most popular restful activity, and ending with number one. I'm happy to tell you from the outset that the most popular activity turned out to be reading. You know what they say about the wisdom of crowds: 18,000 people can't be wrong. Enjoy the book, things don't get any more restful than reading, it seems, and what could be more restful than reading a book about rest?

MINDFULNESS

Question: What is a mindfulness teacher's favourite food?

Answer: Raisins

This is not a joke, as you've probably noticed. If you go to mindfulness classes then it's likely that at some point a box of raisins will be produced and you will be given a single raisin. I've been handed raisins several times when I've interviewed mindfulness experts for radio shows. I have to admit I find myself thinking, 'Here we go again. Another raisin that I'm not allowed to just eat.' And yet, the experiment with a little dried grape works every time. Despite my scepticism that mindfulness can solve everything, I can't deny that the raisin exercise is fascinating.

Here's how it generally works. First, you hold the raisin between two fingers and examine it very carefully, noticing the wrinkles on its skin, the shade in the creases and the way the top edges of the ridges shine as they catch the light. Turn it around until you've observed all the different colour tones. Lay it on your palm. Can you feel its weight? Hold it up to your ear. Listen to it like a seashell. If you squeeze it, can you hear anything? No, you can't hear waves lapping against the shore. How does it feel between your fingertips? It's probably getting a bit warm and squidgy by now. Can you feel its crests and crevasses? Swap it to the other hand. Does it feel the same or different? If so, how exactly?

You'll have realised by now that this minute inspection of a raisin is taking you through the senses one at a time. Hold it under your nose. Does it smell? Mindfulness teachers can drag this out for a good five minutes before you're finally allowed to put the raisin in your mouth. (Assuming you still want to.) But even then, you can't just eat it. First, you must place the raisin on your tongue and note how it feels. Do this for thirty seconds, ideally. Then, and only then, and slowly, of course, can you begin to chew the raisin, taking in everything that happens in your mouth: the sweet taste, how your saliva flows, the sensations of chewing and swallowing.[1]

You can stop now. Congratulations. You have just eaten a raisin mindfully. You can apply this technique to anything. Travelling on a train mindfully, walking the dog mindfully, doing the washing up mindfully (no need to go as far as tasting the washing up liquid), all the while paying attention to all your senses and, crucially, to your breathing. If other thoughts start to pop into your head to distract you, observe those thoughts without judgement and accept them, instead of trying to suppress them.

You may be someone who practises mindfulness every day, or someone who has been meaning to give it go. Or you might be a person who thinks it's a lot of new-age mumbo jumbo and finds the idea of eating a raisin in slow motion cringeworthy. As I've already said, I'm somewhat sceptical about mindfulness as a cure-all. It's instructive, I think, that although mindfulness is now a multimillion-dollar business, it only came tenth in the Rest Test. It's clear that it's not for everyone and, as we'll discover, it certainly isn't the panacea that it is sometimes claimed to be. But even if you don't want to immerse yourself in it regularly there is still plenty that mindfulness can teach any of us about how to rest.

Of course, there is a strong argument that mindfulness is nothing new, that various Buddhist meditation practices from 2,500 years ago have been repackaged for the modern age without the ethical, spiritual, compassion-focused parts, and then repurposed as something that just helps us personally rather than helping anyone else. And it's also true that the word 'mindfulness' is used as a catch-all term to cover a host of practices. Even just one branch of meditation, that of Tantric Buddhism for example, includes a multitude of different meditation techniques, any of which mindfulness practitioners and promoters might adapt. If you add to these the many other traditional meditation practices, plus therapeutic programmes developed to improve mental health, mindfulness apps, books and classes at your local gym or at work, it's not surprising that the one thing everyone agrees on about mindfulness is that it *isn't* one thing.

If someone says they practise mindfulness, they might have spent many thousands of hours practising an ancient form of meditation practice, they might or might not include elements of thinking compassionately about themselves or other people, they might be someone who regularly uses an app at home or they might simply be attempting to stay in the moment more and pay attention to the sensations around them in their body. And even this list of different ways of being mindful doesn't scratch the surface of all the possible incarnations of the art or science or philosophy or religion or regimen of mindfulness.

I'm less interested in debates about different forms and definitions of mindfulness than in the solid, reliable research on when it is and isn't effective. So, for the sake of this chapter I'm going to define it simply. Childishly so, perhaps. *The Ladybird Book of Mindfulness*, which someone gave me for Christmas, describes it as the 'skill of thinking you're doing something while you're doing nothing', which I quite like. A more serious definition, and one that is most often used today, comes from someone who is a hero to many in the field, Jon Kabat-Zinn. He spearheaded a resurgence of interest in mindfulness in the West, beginning in 1979 with the development of the mindfulness-based stress reduction programme. He says mindfulness is 'the awareness of paying attention in a particular way: on purpose in the present moment, non-judgementally'.

But how exactly might doing this help us rest?

The Path to Ultimate Stillness

As we all know, when our minds are left to their own devices they tend to wander. Sometimes we enjoy letting our thoughts drift, but at other times these thoughts are more troublesome: we find ourselves being self-critical, we pick over the past or we worry about the future. Here's when mindfulness is at its most useful: it helps to keep us in the present. The more people practise doing it, the more they find they can return to this state, even at the hardest times when they're feeling stressed or emotional.

The nineteenth-century philosopher and psychologist William James said: 'Human beings, by changing the inner attitudes of their minds, can change the outer aspects of their lives.' Some compare mindfulness training with strengthening a muscle, and of course that takes work. It's true that early practice at being mindful can be far from restful. When I attended a meditation weekend at a Buddhist Centre when I was a student, I spent most of the two days thinking how bad I was at meditation, how much my knees hurt and that everyone else seemed to be really good at it. At the end of the weekend, I didn't feel blissed out – I felt stressed out. I gather my experience is not uncommon.

But its advocates urge sticking at it. Do that and mindfulness will bring you rest in the end. It is the same with many eventually restful activities. When I began gardening seriously it involved concentration, planning, decision-making and of course plenty of physical effort, all of which sound more like work than rest. Yet now I find any part of that process, even the strenuous parts, which of course in gardening are repeated every year, immediately restful. Within moments of going into my tiny, standing-room-for-just-one, greenhouse, I feel better. Almost as soon as I am digging in my raised beds, or planting out in my small front garden, I am relaxed and happy.

Jon Kabat-Zinn is unapologetic about the hard work involved in practising mindfulness. The influential course he devised consists of weekly two-hour sessions for eight weeks, along with an all-day retreat near the end of the course. But the most demanding part is the homework. 'The contract is that you've got to carve out forty-five minutes a day, six days a week to practise non-doing. OK. We don't care where you find that forty-five minutes, but you have to make it happen. And, you don't have to like it. You just have to do it.'[2] To do it properly does require dedication. I have tried it many times, strangely often en masse when chairing public events on the topic of mindfulness, but also on my own at home. Although I started out with the intention of doing regular practice, I've never kept it up. I suspect that the mindfulness trainers I've interviewed disapprove of the dabblers like me, although they're far too nice ever to say so because they are never judgemental.

To reach a state of peace takes a lot of work, but Jon Kabat-Zinn is surely right to insist that it's worth it, 'Just to experience such sustained elemental stillness outwardly and the interior silence that can accompany it, is ample reason for arranging one's life to cultivate and bathe in this possibility from time to time.'

Why is Mindfulness Restful?

Ultimate stillness sounds supremely restful, but there's still a paradox here. If it's such hard work at first, does it really count as restful? Shouldn't something be restful right from the start? Nine other activities might have beaten mindfulness in the Rest Test, but still more than 4,000 out of 18,000 people consider it restful. Why this level of support?

For a start, mindfulness imposes strict discipline. It forces you to stop. If you practise mindfulness properly, while you are doing it, that's *all* you are doing. Nothing else. No radio or TV. Your phone is on silent. Your laptop is turned off. There is no music in the background. The noise and insistence and distraction of modern daily life is shut out. That in itself can be restful, even as you struggle to be truly mindful.

Practitioners can stop reliving conversations where they think they said the wrong thing or imagining the meeting they are dreading the following day. They become less self-conscious and briefly stop worrying about how others might view them. Mindfulness allows them to acknowledge rather than fight the chatter in their heads. It's there but they tune it out. Thoughts that come and go are observed and accepted, rather than judged. They are not bad thoughts or good thoughts; they are just thoughts. Mindfulness can also allow people a break from their own emotions.

With a list of benefits like this, it's hardly surprising that for some mindfulness can feel like the best form of rest.

Despite practising mindfulness in any disciplined way less than once a year, I can't deny that I have felt the power that paying attention in the present moment can have. I was once asked to interview the comedian Ruby Wax on stage in front of a large audience at the Barbican theatre in London. Unlike many people, I like and am quite used to being on stage. I have done tens of thousands of interviews, though mostly in radio studios. This was going to be different. I was going to be interviewing someone who was not only a celebrity, but exceptionally quick-witted.

Before the event began, we walked out onto a stage large enough to fit a choir and a full orchestra. In the middle of the stage were two chairs for us, and opposite were 1,500 seats. I started to feel nervous. Why had I agreed to do this? Was there any way to get out of it? We returned to the green room while the audience was let in. When we were about to go on stage, we stood waiting beside the longest line of vertical mirrors I've ever seen, which allow a whole orchestra to look in the mirror and adjust their clothes all at once before going on stage, and there was a screen where you could see and hear the people settling in their seats. Hundreds and hundreds, yes, and hundreds more of them.

We were there to discuss depression and how Ruby Wax had studied mindfulness in order to diffuse it, so in the middle of the event a mindfulness teacher was going to join us on stage to take the audience through some exercises. The stage manager said we had one minute before we were on, so to calm us both down (and it was reassuring to know that very famous people get nervous too) the teacher took us through a short mindfulness routine standing next to the door to the stage. We turned our attention to our feet and the way their contact with the floor gave us a firm base. We focused our awareness on the sensations we could feel in our legs and the trunks of our bodies. We observed our breaths going in, and then out. We paused. We waited for just a few seconds, breathing, waiting, being. Then it was time to go on. The effect was remarkable. From feeling anxiety bordering on panic about talking to a celebrity in front of such a large audience, I felt a sense of calm wash over me. I walked on the stage, took my seat and felt what I can only describe as 'at rest'.

As well as mindfulness bringing a sense of restfulness to difficult situations, there is a wider point. It can also teach us when we need to rest. By tuning into your body and mind you might be able to pick up hints; maybe you are holding your shoulders up stiffly or perhaps you're feeling irritated with everyone around you. Increased awareness might tell you that the reason for your impatience has nothing to do with them; it's a sign that you're feeling tired or over-whelmed. The sooner you notice these things, the sooner you can decide to make time to rest in some way. That need not involve mindfulness, but being mindful has brought you to this point.

Mindful of the Evidence

The Ruby Wax story was an anecdote, but to measure the impact of mindfulness on our minds we need data. Over the years there's been a rise of mindfulness in workplaces, schools and even prisons. As with everything that becomes this popular, it has inevitably come under great scrutiny. While there is good data demonstrating that some specific mindful-ness interventions work well with specific groups, mindfulness is too often presented as a panacea, when the evidence suggests it isn't. Thousands of studies have been conducted, but many are small and involve people who have chosen to learn mindfulness rather than people who have been randomly assigned to learn it, so we can't be sure that the studies have not attracted a certain type of person, skewing the results.

That said, in the past twenty years in particular some very good trials have been conducted, with some impressive results. The problem is these results are often used to back up the utility of any mindfulness practice, whether alone or in a class, when they only truly apply to the formal, structured courses they were testing. So much falls under the general umbrella of mindfulness that we can't be sure that every type of class and practice is equally effective.

Even a very positive report from the All-Party Parliamentary Group on Mindfulness (yes, there really is such a thing), calling for an increase in the availability of mindfulness in healthcare, education, offices, factories and prisons, admitted that the evidence in the workplace is 'patchy', that there are gaps in the evidence in schools and that the current popularity of mindfulness is running ahead of the research. The parliamentarians also lamented the lack of evidence overall. What we need, of course, is more really good research, particularly on who mindfulness does and doesn't suit.

The good news is that this is starting to happen. Professor Richard Davidson, at the Waisman Laboratory for Brain Imaging and Behavior at the University of Wisconsin, leads a team of more than a hundred who are trying to fill the gaps in the research, but acknowledges that there are still plenty of questions for which they don't have the answers.[3] Larger trials are now underway, including a five-year trial involving 7,000 adolescents in British schools, half of whom will learn mindfulness.

Some of the most influential research in this field to date has been conducted at the Oxford Mindfulness Centre at Oxford University, which developed a specific therapeutic programme called Mindfulness Based Cognitive Therapy or MBCT. Like the American intervention, this also consists of weekly sessions for eight weeks. Randomised controlled trials show that if somebody has had three or more episodes of depression then MBCT can half the risk of their depression returning.[4] It was most successful in those at the highest risk of relapse. It has not proven so effective with people who have only had depression once or twice. This might surprise you, because we often hear that mindfulness is good for all forms of depression. The Director of the Oxford Mindfulness Centre, Willem Kuyken, wonders whether the reason it's more successful with people with persistent depression is that they have more of a tendency towards rumination, going over and over negative things in their heads, and this seems to be something mindfulness is particularly good at tackling.

There is also some evidence that mindfulness can help with chronic pain, ease anxiety and reduce cravings in people addicted to drugs, although other studies conclude mindfulness is not necessarily any better than other psychological interventions. These studies do rightly set the bar high. They are testing to see if mindfulness can ease serious conditions. Achieving relaxation through mindfulness is easier. Some studies have also found improvements in memory, attention, mood, creativity and reaction times, as well as the lowering of blood pressure and boosts to the immune system. According to one study, using mindfulness can even make you a nicer person. After two weeks of using an app or eight weeks of classes, people were more likely to offer assistance to someone using crutches.[5]

When it comes to serious rest and escape from both our feelings and the incessant chatter in our minds, the most interesting studies come from neuroscience. Reductions have been shown in activity in the amygdala, the walnut-shaped area deep inside the brain that is at the heart of our response to fight or flee when we're afraid.[6] But here we must remember that these studies have often been conducted with experienced Buddhist meditators who have spent thou-sands of hours meditating over many decades. Richard Davidson's team has studied yogis, who have an average of 27,000 lifetime hours of meditation, and the researchers discovered something extraordinary. When their brains are at rest and they're lying in a brain scanner not meditating or doing anything in particular, they show the same kind of activity as someone who is meditating. For these yogis mind-fulness has become an effortless state.

If you haven't got a spare 27,000 hours to spend medi-tating, take heart from the discovery that some differences in brain activity are apparent after just two weeks of prac-tising mindfulness. In a study in 2013 Davidson and his team randomly assigned people to follow one of two daily thirty-minute audio guides. The first guided them through a form of meditation focusing on compassion. They would think of a close friend, imagine their suffering and concen-trate on wishing them free from that suffering, before trying the same with themselves, then a stranger and then someone they find difficult. The other audio guide used classical techniques from cognitive behavioural therapy where people were instructed to recall a stressful event and to describe in detail their feelings and thoughts about the event, before moving on to viewing the event from the perspectives of the other people involved. After two weeks the brain of each person was scanned while they looked at pictures of people suffering. The group who had been practising meditation showed altered activity in various areas of the brain, including the inferior parietal cortex and the dorslat-eral prefrontal cortex, both areas implicated in understanding others' feelings and in regulating your own emotions. And if that weren't enough, the meditators also behaved more generously in a game where you could decide how to allocate money to other people. But Davidson does warn that these kinds of improvement are fragile and will disappear if you don't carry on meditating.[7]

And mindfulness is not for everyone. Even among those who are attracted to the idea in the first place, roughly 15 per cent of people who embark on an eight-week course drop out and presumably some others give up after a few months or years. It would be useful to know what type of person benefits most from the technique, so that you could assess whether you are the type who should give it a try, but very little research has been done on this.

Everyone varies in how mindful they are in the first place. You can measure this using questionnaires which ask people, for example, how much attention they pay to sounds such as clocks ticking or cars passing or whether they 'stay alert to the sensation of water' on their bodies when they shower or bathe.[8] It seems to come down to personality type. People who score high on conscientiousness have higher levels of mindfulness than those who score high in neuroticism (people who tend to worry a lot).[9] Of course, we can't know which comes first. Does being mindful make people less neurotic or does feeling worried interfere with mindfulness because people don't like paying attention to their own self-doubting thoughts? Some studies found that people with lower baseline mindfulness benefited more from a mindfulness course.[10] Others have shown the opposite.[11] So until more research is done the only real way to find out whether mindfulness is for you is to have a go.

David Creswell from Carnegie Mellon University in

Pittsburgh has studied mindfulness extensively and thinks of it as a buffer against stress. Inevitably we all experience stressful events, but we all deal with them differently. He believes that if people have already trained in mindfulness, then when something bad happens they find it easier than the rest of us to step back and see the situation from a wider perspective, which in turn makes it easier to cope. This fits in with a study involving university postgraduate students at Cambridge University which showed that those who'd done a mindfulness course were more resilient and coped better when it came to handling the stress of exams.[12]

Everyday Mindfulness

The best thing about mindfulness is that you can incorporate it easily into daily life. I once had a lovely lesson from a mindfulness trainer on walking to the bus stop mindfully. I had to stand and ground myself at the beginning, feeling the connection between my feet, the soles of my shoes and the pavement. Then we began to walk, focusing on one sense at a time, observing the background traffic noise, the shrieks of children in a playground in the distance, the urban smells, the grey stains on the paving slabs. I've often done it since, particularly if I am facing a busy day ahead. These simple techniques of slowing yourself down, focusing on the task at hand but being open to all your senses, can be applied to almost anything you do.

My favourite mindful breathing technique is called square breathing and it was taught to me by Mandy Stevens. She was a senior mental health nurse, managing a lot of staff as well as dealing with very unwell patients. One day she became overcome by anxiety and depression and found herself admitted to a mental health ward. She had taught her patients square breathing many times and now used it on herself. I find it helpful too. This is how it works.

If you feeling the panic rising, then look for a square. Or a rectangle. If you're in the back of a car, maybe it's the window frame. If you're in an office, it might be a sign on a wall. At home, it might be a picture. Wherever you are, there is usually some kind of square or rectangle nearby. You stare at the square and, starting in the top left corner, imagine tracing a line along the top to the corner on the right, meanwhile taking a breath in. Then hold that breath as you trace down the right-hand side, let it out as you mentally trace along the bottom of the square, hold as you trace back up to the top and then start again, taking a breath in across the top. You can do this as many times as you want to until you feel calmer.

Although I don't set time aside to practise mindfulness, finding my rest through gardening and running instead, I do try to reframe frustrating waiting times as opportunities to practise mindfulness. If the train is late, or I'm kept on hold on the phone, or that tiny wheel of death starts spinning on the computer, then I try to take it as a cue to practise some mindfulness, focusing on my breathing, going through each of my senses one at a time and attending to what I find, while noticing other distracting thoughts come, and hopefully go. I say, I try. I don't always do it. On the phone I might be poised ready with my query, or complaint, and I want to hold it in mind, so that I can explain it as well as possible. But if I can overcome that, mindfulness *does* transform the feeling that I'm wasting my time, or worse, that someone else is, into a welcome opportunity to pause and get some rest.

The US social psychologist Ellen Langer believes that doing even less than this can still bring benefits. In her view we don't need to sit still doing formal meditation. Instead 'the simple act of noticing things' can improve our well-being. By deliberately paying our attention to anything that changes – at work, in people we see, or the streets we walk along – we remain engaged and interested. She also believes this helps us to feel calmer and less frustrated because we begin to accept that few things are constant; most things change.[13]

Ten years ago I doubt that mindfulness would have made it into our top ten, but it was no surprise to see it in the list now. The evidence that all mindfulness works as well as its many advocates claim is mixed. Whether or not it is a good way to achieve rest is also open to dispute. But the benefit of mindfulness coming tenth in our survey and therefore first in this book is that it has lessons relating to many of the other activities we will be considering. Many of these activities bring about some kind of change in our awareness. We head out into countryside, we listen to music, we become absorbed in a novel and, as a result, we adjust our focus. Our chattering minds begin to quieten. Our bodies start to relax. We slow down. We aren't practising mindfulness per se, but even so there is something mindful about these activities. And there is another powerful lesson we can learn from mindfulness practitioners – that putting time aside for rest is beneficial. By turning your phone to silent and living without interruption for fifteen minutes you can start to find restfulness.

Mindfulness may or may not be for you. On balance, I would say give it a try, but don't expect it necessarily to change your life.

9

WATCHING TV

It's a decompression chamber, immersion in a fantasy world for a few moments, a few hours. Delightful.

I don't think about anything. I don't think about my kids, my wife or anything. I'm not there. I'm not at school and I'm not at home. I'm in the TV screen. I'm in there with them.

I feel refreshed. I haven't done anything for two hours except rest my bones and my mind. Then I go out . . . I'm ready to do another five hours of work.

I become serene and relaxed. It's almost as if I took a tranquiliser.

D o you identify with these comments? They come from four different people who took part in focus groups held a quarter of a century ago by the American researchers Barbara Lee and Robert Lee.[1] Although technology has changed the way we watch TV since then, many of us still find an hour or two in front of the television just as restful and relaxing.

If I'm honest, TV is the form of culture I enjoy the most and it is also the main way I relax. The more tired I feel, the more likely I am to turn on the television. I get to sit with my feet up. It requires no physical effort. It requires almost no mental effort. And when the programme is any good, it's completely absorbing. I immerse myself in other people's lives and forget my own. I get transported around the world without leaving my living room. And on top of all that I get to share the experience with my partner. We can sit in happy companionship, not talking unless we feel like it. In many ways it's the perfect form of rest.

This is the secret to the enduring popularity of TV; it induces restfulness. Yes, viewing habits are changing. Yes, it's true that now we watch on smartphones and laptops as well as large screens. Yes, we can now choose what to watch and when, taking seconds to summon up programmes from vast video libraries. But whether it is BBC One or Al-Jazeera or Netflix or YouTube, it remains essentially the same: moving pictures which unfold in front of us, while we simply watch and listen. And for the purposes of this chapter, all of this I am calling TV.

Worldwide it's estimated that we consume 3.5 billion hours of TV each year. Indeed, television drama in particular is experiencing such a golden age that Hollywood's top film stars are suddenly happy to head for the small screen, along with the best writers and directors. I'm sure I'm not alone in watching TV as my default mode of resting. Does this sound like a regular evening for you? Get home from work, cook the supper, get the kids to bed, clear up and then, at last, plonk yourself down on the sofa and turn on the television. And even after an evening out doing some other kind of recreation – a drink with friends, dinner in a restaurant, a trip to the cinema – what do you do when you get back home? Watch a quick comedy to wind down before bed. Turning on the telly is what you do at the end of a long day, if you are under the weather or feeling a bit low. You turn to it when you are alone or with the family. It is easy, it is ubiquitous.

So I was intrigued to see that TV only came ninth in the Rest Test. Perhaps it's because watching TV doesn't have a good reputation. It doesn't have the cultural cachet of other art forms. I grew up watching the kids' programme *Why Don't You?*, a show which ran for more than twenty years and whose full title was *Why Don't You Just Switch Off Your Television Set and Go Out and Do Something Less Boring Instead?* There is something gloriously Reithian about this title: a BBC TV programme that suggests in a high-minded way that TV is bad for children.

When the comedian Bob Mortimer was on the famous radio show *Desert Island Discs* recently, he said one of the things he would most miss when he was marooned on the island is watching the television. The format of this flagship Radio 4 programme, unchanged in nearly eighty years, speaks volumes. Guests are allowed to take along eight records, they can take a book in addition to *The Complete Works of Shakespeare* and *The Bible* and they also choose a luxury. Though I suspect most of the celebrity castaways enjoy television as much as Bob Mortimer, and quite as much as their chosen records and book, few mention it and hardly any choose it as their luxury.

We've long assumed that TV is bad for us. We've been told that if we indulge in it too much we'll end up as couch potatoes with square eyes and rotted brains. Groucho Marx once said, 'I find television very educating. Every time somebody turns on the set, I go into the other room and read a book.' So maybe this kind of negativity about TV has made people wary of admitting they enjoy it and find it restful. Though it's interesting that more women than men did put TV down as one their top three restful activities, as did more young people than older people (which might reassure TV companies who constantly fear that they'll never attract the next generation).

But regardless of what we might admit to, viewing figures tell the true story. TV is undoubtedly still a hugely popular way of spending our spare time. Studies of time use conducted in the USA reveal that by the age of seventy-five the average person will have spent a total of nine years watching television – that is more time than we spend doing anything apart from sleeping and working, which is a sobering thought, even for people like me who stick up for TV.

But then hasn't that time in front of the screen passed rather deliciously? And who said we must make the most of every minute we have on earth doing things that are active and challenging and worthwhile and memorable? The central argument of this book is that it is *good* to rest and we should try to rest more often. In coming chapters, we will look at ways of resting that are less sedentary and arguably more fulfilling. We could practise mindfulness, but there's nothing wrong with a bit of mind*less*ness. Nothing wrong with zoning out rather than zoning in. Watching TV is escapist and easy. No going to classes to learn how to do it. No paying to go to a spa. No practice needed. Just switch on the screen and switch off the brain. Binge watch that box set. It is total immersion. Totally mesmerising. Totally relaxing.

TV as Tranquiliser

Strangely, the extensive body of research on watching TV rarely focuses on rest. It tends to concentrate on the deleterious impact of TV viewing. On second thoughts, perhaps that's not surprising. Applying for a research grant to investigate whether TV is restful might appear a bit 'No shit, Sherlock.' (A great recent TV series, incidentally: *Sherlock*, I mean, though doubtless someone's also made a programme called *No Shit, Sherlock* too.) Seriously, I can see why funders prefer to finance studies on whether or not watching violence on TV affects children. It is an important thing to establish. By contrast, whether or not, and to what extent, TV relaxes us might seem rather trivial. Fortunately, though, there are some studies to which we can turn.

The psychologist Mihaly Csikszentmihalyi has been hugely influential in researching the ways we choose to spend our leisure time and the types of activities which bring us joy. In 1981 he recruited a large group of people from five different Chicago-based companies and paged them at random fifty-four times in a week during waking hours. Each time the beeper went, the participants were required to make a note of what they were doing at that moment and answer a series of questions about how they were feeling. Previous research had tended to assume that TV was at best boring and at worst harmful, but that's not what Csikszentmihalyi found.

People reported that watching TV was more relaxing than playing sport or going to clubs. Which is understandable. But they also found it more relaxing than eating meals, or even idling. It made them feel drowsy and passive, but also moderately cheerful. What more could you want after a hard day's work! People said that they liked spending time watching telly because they didn't feel obliged to do it. And they said the reason they found it enjoyable was that there was virtually nothing at stake. All this sounds like a perfect description of rest.

From the US to Kyrgyzstan, studies show that one of the main attractions of watching TV – and in many cases *the* top attraction – is to relax. As one research paper puts it we use 'TV as a kind of Valium'.[2] Apart from doing nothing, which as we'll discover later in the book is harder than it sounds, there are few activities that could involve less effort.

Television provides an escape from ourselves. It stops our minds from reliving a bad day or worrying about tomorrow. Just for a while, watching TV can distract us enough to put such thoughts out of our minds. A study from 2008 suggests that this kind of emotional escapism works particularly well for people who often have low moods or experience social anxiety. These people felt most transported by watching TV, as well as feeling closest to the characters.[3]

Perhaps we can learn something about the TV and rest by looking at the programme that was downloaded more times than any other in 2018. It was *Friends* – the sitcom about the twenty-somethings living in unfeasibly expensive flats in Manhattan. It started back in 1994, when the cast all had bigger hair and weren't quite as groomed as they became once they were super-famous. As I wrote this, news of the continued popularity of *Friends* had just been released. Every radio programme was covering it and presenters were wondering why it was still so popular despite some of its dated attitudes. I was struck by the fact that critics were saying the reason *Friends* had endured is that it is the perfect escapist programme which you can flop down and watch when you're tired, without making any effort whatsoever. As well as summing up the popularity of *Friends*, I wonder if these critics have also summed up the popularity of TV in general as a means of achieving restfulness?

(Incidentally, in the 2008 study I mentioned on the previous page, the participants were asked to name their favourite character on TV, real or imagined, and the women's favourite was Rachel from *Friends*, while the men chose Homer Simpson, which I'm sure reveals something interesting about the difference between men and women's personalities, though goodness knows what!)

Back in 1959 when fears about the risks of watching TV were already being voiced, a sociologist called Dr Leonard Pearlin was ahead of his time. He interviewed more than seven hundred people in an industrial city in a southern state of the US about their viewing experiences. More than 90 per cent said they liked TV programmes which helped them to forget their troubles. The more stressed people felt, the more they enjoyed this kind of escapist viewing. Dr Pearlin concluded that watching TV can provide a 'day-to-day safety valve' to help people cope with life.[4] Three decades later more research has confirmed that we often turn to TV for distraction when we're feeling anxious.[5]

Social Grease

TV provides an escape not only from our own thoughts, but also from the demands of dealing with other people, even when they're with us. People who don't live alone tend to watch TV with others, but do so without any pressure to keep up a conversation. No effort is required. It's perfectly acceptable to say nothing for long periods. You don't even need to make eye contact. Yet you share the activity, you share emotions, you share your humanity as you react to whatever you're watching.

When I was involved in a large research project on loneliness last year, I noticed several people who lived alone commenting that the element they missed most about not living with someone else was having no one to watch TV with. They missed that sense of restful companionship.

The television has been dubbed the 'electronic hearth'.[6] While our forebears sat around the fire sharing stories, we gather around a screen to share tales which have been filmed for us. We discuss and debate them while we watch and discuss them again the following day around the water cooler. And now that we often watch programmes on different days, it's common to hear cries of 'No, no spoilers! I've not seen the last one yet. Don't tell me!'

The Lees, who conducted the focus groups from which I quoted earlier, believe television is a form of 'social grease'. It provides discussion without demands. The joy of watching TV in company gets neglected; adverts for large screens have tended to emphasise the individual privacy and personalisation of the home cinema experience. And for a long time scholars had assumed that watching TV meant not socialising, when in fact back in 1990 research had already demonstrated that people like watching TV even more when they have company, and that far from sitting in total silence 20 per cent of the time while they watched people were also talking.[7]

The TV programme *Gogglebox*, in which we watch people watching the same programmes we watch, reminds us of the comments being made in living rooms up and down the land.

What is she wearing?!
Ahhhhhh – the poor monkey's feeling all left out. It knows the others don't like him.
Why do TV detectives always go down into cellars without turning the light on? Don't go down there! Don't do it! Why would you even do that?!

And of course, these days there is Twitter. If a politician says something particularly obnoxious on *Question Time*, or a Scandi noir drama has a ridiculously implausible ending, yes, you can shout at the television, and yes, you can share your outrage with your partner, but you can also tell the world, or feel as though you're telling the world.

Television can be a restful distraction even at the most traumatic times in our lives. Our neighbour and friend Jerry had a senior job in the NHS. He cycled often and played badminton. He loved literature, particularly poetry, particularly Seamus Heaney, and he was a committed socialist. He loved good food and wine. He loved his family and was chatty and funny and always good fun to be around. Then, aged fifty-five, he was diagnosed with bowel cancer. At first there seemed to be a good chance he would survive, but eventually he knew, and then we knew, that his cancer was terminal. He talked very openly about dying, typically taking care of the rest of us in conversations, trying to make it easier for us to talk comfortably about such a distressing subject.

In the last couple of months of his life a close family friend visited on Saturday evenings. They didn't spend the time having deep and meaningful conversations about death or the meaning of life. Instead the whole family including the adult children watched *Strictly*. It became a focal point for all of them, a new Saturday routine, a new indulgence which drew them together.

At Jerry's memorial service this friend recalled how Jerry's most frequent comment about the sequinned outfits was 'bizarre' while on the judges' scoring decisions he would often shout out 'outrageous!' Here was a cerebral man, known for reading the *London Review of Books* cover to cover, finding solace in the shared pleasure of watching a celebrity game show. And for all of them, it was the perfect distraction from his prognosis, a rest from his cancer.

Eventually, inevitably, the Saturday night came where Jerry was too ill to leave his bed to watch TV on the sofa downstairs. It was clear that he only had a matter of days left to live. As his friend said at his memorial, 'It was bizarre. It was outrageous.'

It's not uncommon for TV to begin to fill people's days nearer the end of life. In nursing homes the perpetually switched-on, volume-turned-up-to-the-max television is a fixture of the day room. On average, retired people of any age still watch more TV than younger people. We might think millennials invented binge watching, and it's true that they have been the first generation to grow up with the opportunity to watch an entire series or three in a sitting, without having to wait a week for the next instalment. But many retired people have been expert at binge watching for decades now, engrossed in many hours of daytime TV interspersed with the occasional snooze. Research shows that on average TV can occupy half of an older person's leisure time.[8]

So it interests me that in the Rest Test older people didn't rate TV to be as restful as the younger people did. I wonder whether this is because for them TV is a major part of the day, rather than a way to rest at the end of the day. It relates to a question that we will keep returning to in this book: to what extent is the restfulness of an activity dependent on the activity that precedes it? Maybe for the younger and middle-aged people TV feels most restful because it comes after a busy day at work. The preceding busyness grants permission to lounge and luxuriate, and what better way to do that than watching some telly? By contrast, for many older people television is all they have, so it is not such a treat or luxury.

Empty Time

So far this has been a call to celebrate or at least defend resting through TV-watching instead of feeling guilty about it. But I can't escape the fact that psychologists tend to be more negative about TV viewing, especially if it becomes compulsive.

One of the fears expressed by some psychologists is that TV does too much of the work for us. If we are reading a book or listening to the radio we are required to paint the pictures in our minds to create an imagined world. By contrast, TV does it all for us, giving us a sense that it might stunt our imaginations, preventing us from daydreaming or conjuring up images of our own. And as we'll discover later, if you want to achieve restfulness, daydreaming can help you on your way, so it would be a shame if TV put a stop to it. But fear not. The evidence does not really support this idea. In fact, we're perfectly capable of drifting off into another world while we watch TV.[9] It's not surprising when you think about it. If we can manage to go on social media, chat, eat or iron while we watch TV, then letting your mind wander a bit shouldn't be hard. And splitting your attention between the TV and another activity is no twenty-first century phenomenon. Back in the 1981 study, people were found to be carrying out a second activity 67 per cent of the time while they were watching TV. They may not have been multi-screening, but they were eating, doing housework or even reading.

Another concern that is expressed is that television viewing can have a negative impact on our perception of time passing. The hours spent watching TV are sometimes referred to as 'empty time'. Part of the problem seems to be that, in terms of memories created, any hours spent watching TV are poor value. We might enjoy programmes at that moment, but unless they're exceptional (here I'm going to defend the many hours I've devoted to watching *Breaking Bad* and insist that there were scenes which will stay with me for years to come, not necessarily in a good way), we forget most of them. This is problematic because we use the number of new memories we've made as a way to judge how much time has passed. So if we watch a lot of TV, and don't remember much about it, then time will speed by, and life will feel as though it is passing us by, something none of us like.

Perhaps the biggest concern is that TV is so addictive that

we tend to overindulge in it. Of course, spending every evening or whole weekends bingeing on box sets is not good for us, not least because TV watching is a passive and sedentary activity. Yet TV watching seems to be judged more harshly than other cultural pastimes. No one spending a whole weekend reading *War and Peace* cover to cover would be accused of binge reading. And spending a full fifteen hours attending Wagner's *Ring* cycle is not condemned as binge opera watching. There is no doubt that a certain cultural snobbery still attaches to watching TV, along with an assumption that it is a mindless and shallow activity. Again it's the same anxiety that has accompanied each new technological development. Novels rotted the brain, then it was films, then TV. Now it's gaming and social media we worry about.

But very new research conducted with American students found that when they binge watch the hour upon hour of viewing doesn't put them into a passive stupor. Rather the students are engaged with characters and absorbed in the action.[10] As the study's authors sum up, 'Marathon television viewers are active cognitively and emotionally, during and after the media exposure. They form meaningful bonds with characters beyond the moment of exposure. They are not merely entertained but feel compelled to continue watching as they engage in deep reflection.' It strikes me that is the kind of description that might also apply to reading a novel, yet reading for the most part escapes the same kind of moral judgement.

And this engagement with the characters might explain one of the benefits that watching TV has been demonstrated to bring. Like reading, it improves empathy and makes us better at seeing things from other people's points of view.

Other research has found that the lonelier people feel, the more likely they are to binge watch, which – typically – researchers tend to view negatively.[11] But I wonder whether we should reframe such marathon TV sessions as a short-term coping strategy instead. It isn't a long-term solution to loneliness of course, but loneliness is often temporary, and when it is, television could help by distracting us from painful feelings and providing a sense of companionship.

Does Watching TV Make Us Unhappy, Unhealthy and Anti-Social

If you ask people to rate a list of different activities according to the happiness, cheerfulness and friendliness they invoke, TV comes low down on the list. This seems like bad news for TV fans, though reading and idling, which are also popular ways of resting, received similarly low ratings.[12] And remember, our main concern here is what helps us feel rested, not what perks us up or makes us popular.

That said, it would be a pity to indulge in an activity which, however restful, makes us unhappy. So *does* TV do that? An obvious answer to the question is that it depends on what you watch. A diet of violent thrillers or true crime stories is not likely to lift your mood or make you view the world optimistically. One of my favourite programmes at the moment is the documentary series *Hospital* which follows doctors and nurses struggling to save patients in the face of budget cuts. While in one sense I enjoy these programmes, inevitably I cry when a patient doesn't make it and I feel cross when I see the efforts staff have to make to find a free bed. Watching the news can also make us feel miserable. So much so, in fact, that the authors of one study recommend we do relaxation exercises after every bulletin to help us to recover. Perhaps a quick class could be played after the news. The authors concede that it might seem excessive to suggest relaxation techniques in order to cope with watching the news, but insist that if you don't do them you can be left with negative after-effects – a kind of nasty news hangover.[13]

But we do all have a choice about what we watch, so I'm more interested in any general link between our well-being and the number of hours we spend watching television each day. The bad news is that many studies find that people who watch a lot of TV do have lower levels of well-being on average. To take just one example, a major study of more than 60,000 Brazilian adults found that watching more than five hours of TV a day was associated with a higher risk of depression.[14]

But, of course, this does not prove that TV per se is the problem. It won't surprise you to learn that people who are unemployed or stuck at home because they're unwell tend to watch more TV on average.[15] It's cheap, ever-changing, doesn't require physical fitness and can provide hours of distraction. Those same people also have lower levels of well-being than people in good health or with jobs. So we are left with a perennial research issue – correlation versus causation. We don't know which came first – the unhappiness or the TV watching.

Staying in all day watching television might well isolate

people and make them feel worse. Alternatively, they may already be feeling unhappy and are using TV to cope, like the lonely people we heard about earlier who binge watch box sets. If this dependence on TV becomes habitual then it may store up other problems for the future. But as a temporary means to combat isolation it certainly shouldn't be condemned. An interesting and encouraging study among older people found they not only used TV as a coping strategy, but also learned to use their own viewing habits as a way of monitoring their personal well-being. The researchers found that when the older people realised they were starting to watch TV for many more hours than usual, they knew from experience they should be wary.[16] So in this study some people were using TV effectively to boost their mood, such as the seventy-one-year-old widow who commented, 'You watch television and you get happy, you get hungry. You get many emotions when you take television, and usually I take the news and have many emotions so I forget my problems.'

I should add that in the Brazilian study I mentioned the researchers found there was another group of people who seemed to have a higher risk of depression: people who watch less than an hour a day of TV. It seems a curious result, but it is almost certainly other factors that were to blame, not the lack of television. Perhaps these people were so poor they couldn't afford a television or so busy working and caring for others that they never had time to rest and watch it, in which case, of course, it was the lack of any free time and the overwhelming stress of their lives making them unhappy rather than the lack of an hour's television watching.

To get around the correlation versus causation issue,

researchers in the US examined data from 50,000 nurses, who were followed over a ten-year period. Did long hours spent in front of the television precede depression several years later? For many of the nurses it did. And the reason? Watching lots of TV meant they did less exercise, and the authors think it's that rather than anything about watching TV per se that was the main problem.[17]

It is obvious that watching a lot of TV is not good for us physically because it generally involves a lot of sitting down. So you won't be surprised to hear that a strong association has been found between high numbers of hours spent watching TV and obesity, heart disease, high blood pressure, diabetes and bowel disease.[18] Again we have to be a bit cautious here in case people are already unwell before they become heavy viewers. After all, if you're too ill to go out then it's not surprising if TV becomes one of your chief pastimes. But then it must be said that a Japanese study from 2016 found that if people watched more than five hours of TV a day, their risk of dying from a pulmonary embolism was doubled, an effect that was independent of how much other physical activity they did. And very new research using data from over 3,500 people over the age of fifty found that those who watched TV for more than 3.5 hours a day had a greater decline in their scores on memory tasks six years later than those who didn't. What we don't know, of course, is whether people were already in the early stages of cognitive decline, which prompted them to decrease their activity and fill their time with television. And the study hasn't gone on long enough for us to know whether the TV watchers were more likely to go on to develop dementia. As the eminent Professor Til Wykes commented, 'A lot more research is needed before we panic and closely measure TV time like a step counter'.[19]

Another problem associated with watching a lot of TV is that people are tempted to stay up late. Not surprisingly, studies have found that this can have a detrimental impact on the amount of sleep people get, although the internet is now regarded as a more disruptive factor here.[20] Having a TV in the bedroom is often seen as a bad thing. But studies in India and the US have found that although people ended up going to sleep later if they had a TV in their bedroom they also tended to get up later next day to compensate.[21] Of course, the bright lights from a TV screen and exciting programmes that stimulate you, making you feel wide awake late at night, are not going to help you get to sleep either. But your tendency to view late-night TV watching as negative may depend on your attitude to late nights and early mornings.

Of course, us TV fans can learn from this research. Yes, we should certainly avoid becoming couch potatoes, scoffing TV dinners while glued to the box for hours. And perhaps it is not a bad idea to avoid watching television in bed. But we don't have to give up that brilliant drama or great comedy altogether. Perhaps we could watch our favourite programme while doing some vigorous exercise on the running or rowing machine. Or less strenuously, as I sometimes do, we could stand up and do the ironing.

As for the wider social impacts of television watching, in his seminal study, *Bowling Alone*, the Harvard political scientist Professor Robert Putnam indicted TV for the devastating effect he felt it had had on social capital in the US. Simply put, Putnam found that increased TV consumption had led to more and more Americans staying home in the evening rather than engaging in social activities, such as bowling or, more seriously, civic activism and local politics. And any advocate of the benefits of TV watching cannot escape from the fact that huge data sets have shown an association between low life satisfaction and high TV consumption. We have to acknowledge that having a box in our homes that brings us so much information and entertainment is likely to tempt us to stay in rather than engage in more social activities out in the community. But a re-analysis of the data on TV watching and life satisfaction from more than eighty countries shows that hours of TV watching still have a far lower impact on satisfaction than factors such as their health, their freedom or unemployment.[22]

Getting the Right Balance

By now you can probably guess my conclusion on using TV as an aid to rest. Moderation in viewing is what's needed. A couple of hours of TV can certainly help you relax, but five hours a day is almost certainly too much. Though it might depend on the circumstances. The trick is to give yourself the right dose at the right time and not to allow it to deter you from going out.

There are occasions where a decent dose of telly is just what's needed. Csikszentmihalyi found that if people were in a bad mood in the afternoon, a few hours of telly later on left them feeling much better by the end of the evening.[23]

We've seen that habitual heavy viewing is bad for us, but we must resist the notion, still prevalent, that TV per se is a problem, that it would be better if we watched none at all. A 2005 study did include people who don't watch any TV, a group now so rare that the researchers had to advertise in order to locate them. What the team found was that in terms of loneliness, shyness, self-esteem, depression or satisfaction with life, there was no difference between the no TV people and those who watched moderate amounts (roughly two hours a day).[24]

So there is no reason to feel concerned about moderate TV viewing. Indeed if we want to watch television, we should actively guard against feeling guilty when we reach for that remote. A German study entitled 'The Guilty Couch Potato' found that the more mentally exhausted we are, the guiltier we feel about watching TV and the less refreshed we feel afterwards.[25] So we're left with a situation in which a medium that can relax us is causing stress because of a reputation it doesn't really even deserve.

Perhaps it would help if we reframed watching TV in the evenings as a due reward for a hard day's work rather than a manifestation of our idleness. Yes, there are probably things we should be doing instead, but there will *always* be things we should be doing instead. Don't watch TV all night, but, to get the benefits and to feel refreshed, we need to allow ourselves to go with it.

8

DAYDREAMING

The Daydream Catcher

I can remember 11 January 2016 especially well. It was a Monday. You may be expecting me to say it was a special day or that something unusual happened. It wasn't my birthday or my wedding day or a day of holiday or celebration. And it wasn't one of those days captured in what psychologists call flashbulb memories – where you know exactly where you were when you heard the news that Princess Diana had died (I was in bed), or that the UK had voted for Brexit (I was in bed), or that Donald Trump had won the US presidential election (I was in bed). No, this was an ordinary day; the sort of day I would ordinarily completely forget.

Yet several years on I can tell you that our boiler had broken down, meaning I had to have a cold shower; that fortunately the weather was fairly mild for the time of year; that I was offered a choice between orange and apple juice while I sat in a booth reading out loud for the audio version of my previous book; that I ran part of the way home from the recording studio and on the way squeezed through a narrow gap between a wall and skip; that later, on the train,

I looked at the hexagonal-texture of the red fabric of my running bag; after I got home, I danced to David Bowie's 'Starman' while tidying my room;[1] then, finally, my husband came home and greeted me with a kiss.

Okay, some pretty mundane things happened and for some reason I can remember them all. But what's this got to do with daydreaming? Here's where my recall of that day gets more impressive. For I can remember not just things that I did that day, or incidents that occurred, but also the thoughts I had at those moments.

Here's the list:

I was disappointed that the producer hadn't sounded more sympathetic when I said we had no hot water. I wondered whether I'd get marks on my top while squeezing through a narrow gap between a wall and skip; I wondered whether it mattered since the top would need to go in the wash anyway. On the train I wondered whether the hexagonal texture on my running rucksack was the designer's first idea. Or did they go through various iterations of squares and octagons and had a final meeting where they settled on hexagons as the ideal textured pattern; I was on an escalator marvelling at how many of the people riding up the other way looked familiar and wondered whether this was because I had been around for so long and met so many people that now almost everyone resembles someone. I was thinking how sad it was that David Bowie had died and of the songs he might have written in the future which now we'd never hear. I wondered whether my step counter counts dancing. Life and death and the insignificant all at once. I was amazed at how, at the exact moment my husband's lips touched mine, the lights went out. How did he do it?

The reason I remember so much – both things I did and things I thought – was because I was taking part in an experiment designed to capture what is usually lost from our memories as our minds rush from one thing to the next. The psychologist Russell Hurlburt had given me a small black box to clip on to my belt. He had come over from the University of Nevada in Las Vegas to do research with the Hubbub team in London. The box was attached by a pale pink lead to a pink earpiece. At random intervals during the day, a series of sharp beeps were transmitted from the box into my ear. My task was to write down as precisely as I could what I had been thinking or experiencing in the moment before the beep happened. The following day Hurlburt interviewed me about each moment, referring to them as Beep 1, Beep 2, etc. He asked detailed questions. Endless questions. Every time I thought he had finished he would quiz me further.

Could I see the thought? Was the thought in words? Was it in colour? Where was it in my head? Or could I see it in front of me? Could I see any words written? Could I hear them? Whose voice was speaking the words? Was I seeing myself in these thoughts or looking out from my head?

These were often hard questions to answer, and the temptation was sometimes to make something up or slightly embellish an answer. But whenever I tried this, Hurlburt spotted it immediately. He has been doing this for forty years; forty years questioning people in detail about single moments in time. Gradually I found myself giving more honest, if dull answers. And this was how it should be. It's an iterative process, and like everyone I got better at it.

His method is called Descriptive Experience Sampling or DES and through it he has found that five particular elements turn up a lot in people's mind wanderings. He calls them the 'five frequent phenomena' – visual imagery, inner speech, feelings, sensory awareness and unsymbolised thought. I scored high on visual imagery, apparently – seeing thoughts in pictures. Hurlburt said my thought patterns were almost kaleidoscopic, with thoughts coming in one after another in a more complex way than most people describe (from the way he said it, this probably isn't a good thing). I learned that I have some thoughts without words, which some people have a lot, and others, like him, never have.

Why does he do it? Well, he wouldn't put it this way, but I like to think of him as a daydream catcher. Through an exhaustive process he captures that most elusive of things, a random thought, a thought that pops into our heads for a moment, for no apparent reason, and then is gone – and some of these thoughts are daydreams.

Think of it this way. Hurlburt has a big net. In it he captures plodding events, like taking a shower or running home from work. These are easy prey, and he is not interested in them. They are just context. He also nets big, worthy thoughts. The things we like to think we are thinking about, like the work we are doing at the time or a problem we have long been wrestling with. But he also wants to catch what normally falls through the holes: the fleeting, flashing, unconnected, all-over-the-place, coming-out-of-nowhere, disappearing-as-fast-as-they appear, quicksilver thoughts we all have. All the time.

He listens with an astonishing level of attentiveness. I was boring myself in the end with the disappointing banality of my own thoughts (not once was I thinking anything deep or even thinking about work, which I'd have guessed occupied a lot of my thoughts), but he listened as though every word I said was fascinating. To him our thoughts are like treasure – windows into our interior lives.

These thoughts aren't rare or valuable or interesting in themselves, but they are hard to collect – which is what makes them fascinating to a collector like Hurlburt. The main problem he has to deal with is contamination. The contamination that comes from the fact that the thoughts are reported to him by the person who experienced those thoughts. The natural tendency of participants in his experiments – as I did – is to try to polish the thought, to make it sound more interesting than it actually is. Hurlburt uses the random beeps to catch our thoughts unawares, as it were; in the purest possible state of unself-consciousness. And banal is good, inconsequential is as it should be, for this is the stuff of most of our thinking. One of the things he's been investigating is the experience we have in our heads at those moments when we're supposed to be doing nothing, resting.

Problems remain, however. The developmental psychologist and writer Professor Charles Fernyhough, who was part of the team who created the Rest Test, is someone I think of as a big fan of DES, but even he warns that the very fact of observing your thoughts as soon as you hear the beep can change the thought experience you've just had, while discussing those experiences later can change them again.[2] It's true that this kind of introspection suffers from the problem of subjectivity which Hurlburt acknowledges, but what fascinates me is that, even though I was initially sceptical about Hurlburt's method, when I occasionally meet someone else who's tried it I discover that the patterns that showed up in my thinking are completely different from theirs, suggesting that Hurlburt is at the very least capturing something about the way we think that no other method can. He's not setting out to study daydreams in particular, but he catches them in his net nonetheless.

The Restlessness of the Resting State

Of course, DES is not the only way to study daydreaming. There is a method that avoids reliance on subjective experiences. Instead of writing down your thought experiences and then being quizzed in detail about them, you lie on a hospital mattress with ear plugs pushed deep into your ears while you are reversed into a brain scanner.[3] Then you stare at a small white cross on a black background. The idea is that the cross allows people to think of nothing in particular, wiping the mind clean of previous thoughts and leaving it a blank slate. Over the years this crosshair has been used in thousands of neuroscientific studies to reset the brain to neutral, ready for the next task. In a typical study you might be given some sort of task while you're in the scanner – mental arithmetic, say, or looking at photographs designed to elicit different emotions. The scan can then reveal which parts of the brain become more active when doing such a task, and which less. This is how it's been possible in recent years to work out which parts of the brain or combinations of parts of the brain are used for different activities, and what happens to the brain when we rest.

I had a go at this too, as part of a trial at the Max Planck Institute for Human Cognitive and Brain Sciences in Leipzig. People had warned me about the periods of banging sounds in a scanner as the magnet is turned on, bursts of repetitive hammering. Some people hate both the noise and the sense of claustrophobia, but I had chosen to have the scan, rather than needing one due to serious illness, which must make it easier. And although the hammering was loud, the noises were so rhythmic that I found them almost hypnotic, like a piece by the minimalist composer Steve Reich except that that gradual shifting change in repeating rhythms never came. As a result, I found it quite cosy and relaxing. It was nice to be allowed to lie down in the middle of a working day and think of nothing in particular.

Not that this continued for long. Although there wasn't any detailed questioning, after each session of thinking about nothing in particular and while still in the scanner I had to answer a questionnaire about my mind wanderings which was projected on the screen in front of my eyes. Yet again, I found I wasn't having deep thoughts; again, what I was thinking was apparently banal and inconsequential. But for all the vapidity of my thoughts, I was definitely feeling relaxed; indeed I had trouble staying awake.

Within neuroscience, this is known, appropriately, as the resting state. I wasn't really thinking, certainly not in a focused or concentrated way, I was just daydreaming and that is presumably restful, right?

There's a problem with this thesis. Twenty years ago a student called Bharat Biswal was studying for a doctorate at the Medical College of Wisconsin in Milwaukee. He was investigating how to obtain a purer signal from a brain scanner when he noticed that the so-called resting brain didn't appear to be resting. In fact, it was as busy as ever. Indeed, often more busy.

People in the scanner had been asked to stare at the white cross, clear their minds and think of nothing. And like me, they often experienced a feeling of relaxation and restfulness. While they might not be thinking of nothing, they weren't thinking anything in particular. They were day-dreaming lazily. But their brains hadn't in any sense stopped working. Indeed, their brain activity wasn't even random. Brain scans revealed a degree of coordination between different parts of the brain.[4]

Around the same time, there was another discovery. This time it came from a different type of scan known as a PET scan.[5] A researcher called Gordon Shulman combined the results of nine studies, hoping to find the brain network that comes to life when people pay attention. But he discovered the opposite – the network which is activated when we do nothing. In these studies, when the participants stopped resting and began concentrating on a task, instead of the brain jumping back into life, some parts even showed a decrease in activity.

To start with, there was some resistance to these findings in the neuroscience community. For many years, neuro-scientists had believed that brain circuits were switched off when they weren't needed. After all, why waste energy on unnecessary mental processes? Some sceptics even thought there must have been a mistake, with a referee rejecting a paper written in 1998 by the neuroscientist Marcus Raichle, now one of the leaders in this field, because they felt the apparent activity must surely be down to an error in the data.[6]

Now, however, the idea that the brain is always busy is the standard view. Mark Lauckner, a neuroscientist at the Max Planck Institute, put it bluntly during my visit to Leipzig. 'The brain only really rests when you are dead.'

So even though many respondents in the Rest Test claimed they found or sought rest in 'a calm state of thought' or in 'mental stillness' or in 'clearing the head' or in 'quietening' or 'slowing down' or 'emptying' or 'shutting down' the mind or in 'exerting no mental effort' or in 'stopping thinking' or in 'turning my brain off',[7] there might be no state of mind where this literally happens.

Instead of 'daydreaming' scientists tend to use the term 'mind wandering'. Wandering (and indeed, wondering) is the brain's natural state, not rest. Off it goes in search of things, endlessly inquisitive, another thought occurring, another interesting idea to be pursued. Does this sound tiring? Only if you endlessly chase after it, following and trying to impose order. But not if you let it go – like a toddler or a puppy racing around the garden while you relax in a deckchair.

This is what we mean when we say daydreaming is restful, I believe. The mind never stops, but if we relinquish control, let it go wherever it will, we feel less stressed, less put upon. Traditionally, from a young age, we are urged not to daydream but to concentrate. The recent trend for mindfulness is a variation on this and there's no doubt that some people do find it restful. That's fine. A leitmotif of this book is 'whatever works for you'. But if you are among those who find daydreaming restful, don't beat yourself up about it. Not least because, as it turns out, while you might be doing nothing much while you daydream, your brain is still engaged in useful tasks and that in turn can benefit you.

As we've seen, the so-called 'resting state' is a bit of a misnomer, which is why some scientists prefer to refer to the areas of the brain which remain active while we are supposedly mentally inactive. This is called the 'default mode network'.

The phrase captures rather better the fact that the brain defaults to activity in certain areas when it is not being called on to do anything else.[8]

More than 3,000 scientific papers have been published investigating this default mechanism. These methods have their critics, of course. Even with millions of pounds of brain scanner we can't be certain that people are daydreaming; maybe they're looking at the inside of the scanner or pondering the noises they can hear.[9] But neuroscientists do now believe that the idling brain is not only surprisingly busy, but that all this activity is far from random.[10] All this busyness could explain, by the way, why the brain uses 20 per cent of the body's total energy when it would appear to need only about a quarter of that to perform its functions. Marcus Raichle calls it the brain's dark energy. Like the dark energy that mystifies physicists, to the best of our knowledge it's there, but we can't account for it.[11]

We can ask some other obvious questions about mind wandering too. Is mind wandering when you are trying to concentrate but become distracted, different from mind wandering when you have been asked specifically to think of nothing?

And why does the brain remain so active all the time? Does this activity have wider benefits or is it only relevant to the internal workings of the brain?[12] Perhaps the 'resting' brain is like a car parked at the side of the road, idling in neutral but with the motor still running, which the driver (us) can jump in and drive off immediately whenever we need to. Or it is possible that different parts of the brain are simply using the time when we don't need them consciously to practise working together. Or is our brain using our mind wanderings and replays of our day to help us to consolidate our memories? We know that during the night dreaming seems to play a part in doing that, and now there is evidence to suggest that (in rats at least) this happens during the day too.[13]

Another feature of the mind is that when left to its own devices, unoccupied by more immediate tasks, it often focuses on the future. The three chief areas of the brain involved in imagining the future are all part of the default mode network. So when we daydream we often start to think ahead, even about highly unlikely, life-changing scenarios.

Moshe Bar from Harvard Medical School has an interesting theory about this.[14] The reason we daydream, he argues, is to create 'memories' of possible future events; if these events *did* actually happen we could then usefully draw on these 'memories'. It is a rather neat idea. Anyone who has travelled by plane has wondered what it might be like to crash. If Bar's notions are right, then if that did happen, we could use our daydreamed experience of plane crashes to help us, both practically and emotionally, as we have already imagined what it is like to fix our oxygen mask, use the lights on the floor to guide us to the nearest exit and slide down the safety chute.

We know now that while we might experience a resting state in which we are not doing any hard thinking, our brains are still working hard. It is a bit like a trip to a spa. In order for us to enjoy a day of R and R, a team of receptionists and masseurs and pool technicians are constantly on the go. Meanwhile, research on daydreaming shows it not only brings the benefits of allowing us to plan for the future and even practise for emergencies, but allows us to do much more. The psychologist Jerome Singer was singing the praises of daydreaming back in the 1950s. He and others have demonstrated an impressive list of benefits: increased creativity, improvements in planning, better problem solving, relief from boredom, increase in patient rather than impulsive decisions, enhanced social skills and higher levels of curiosity. Daydreaming helps us to gain a better understanding of ourselves, our relationships and our place in the world. We mentally time travel back into the past and forward into the future, imposing narrative and meaning on our lives. As Jerome Singer and his colleagues put it in a paper in 2014, 'Arriving home from the store without the eggs that necessitated the trip is a mere annoyance when weighed against coming to a decision to ask for a raise, leave a job, or go back to school.'

Mind Wandering into Dark Places

Of course, our experience of daydreaming isn't always positive. In around 420 AD, in the form of dialogues with his friend Germanus, the Christian monk John Cassian, also known as John the Ascetic, wrote of the struggle to keep the mind on godly matters: 'We work to bind it with the most tenacious attentiveness of heart as though in chains, but in the midst of our attempts it slips away, swifter than an eel from the recesses of the mind.'

Centuries of medieval monks, as the historian Hilary Powell has shown, were also plagued by mind wandering, their greatest fear and obsession being that their thoughts might lead them towards 'the harmful shoot of fleshly lust'. Despite living in a tranquil sanctuary free from outside disruption, the monks constantly struggled to concentrate. They viewed the quelling of worldly thoughts as a task requiring hard work.[15]

While both Cassian and the medieval monks studying his writings 600 years later despaired at their wandering minds, it was clear from the Rest Test that today, as long as we can choose the timing, many of us love nothing more than an opportunity to follow our train of thought wherever it might take us. The monks viewed mind wandering as a constant danger; we are more relaxed in our attitude to it, viewing it as restful.

But, of course, there are two situations where daydreaming is not a good thing. The first is when, like the monks, you need to concentrate on a task, but can't because your mind is busy wandering off. The second is when it makes you feel miserable. In research where more than 2,000 people were sent random alerts on their iPhones and then asked how they were feeling, what they were doing and whether they were thinking about something other than what they were doing, it turned out that 47 per cent of the time while their minds were wandering they felt unhappy.[16] And worse, if their minds had been wandering when they received the alert, the data showed they were more likely to feel unhappy the next time they were beeped too.

But looking across a range of studies the cognitive neuro-scientist Jonathan Smallwood, who's become something of a leader in this field, concluded that it's not just the context that matters (you're trying to revise, but keep losing your concentration), but the content of those daydreams.[17] Sometimes your mind wanders back to conversations where you embarrassed yourself or said something you feel guilty about. Or you find yourself feeling anxious about the future and what might go wrong. This combination of rumination about the past and worry about the future is known as perseverative thinking and it has implications for our health. In an American study, people were phoned up early every evening for just over a week and asked detailed questions about how their day had gone and the kinds of emotions they had experienced. When the researchers followed the people up ten years later they discovered something which might make anyone prone to worry, worry a little more. The people who had brooded over the everyday stressful events, often continuing to worry about them for days after they had happened, were more likely to suffer from ill health a decade on.[18] Dwelling on things that have gone wrong appears to reactivate the body's response to the stress you felt at the time, thereby interfering with long-term health.[19]

People who are feeling depressed or suicidal ruminate more, and – as well as negative thoughts intruding on their thinking – it's been shown that they find it harder than others do to recall happy memories. It's as if the joyful thoughts have been locked away in a filing cabinet upstairs, while the unhappy thoughts are spread all over the kitchen table, always to hand.

So if your mind's meanderings are mainly negative, it's not

surprising that daydreaming can make you feel worse. But when people rate their thoughts as interesting and personally relevant, especially if they're about the future rather than the past, then their mood doesn't dip in the same way.[20]

The titles of some of the scientific papers on this topic give you some sense of the debate on the pros and cons of mind wandering within the world of psychology: An Ode to Constructive Daydreaming; A Wandering Mind is an Unhappy Mind; Not All Minds that Wander are Lost; Finding the Balance between Mindfulness and Mind-wandering. This latter paper is Jonathan Schooler's call for a middle way. If your thoughts distract and trouble you, then coping with those mind wanderings by turning to a technique such as mindfulness might help, but if your thoughts are nice and it's not essential that you concentrate on what's in front of you, then allow yourself to rest by floating away with them.

Quietening the Mind

Even if we are not great worriers, bedtime is a time when many of us wish we could quieten our thoughts. Research shows that 40 per cent of adults say that several times a month they can't get to sleep because thoughts are whirring round in their head – and of course for some people it happens more often than that.[21]

Various techniques can help distract you from troubling thoughts or anxiety about all the things you need to do. Some people practise mindfulness, focusing on their breathing and carefully watching their thoughts come and go. Others do what is known as a body scan – an exercise where you focus on, tense and relax each part of the body in turn, starting with the tips of the toes and ending with the top of the head. We'll hear more about that in Chapter 5 on doing nothing in particular.

I do maths in my head. I pick a number and play with it whenever I can't sleep. At the moment the number is 314. I work out what numbers it can be divided by or how you could combine the figures in that number adding, multiplying, subtracting and dividing *Countdown*-style until I get to 314 again. I find the arithmetic needs to be difficult enough to force me to focus on the figures instead of my thoughts, but not so hard that it stimulates my mind and keeps me awake.

If you're good at summoning visual imagery, you might prefer the techniques trialled by the Dutch clinical psychologist Ad Kerkhof.[22] After working to reduce rumination in people who were feeling suicidal, he developed similar techniques for use by anyone who would like to worry a little less. One method of stopping those thoughts circulating in your head at night (or during the day) is to imagine locking them in a box and putting it under the bed. Each time the thoughts reappear in your mind, you send them away; they're safely locked in that box and they cannot come out. Or if under the bed feels a little too close for comfort, you might prefer to imagine the thoughts whirling around in a colourful cloud (the choice of colour is yours – my cloud is purple) which then floats away on the wind or is whisked up into the air in a *Wizard of Oz*-style tornado.

Any of these techniques are worth a try and not everything will work for everyone, but in trials they do work for a significant proportion of people, as does this new technique from Michael Scullin, Director of the Sleep Neuroscience and Cognition Laboratory at Baylor University in the USA. At first sight, bedtime might sound like exactly the wrong moment to write a to-do list. Why risk making yourself feel anxious by reminding yourself of all the things you need to do the following day? On the face of it, this seems guaranteed to stop you getting to sleep while you worry about how you can possibly manage it all. But in trials just before bed in which people were required either to write a to-do list or a satisfying list of everything they had achieved that day, those prescribed the to-do list fell asleep an average of nine minutes faster.[23]

The theory is that once the items are written down on a list they have been off-loaded from your mind. You no longer need to make the effort to keep them alive in your thoughts because they are safely on your list, ready to be both remembered and dealt with when you get up. They also look a bit more manageable written down than whirling around at random in your head; you've quantified them. You might expect the busiest people with the longest lists would still find it hard to get to sleep, but the study found that busy people who created lists of more than ten tasks did better, falling asleep an average of fifteen minutes faster. It is better to be specific when you compile your list, even though you end up with a longer list, rather than simply listing 'chores' or 'work stuff'. And if you're thinking of doing this mentally to save you the trouble of making an actual list, bear in mind that it probably won't work. If you want your thoughts about tasks to stop disturbing your peace, you need to offload them by writing them down. Holding the list in your head could even prove counter-productive, encouraging your brain to recycle those items and keep it to the forefront of your mind, so you don't forget to do them.

In Praise of Mind Wandering

These techniques and others serve the purpose of stopping our minds wandering into dark places or putting our minds in a place where we can achieve the ultimate rest of a good night's sleep. They have their place and can be helpful. But generally speaking, we should not be too concerned about daydreaming or mind wandering. Obviously, we can't spend our whole lives in this state. But as with other aspects of rest, we probably should allow our minds more time to mind wander than we do now.

This is a relatively under-researched area and as yet science can tell us little about why we daydream and even less about why it seems to many of us to be a good way to get some rest. As we've seen, we may feel as if we are resting but the brain never stops, and in some ways is busier than ever while the mind wanders. For those people who feel a bit guilty about letting their minds wander, who think it is being lazy, the neuroscience is perhaps helpful. When we are daydreaming we are not just switching off, but rather slipping into a different form of mental activity. In this sense, daydreaming is closer to going for a walk than sitting in an armchair.

But just as with the most relaxed of country walks, it is not to any particular end, but for the intrinsic joy of the exercise; it is not the destination but the journey which matters. Mind wandering at its best involves a gentle ramble, enjoying whatever we see along the way.

The ability to daydream is just as crucial as the ability to stay on task. In terms of research, this is a very new field, but perhaps if we understand it better and discover more about how to promote beneficial mind wandering, rather than worry and rumination, then one day we could have prescriptions to daydream.

For the time being, it seems to be something we like to do, but feel guilty about, and something we don't understand very well or do very well. And yet, for all that, we find it restful. The problem is that daydreaming is at odds with so many of the preoccupations of modern life. It is a natural state and can be done anywhere, yet we seem to need to give ourselves permission to lapse into it and to find places of sanctuary where we can do it safely.

We turn to one such place next – the bath.

7

A NICE HOT BATH

Eighty-year-old Amou Haji hasn't had a bath for more than sixty years. Or indeed washed at all in that time. If anyone dares to suggest he should bathe, he becomes angry because he believes that 'cleanliness brings on illness'. His face and beard are caked in mustard brown earth. He blends in so well with the barren landscape of southern Iran, where he lives in the desert, that when he sits still he resembles a rock sculpture. He survives by eating rotten porcupine carcasses, and he likes to smoke animal dung in his pipe. And when his hair gets too long he burns off the excess length with a naked flame. Not surprisingly, Amou lives alone. But when his story was reported online in 2014, he said he was looking for love.

Who knows if he found it? But if Amou is now living with a soulmate, he and his partner would stand out as a most unusual couple in the modern world. For most of us, as the results of the Rest Test show, *love* a bath, not just as a functional way of getting clean but as a great form of pampering and relaxation.

First comes the delicious shiver of anticipation as you run the bath, steam filling the bathroom. Then, after dipping your hand or foot into the water to test the temperature, comes the sensuous luxury of slowly easing yourself into the hot water. Next, you slide down until only your face is above the surface. And after that . . .

Well, you just lie there.

Apart from doing nothing (which as we'll discover in Chapter 5 is harder than it sounds) having a bath is perhaps rest at its purest. If you think back to the words people gave when they were asked what rest means to them, it's striking how well they describe the experience of having a bath.

> *Free Fulfilling Warm Restorative Recumbent Quiet Dark Dreamy Delicious Cool Clarifying Necessary Mindless Sublime Safe Serene Healing Precious Private Yearned for Unthinking Undisturbed Uplifting*

One reason for this is that while you're in the bathroom, particularly once you're in the bath itself, you're cut off from all those things that need doing around the house. That letter needs posting. Not now. There's a pile of ironing. Let it wait. Perhaps the one place in the home where you don't take your phone or laptop is the bathroom, so you can't attend to all those messages and emails. Okay, you can listen to the radio or read a book, but why bother?

What makes doing nothing difficult is that we feel guilty about it. It is a waste of time; we are being lazy. This is why many of us find we can't sit in a chair for long without feeling the need to jump up and do something. But a bath gives us the perfect get-out from our guilt. Yes, we are just lying there in the hot, steamy water, but at the same time we are getting clean. And we have to do that some way or another, don't we? So a bath isn't a waste of time, and it is more than an indulgence. It is in some sense a necessary task.

There are limits to this line of argument, of course. These days, the shower has replaced the bath for most people as the quick and hygienic way to wash, while a bath has become more obviously a treat. Even in our own homes, more and more of us take a bath in water infused with oils or crystals, or surround the bath with scented candles. A few have even had a spa bath or hot tub installed. So strictly speaking we might not really *need* a long hot soak, perhaps we simply find a bath lovely and restful at the end of the day.

Sharing a Bath With 18,000 Other People

In pre-history, Amou Haji's attitude to personal cleanliness wasn't the exception. It was the rule. He wouldn't have stood out among early humans. But bathing has featured in human life in civilisations around the world, though often as a largely public rather than a private activity. And attitudes to it have fluctuated over the centuries. Personal hygiene has always been a reason to bathe. But in different times and cultures, bathing has also been seen as important for health giving, as a religious obligation, as a social pastime, or as a form of sensual or even sexual pleasure.

The Ancient Greeks living in the Homeric age made frequent visits to public baths, chiefly as a way of getting clean. But spin forward some 600 years, to after 460 BC, in the time of Hippocrates, and the Greeks were taking the waters more in the hope of improving their health. By the time of the Roman Empire, public bathing was taking place on a vast scale. The Roman Baths of Caracalla were said to have held as many as 18,000 people, although some historians argue this is a daily visitor total rather than implying that 18,000 simultaneously crowded into the baths and that the true capacity was closer to 6,000. Either way, having a bath in Roman times must have been more like going to a major sporting event than the quiet and private experience we enjoy today. And at the time of peak bath enthusiasm, each resident of Rome was said to be using a staggering 1,400 litres of water a day.[1] No wonder the Romans became so adept at building aqueducts.

In the early days of the Roman Empire, the public baths were primarily places where soldiers could recuperate after battles if they were injured or exhausted. But in time, the baths also became places where the general populace went to rest and relax, and bathing was highly valued for its hygienic and physiological benefits. And of course bathing with several thousand close friends provided plenty of opportunity to socialise.

But as the baths became more geared towards relaxation, so they also became places of sexual practice, and it was the fear of public licentiousness which led the Christian church to ban bathing altogether after the fall of the Roman Empire; some bathhouses were converted into churches.

Despite this, bathing continued on a smaller scale through the so-called 'Dark Ages', when people were perhaps not as filthy and smelly as history books like to suggest. For instance, there is evidence that the monastic orders in the West took personal hygiene quite seriously, and of course other major religions have long used bathing as part of ritual purification, whether in fountains or in the sea or, in the case of Hindus, the River Ganges. The expression 'cleanliness is next to godliness' is attributed to the Methodist Minister John Wesley, speaking in the late eighteenth century. But the notion goes back to much earlier times and is shared to some extent by all major religions.

By the sixteenth century taking the waters in Europe was once again considered both health giving and fashionable, with the French essayist Montaigne devoting much of his famous travels in 1580 and 1581 to visiting mineral baths in Germany, Switzerland, Austria and Italy as he sought relief from the kidney stones that plagued him. The extent to which the minerals in the water could ease or even cure pain and suffering was disputed at the time and still is. But throughout the seventeenth, eighteenth, nineteenth and even early twentieth century, almost every Grand Tour of Europe or indeed local excursion by the upper or middle classes involved spas or baths of some sort. Just think of how many novels, from Jane Austen to Leo Tolstoy to Thomas Mann to Henry James, feature episodes in which the wealthy protagonists take the waters. By the nineteenth century, there were numerous grand and glamourous spa resorts across Europe and the USA. In some, the emphasis was very much on luxury and self-indulgence, and the resorts featured theatres, dance halls and even casinos. Others prioritised medical treatment using stringent and rigorous techniques which were sometimes far from restful. Charles Darwin famously visited a doctor in the English spa town of Malvern in 1849 in search of a cure for his nausea, dizziness and chronic headaches. For many weeks he endured vigorous rubbing with cold, damp towels and packing in freezing wet sheets, interspersed with perspiration baths.[2]

For poorer people, a public bathhouse was generally the only place they could go for a proper soak, but there was nothing luxurious or relaxing about the experience. Only in the last century, and only then in the developed world, have most people come to expect to have a bath in their home. And yet it seems the era of the ubiquitous private bath, with most of the population bathing at home several times a week, if not daily, might prove quite short-lived.

Back in 1938, in Shoreditch in east London, only one in seven homes had an indoor bath. These days, the district has given its name to a phenomenon called Shoreditchification. That is to say, the rapid gentrifying of an inner city, working-class neighbourhood in which greasy spoons have been converted into smart cafés selling smashed avocado on sourdough toast and corner shops have been turned into fancy boutiques selling £300 cashmere sweaters. If you want to buy a house or even a good-sized flat in the area, you are looking at paying a minimum of £1 million. You will certainly get a nice bathroom for that. What you aren't necessarily guaranteed is a bath.

Many new-builds, chiefly because of space, partly for environmental reasons, but also because of changing preferences, have bathrooms that only include a walk-in shower or wet room. After only a few decades, we are returning to a time when having a bath in your home in crowded inner-city neighbourhoods is not the standard. This development perhaps explains why this small area of London contains seven luxury spas. In places like Shoreditch, the public bath is back, as once again we see this see-sawing between bathing as an instrument of hygiene and bathing as an instrument of relaxing me time.

Keeping it Simple

I open today's Sunday paper to find an entire travel supplement devoted to health spas, thermal baths, hydrotherapy pool complexes and balneotherapy centres. If you can afford it, you can lie down and detoxify in a vaulted cellar of tactile limestone. You can luxuriate in a foamy wash down. You can slather yourself in seaweed-based organic products. You can take a dip in a bijou wild spa (which in the picture looks more like a muddy pond). You can enjoy spa experiences featuring hand-harvested herbs. You can feel the therapeutic power of a salt micro-climate. And if you feel in need of a rest after all that, you can lie back and gaze at intricate glazed brickwork and painted ceilings in rooms that draw inspiration from traditional Turkish bathhouses.

Despite my love of baths, I have made very few visits to anything that could be called a spa, but during these rare experiences I have been struck by how the experience oscillates between relaxation and a stricter kind of paternalism of the doctor-knows-best kind. There tend to be a lot of rules, rules which I tend to break unknowingly, including the issue of which items of underwear to take off and which to keep on. Everyone else seems to know what they're doing (clearly, they are spa regulars), but I seem to misjudge it, resulting in occasions like one in Austria, where the therapist said sharply, 'Knickers off! Now!'

Some may see having a bath as idling in your own warm filth, but I like nothing better. Somewhat surprisingly, the Rest Test suggested baths are particularly popular with one group to which I no longer belong – the young. Almost twice as many eighteen- to thirty-year-olds listed having a bath as restful compared with those over the age of sixty. Who knows why this is, though perhaps younger people find baths more of an indulgence than older people having grown up in the era of the power shower? Whatever the explanation, my young friends and I are on to something, because bathing is not just lovely and relaxing, it is good for you. And there is evidence to prove it.

Evidence on Tap

As Sylvia Plath wrote in *The Bell Jar*, 'there must be quite a few things a bath can't cure, but I don't know many of them'. I doubt the great American poet had read up on the scientific and psychological evidence, but, as I say, the evidence backs up her contention. I should start by saying that the bigger studies have tended to focus on the positive effects of taking thermal baths rather than bubble baths at home, but, as we shall see as we go on, there is research suggesting that a private bath can have positive effects too. Let's start with a major review of fifteen studies which concluded that thermal bathing can temporarily reduce levels of the stress hormone cortisol.[3] The researchers in this case concluded that the special minerals in the water were having their intended effect. But they also argued that the whole ritual of taking time out from a busy schedule to have a hot bath was also likely to play a part in lowering stress.

One of the studies reviewed found taking a spa bath was more effective in relaxing people than one of the prime relaxation techniques we'll hear about in Chapter 5. That technique is the body scan, during which you relax your body and your mind by starting off thinking about your head or toes and then systematically scan your way up or down the body, clenching and unclenching each muscle, one at a time. For some people this really works, but a spa bath may be even better.[4]

Then there is a curious study which focused on Lithuanian seamen. The seamen sat in baths of hot salty geothermal water that came from a bore hole more than a thousand metres underground, in rocks formed in the Lower Devonian period, roughly four hundred million years ago. The sailors had one of these special baths for fifteen minutes, five times a week, for two weeks. And a fortnight later, compared with control groups who either took part in music therapy or no particular activity, the bathing seamen had lower blood pressure, less pain, improved joint mobility, more positive mood and higher well-being.[5]

Finally in this quick tour of the best research on spa baths, there is the study I'd very much like to have taken part in. It took place at a spa just outside Freiburg in Germany. The participants not only soaked in a forty-degree Celsius pool for half an hour, but were then wrapped up in warm blankets with a hot water bottle to rest for another twenty minutes. Had no long-term benefits emerged from this activity, it would have been nice enough. But researchers found that eight weeks later depression had reduced in the thermal therapy group just as much as in an equivalent group who took part in a group exercise class twice a week instead.[6] Now, I'm not going to suggest that regular exercise isn't important, but it is rather delicious to find that a bath and lie down can be as good for your mental health as an aerobics class or a park run.

Of course, most of us don't live next to a natural hot spring and have to make do with what comes out of the taps in our bathrooms if we are to enjoy the psychological and physical benefits of a bath. And here the research, much of it from Japan, tends to focus on the impact of a hot bath on relaxing us ahead of going to bed and, eventually, to sleep.

But if you're assuming this is because the hot bath makes you feel warm and cosy as you prepare for bed you'd be wrong. In fact, counter-intuitively perhaps, a warm bath helps to induce our core body temperature to *fall* and it is this which aids sleep because in order to sleep well we need our body temperature to drop by about one degree Celsius from our waking state. This is also why you should never overheat your bedroom and why it's easier to fall asleep in a room that's too cold than too hot. As sleep scientist and bestselling author Matthew Walker puts it, a cooler room is 'dragging your brain and body in the correct downward temperature direction for sleep'.[7]

All this explains why if you tuck children snugly into bed, when you check on them later on you'll often find they've flung their arms and legs out from under the covers. What they are doing is cooling themselves down so they can sleep better. The hands and feet are rich with specialised heat-exchange blood vessels, so when we're too hot, blood is sent to the extremities where the heat can be radiated out via this web of vessels close to the surface of the skin. But how does having a hot bath help in this process? It does sound odd, but here is how a hot bath before bed helps to cool us down. What the bath does is rapidly heat up our core body temperature, which in turn means blood is sent out to our extremities so as to cool us down. In other words, a bath helps to *accelerate* the natural process of our body temperature falling slightly as we prepare for sleep, by inducing a temperature spike upwards which prompts a temperature spike downwards. Does that make sense?

But there is a proviso here – and you may have already guessed what it is. The help a hot bath provides in cooling our bodies down for sleep only works if we take a bath some time before going to bed. Indeed, research shows the ideal time for a hot bath is an hour or two before you get into bed, so that your temperature has begun to drop sufficiently before you get under the warm duvet.

And impractical as it sounds, a bath in the middle of the afternoon works even better. In one experiment, students who took a ninety-minute hot bath in the middle of the afternoon felt sleepier at bedtime and experienced more slow-wave sleep and more deep sleep (both signs of high-quality sleep rather than the tossing-and-turning kind) than those students who didn't take a bath.[8] Exactly what use we can make of this finding I'm not sure. I doubt many bosses will agree to us slipping away from work for an hour to take a bath in the afternoon. But perhaps it's worth trying at the weekend? And it is certainly worth having that weekday evening bath a little bit earlier than normal if you want to sleep better at night.

This is certainly true for one group of people: insomniacs. Scientists believe that difficulties in regulating body temperature through heat loss from the periphery of the body might be the cause of insomnia for some people. Such people stick their arms and even legs out from under the covers at night, but still the core of their body doesn't cool down enough. To explain why, we need to consider a strange but normal phenomenon. After you've read this next section you could even do some home experimentation and try it out for yourself.

First, put one of your hands in hot water for a few minutes. Of course, that hand gets warmer. But what about the other? It's not been in the hot water, but it gets warmer too. You may not notice but it is measurable. This is the body's way of regulating heat. Not only does the hot water heat the blood which spreads around the body heating it up, but once again those specialised blood vessels in the hands and feet widen in order to radiate the heat out, allowing the body to cool. In the short term, this makes your other hand hotter.

Now, how is this related to insomnia? Well, in a small study conducted in Australia this curious phenomenon didn't happen in people with insomnia. People who didn't suffer from insomnia held their left hand in hot water and the result was that the temperature of the right hand rose by an average of four degrees Celsius. But when the exercise was repeated with poor sleepers the temperature rise in their right hands averaged at a meagre 0.9 degrees. It appears that this impaired capacity to lose heat is keeping them awake at night.[9]

Now, if you want to sleep better but don't want to wait for a bath to run – or you don't have a bath – you could try having a hot footbath or wearing heated bed socks – special socks with removable soles filled with grain which can be heated up in the microwave.

Experiments have shown that your age can influence the effectiveness of these methods. Heated socks help young people get to sleep faster, while a thirty-minute footbath works better for older people.[10] In Taiwan and Japan several studies have tried footbaths specifically to help older people with insomnia to get to sleep, and it did seem to make a difference. Footbaths didn't prevent people from waking up in the early hours, but they did seem to help with relaxation and reaching the correct body temperature in order for people to fall asleep at the beginning of the night.

If you're in too much of a rush to get to bed for even a footbath, how about a quick shower? Some people only shower in the mornings unless it's so hot that they want to drench themselves in freezing water before bed. There is, though, some limited evidence that suggests a quick hot shower before bed can aid sleep. For instance, a study with young football players, who like many athletcs often sleep badly the night before a big match or competition, found a hot shower before bed helped them to drift off an average of seven minutes faster than usual.[11]

Baths as a Cure-All

If all this still isn't enough to convince you that a long, hot soak might be good for you, then how about this next study published in a journal with the simple title of *Temperature*? Researchers showed that an hour in a hot bath led men to burn the same number of calories as they did if they took a half-hour walk. Now, this might seem a little too good to be true – and bear in mind that the water was kept at a consistent forty degrees Celsius, so if you wanted to try this at home you would need to keep topping up the hot water in the bath, but the findings were clear: the glucose monitors worn by the men in the study showed their energy expenditure increased by 80 per cent while they were in the bath.

Is there an argument, then, for giving up exercise and just lying in a hot bath instead? Alas not. The same men still burned far more calories riding an exercise bike, so in terms of fitness the researchers are only suggesting hot baths as a remedy for those with metabolic disorders who can't exercise another way.[12] Even so, the power of good provided by a hot bath is impressive.

There are suggestions that hot baths might be good for your heart too. In a recent study, elderly Japanese people were asked how many baths they took in a week. The answers ranged from zero to a staggering twenty-four! (Up there with the Romans.) But the point is this: those who had five or more baths a week (about average for me) were found to have better heart and circulatory health.

But beware a bath that's too hot for too long. The Austrian philosopher Ludwig Wittgenstein liked his baths scalding hot, boasting about the temperatures he could withstand.[13] It is a strange thing to brag about, and perhaps not surprisingly it isn't a good idea. In bathing-obsessed Tokyo, the Medical Examiner's Office reported that an astonishing 3,289 sudden bath-related deaths occurred in just two years between 2009 and 2011. The majority of the people who died were over the age of sixty and died in winter. Heart problems were indicated in almost half of the cases, and a quarter of people were drunk. But worryingly a third of cases could not be explained. A probable factor in many of them was that people were having baths that were just too hot.[14]

Combine the Tokyo bath massacre with a case study from Korea in 2006, in which a man with diabetes suffered multiple organ failure due to heat stroke after spending three hours in a hot bath,[15] a similar case four years later in China where a patient died after bathing in a hot spring,[16] and an outbreak of infected hair follicles among bathers who used a contaminated hot tub in Alaska in 1985,[17] and you may start to feel baths aren't restful after all – or don't provide the type of rest you are looking for. But thankfully bath-induced deaths are rare.

Still, if you're worried about overheating, how about a nice *cold* bath? An oxymoron? With the recent trend for cold-water swimming, plenty of people are extolling the benefits of immersing yourself in freezing water to clear your mind, to invigorate your body and to raise your spirits. Friends of mine who live in a small town on the Firth of Forth in Scotland have long tried to persuade me to join them for a dip in the sea on New Year's Day. It is a local tradition, they say. And very 'stimulating' – by which they mean, I presume, *bloody agony*. It's okay, I say, I have my own tradition to recuperate after drinking too much on New Year's Eve: a long lie-in.

And it turns out that science is on my side. There's been a long-running debate on the health effects of hot versus cold baths, with most of the research focusing on elite athletes in search of optimal muscle recovery after a competition. But the evidence for the benefits of ice baths, I'm pleased to report, is rather lacking. Britain's star tennis player Andy Murray swears by them. After every match he has a shower, eats some food, has a massage and sits for eight long minutes in iced water kept at eight to ten degrees. He's not alone.

The Olympic Gold medal-winning heptathlete Jessica Ennis-Hill used to stand in a wheelie bin of iced water for the sake of her muscles.

Murray and Ennis-Hill believe that immersing the body in freezing cold water speeds up recovery after exercise by reducing the temperature, blood flow and inflammation in the tissues of the muscles, just as clamping a bag of frozen peas to your leg can reduce pain and swelling after you've pulled a muscle. For the occasional injury this works well, but professional athletes and keen amateurs also want to build muscle. This is where attempts to mitigate inflammation could prove counterproductive. If blood flow is reduced it can slow down the muscle's ability to rebuild itself after strain or injury.

Although some professionals are regularly leaping into ice baths, randomised controlled studies on the practice are rarer than you might think. A team based in Australia, Norway and Japan has compared ice baths with a gentle warm down (which is what many athletes do in practice).[18] The study was so complicated that it wasn't practical to involve large numbers of participants and just nine active men took part. They came into the lab on different days for a complex regime of lunges, squats, ice baths, leisurely cycling, blood tests and even biopsies taken from their thigh muscles.

The tests revealed that markers of inflammation in the muscle increased after exercise just as you'd expect, but ice baths made no difference to these levels and didn't help muscles to rest and recover. This will do for me. No ice baths, no cold showers and no swimming in the Firth of Forth on New Year's Day.

Still Waters Run Deep

I'm sticking up for hot baths then. There's just one more question to answer, the most important of all. Should you have bubbles in the bath? (And just for absolute clarity, I'm not talking about my very favourite batty book title, *Bubbles in the Bath* by Ivor Windy Bottom. No, the question involves the bath products that transform an ordinary bath into a champagne experience.)

The answer is yes – if you want the bath to stay hotter for longer. A layer of bubbles does provide some insulation for the water and prevents the heat escaping. As for whether bubbles in the bath make a bath more restful, I couldn't find any evidence to support the theory – though that doesn't mean it isn't true. The closest study I could find addressed a slightly different question: which is more relaxing – the hubble bubble of a whirlpool bath or a serene, still bath?

To clear up this vital matter a study was conducted in 1990 in a whirlpool showroom in Minnesota.[19] On reading the location of this research, I was instantly picturing customers wandering around the showroom, bewildered to find naked bathers sitting in each of the hot tubs they were thinking of buying. But it turns out the experiment was conducted on a Sunday when the shop was shut. Which is just as well for modesty's sake and for the sake of the shop's sales figures, because the results showed that a still bath is just as good at reducing anxiety and improving well-being as one with fancy jets and bubbles.

There is good news for baths in general from this study. Whether the participants in it had enjoyed their bath with bubbles or without, they all felt more rested afterwards. In reply to statements in a questionnaire they said things like: 'All my muscles are relaxed,' and rather sweetly, 'This is the life.'

Which about sums it up. Excuse me if I pause here. I don't want the bath to run over.

6

A GOOD WALK

Conversion through Immersion

I wasn't a fan of walking when I was younger. This was before I unwittingly went on an epic hike through Torres del Paine National Park in southern Chile. I say unwittingly: I went on the walk deliberately, of course, to see the three vast granite spires, the 'towers' that give the park its name. What I didn't know when I set off was how long and hard it would be. I had trusted my husband. 'It's a five-hour round trip,' he had assured me the previous night, as we lay in our bunks in the dormitory of a wooden *refugio*. Quite a hike, but I could manage that, I thought, before falling asleep.

Next morning our route took us through a flat green valley, then skirted a ridge of scree before following a shallow, rock-strewn river through a forest. At a certain point in the woods we had been advised by another back-packer to leave our rucksacks padlocked to tree trunks. It was harder going from here. We half-walked, half-scrambled up more scree and then clambered over boulders until we reached a lunar plateau and an impossibly blue lake. The sky was a wondrous blue too.

There ahead of us were the three immense, sheer, flat slabs of rock jutting out of the moonscape like giant, jagged paddles. These famed natural towers are so tall that climbers brave enough to scale them must spend the night halfway up, suspended in thin air, wind-buffeted, attached by clips and carabiners to their bracing bivvies, peering and peeing into the void.

It was a stupendous scene. Without doubt one of the greatest sights I have ever seen and well worth the physical effort to get to it. But five hours round trip wasn't quite right. In fact, my husband was out by a factor of two. We were well into the sixth hour as we sat eating our packed lunch, still taking in the awesome view, and we hadn't even started on the return stretch.

To begin with, the journey home was not too bad, and a café selling churros dipped in hot chocolate halfway back was my second favourite thing after the view, but for all the great scenery the last two or three hours were a hard slog. Only one thing kept me going.

Before we set off for the hike, we had chosen and booked a room in a cosy B&B, ready for our return, and this was the exciting bit – it was a room with a bath. All the way back from the three peaks I was fantasising about slipping into the hot waters of that bath, soothing my sore feet, my aching knees and burning thighs. But when we neared the clapperboard house, late in the evening in the darkness, we could see lights on in 'our' room. Some other couple were unpacking their rucksacks in there; one of them, no doubt, was about to step into 'my' hot bath! It was agonising, but perhaps there was an explanation. The explanation was this: we were so late turning up, the owner had assumed we weren't coming and given the room away.

So then we had an extra trek around town looking for another room for the night. I insisted on one with a bath.

I had also experienced a sort of epiphany. I went to bed that night exhausted and aching. I wasn't ready to forgive my husband for miscalculating – or for perhaps even lying about – how long the hike would take. Long sections of the walk had been not just tiring but boring. And yet I was in a blissful state. Yes, it was partly that I was proud of myself for walking so far. Yes, it felt great to have seen one of the natural wonders of the world. But it was more than that. I felt an immense sense of satisfaction and of inner peace. Now I understood why people liked walking. I've been a keen walker ever since, though this remains the longest walk I've ever done.

In my enjoyment of walking I am unusual only because I was a relatively late convert to its delights. Of the people who chose to complete the Rest Test, 38 per cent selected walking as one of their top three restful activities. Of course, many factors account for walking's popularity. In my case, a big factor was the magnificence of those unique rock formations on the three spires walk. More commonly, a large part of the pleasure of a long walk is that often it takes place in the countryside, away from concrete, busyness and traffic. Spending time in nature was the second most restful activity of all, and I'll come on to that in Chapter 2. But in this chapter I'm focusing on the other reasons, the physical and mental factors that make walking feel so restful, despite the effort and exertion it involves, which we tend to assume are the opposite of rest.

Nothing and Novelty

To go for a walk you need very little, apart from some time. One of walking's delights is its simplicity.

But the real key to the restful nature of walking is that it solves two of the biggest impediments facing us when we try to do nothing (much more on this in the next chapter). The first is feeling guilty. However much we might want to rest, however much we value it and feel it is good for us, we know that there are a hundred and one things we should be doing at home or in the office. These tasks are all around us – surfaces to wipe, lightbulbs to change, forms to fill in, reports to write. The moment you leave home or work to go for a walk, however, you have stepped away from all of that. All those things might still need doing, but they will have to wait. For as long as you are out walking, all you can do is walk – as long as you put your phone on silent, of course.

The American poet and essayist *Henry David Thoreau* was one of the early proponents of recreational walking. He observed that one of walking's great benefits is that it takes us away from the demands of the home and the workplace. 'I think that I cannot preserve my health and spirits, unless I spend four hours a day at least—and it is commonly more than that—sauntering through the woods and over the hills and fields, absolutely free from all worldly engagements . . . When sometimes I am reminded that the mechanics and shopkeepers stay in their shops not only all the forenoon, but all the afternoon too, sitting with crossed legs, so many of them – as if the legs were made to sit upon, and not to stand or walk upon – I think that they deserve some credit for not having all committed suicide long ago. I, who cannot stay in my chamber for a single day without acquiring some rust . . . confess that I am astonished at the power of endurance, to say nothing of the moral insensibility, of my neighbours who confine themselves to shops and offices the whole day for weeks and months, aye, and years almost together.'[1]

One of the things I most like about this passage is its inversion of a common assumption. It is not a long walk that requires stamina, Thoreau argues, it is sitting at your desk. This is an argument that has chimed with me as I have laboured over this book. He doesn't say it in so many words, but Thoreau understood that to walk is wonderfully restful. Restful for the mind certainly, but even for the body; stretching those legs is ultimately more relaxing than leaving them unused.

The other impediment to rest that a good walk removes is the fear of boredom. A walk can, of course, be boring in parts, but usually there's the natural scenery to divert you – the scintillating sea and white cliffs, rolling green hills and fields of yellow corn, high hedgerows and dark woods. Or if you're walking in a town, there's an ever-changing back-drop of houses and gardens (always interesting to me) and churches (less so) and public buildings and pubs. (A quick drink? Why not?)

And little things encountered along the way can distract and fascinate. Aren't those footprints abnormally large? That's a very curious stile. What bird was that calling?

But even when there is nothing external to distract you, the repetitive rhythm of walking somehow makes monotony absorbing. You can get lost on a walk, but you can also get lost *in* a walk. Even when a walk is a means to an end – that walk from home to the station, for instance – it can also be an end in itself: a rare time in the day when you are not thinking about something else. I know that I use walks between office meetings in London not as a time to collect my thoughts or mentally prepare for what's ahead but to switch off for a few minutes. And it is the rhythm of walking that allows me to do it.

By seeming contrast, in her book *Wanderlust*, on the history of walking, Rebecca Solnit writes that the only time she felt she had permission to think hard about her book was when she went for a walk, Of course, she could have sat at her desk and thought. But these days thinking in itself is not viewed as a productive way of using our time. It is seen as doing nothing, which the modern mind can't stand even though it is the required state for deep thought. So how can we put ourselves into this deep thinking mode? 'It's best done by disguising it as doing something,' Solnit suggests, 'and the something closest to doing nothing is walking.'[2]

I don't have a car, so walking is how I get to anything nearby – shops, the doctor's surgery, friends' houses, restaurants and bars. The result is an intense familiarity with certain local streets, as I have walked up them hundreds of times. I bump into neighbours and chat. I read the lost cat signs tied to lamp posts with string – Sweetcorn, Leo and Lucy, all missing, all 'much-loved'. If it's dark and houses are lit up, I look in the windows, imagining the lives inside. Late at night I often see foxes sniffing the pavement ahead of me as they scavenge for food. They see me coming, but they're not afraid. They amble off when they're ready.

Of course, when the sky is dark navy, and heavy rain is falling, and my shopping bags are welding creases into my hands, I curse that I live at one end of a long road away from the shops, and fantasise about discovering one day that the road has been miraculously shortened. Not every walk I take in my neighbourhood is restful or absorbing or enjoyable.

But the moment I spend a night in a place where I can't just wander out of the door, I miss having the chance to walk. Sometimes when I've travelled for work, I've stayed in areas where it's not safe to walk out of the hotel, either because of high crime rates or more often because it's assumed no one wants to walk and the busy road has no pavement. I remember once asking the receptionist in a motel in the USA which direction I should head in for a walk and she looked utterly baffled. What was it I needed? Where did I want to go? When I said I just wanted to see the area, she couldn't understand why I didn't just take a drive in my rental car. As it happened, I wish I had. My walk that day, beside freeways and under overpasses and through shopping malls, was not a nice one.

Generally, however, a walk is a great way to discover a new place. Walking speed is just right for taking things in. The pace is perfect for us to absorb our surroundings, leave room for a few distractions, but no space for worrying about other aspects of our lives. The pace is slow enough not to overwhelm the senses, allowing our minds to wander. It's the perfect balance between nothing and novelty.

Slowing the Pace

Another restful aspect of walking is that it changes our perception of time. Or more precisely, perhaps, sets it to a rate that feels natural. We must sacrifice some time in order to take a walk, but that initial outlay is more than repaid as time seems to expand as we walk. It slows down as we slow down – to a walking pace.

When our minds try to assess how much time has passed one of the cues we use is the distance we've moved in space. Modern transport, which takes us across vast distances at great speed, has messed with these cues. It is most noticeable in the case of planes, which go so far so fast that distance and time are out of sync. For all the actual time we've travelled, and the boring length of the flight, it sometimes seems we have arrived before we've set off. Or that we have lost days and nights along the way. Our body clocks struggle to catch up. By contrast, we are so accustomed to car journeys that the fact that they diminish distance and so in effect speed up time now feels normal. It no longer disorientates us. But one positive effect is to make our natural speed – the speed at which we walk – seem slower to us, and therefore to expand our perception of time passing. At the end of a four-day trip walking through part of the Czech Republic, pleasingly wearied by our exertion, we took a bus back to the town from which we had set off. The vast tract of land that had taken us four days to conquer on foot took just twenty-five minutes to traverse on the bus. We were immediately back in the modern mode of life where time seems to speed by. From this town, we took another bus journey to a bus station in Prague, then the metro into the city centre. This transit day was both boring and fleeting. None of the details stick in my mind. By contrast, every part of the walk remains in my memory. So, both at the time and looking back, the act of walking appears to stretch and deepen time. This is why we find walking so restful. So much of life these days is speeded up. Walking slows us down.

In the Footsteps of Giants

'Walking allows us to be in our bodies and in the world without being made busy by them. It leaves us free to think without being wholly lost in our thoughts.' In these two sentences Rebecca Solnit has summed up the unique qualities of a walk. Both the body and the mind are involved and by just the right amount.

Like Rebecca Solnit, Beethoven, Dickens, Goethe, Kierkegaard, Nietzsche, Wordsworth, Kant and Aristotle (to name just a few) were all fans of a long ramble – and for the same reason: because it gave them the opportunity to think. 'All truly great thoughts are conceived by walking,' wrote the philosopher Nietzsche in 1889. Writing a century earlier, Rousseau insisted it was the only way he could concentrate, 'When I stop, I cease to think. My mind only works with my legs.' The rest of us may not have the talent of these great people, but we will have shared a common experience. We are stuck on something. We give up and go out for a stroll. We stop thinking about the thing we are stuck on and – if we're lucky – the solution comes to us. I'm sure many of us have said we're going for a walk to 'clear our heads'. What we mean is that our minds are knotted up with problems. A walk seems to unravel the knots. To sweep away the clouds.

There is good research evidence that walking helps to increase our creativity. Researchers at Stanford University randomly assigned people to four different activities: walking on a treadmill indoors in front of a blank wall, sitting on a chair indoors in front of a blank wall, walking around the university campus, and sitting in a wheelchair while someone else pushed them around the same route through the campus. Then the participants were given a test of creativity. Their task was to come up with as many uses as possible for an everyday object such as a button (one person suggested using it for a tiny sieve, which I think is sweet). To score a point the answers had to be so original that no one else taking part in the study had made the same suggestion. But it's no good suggesting the button could be used as a space-ship because that is unfeasible. In the paper they call it 'the production of appropriate novelty'. They give the example of suggesting lighter fluid could be used as a soup ingredient. This, they say with some understatement, is original, but not appropriate. The researchers found that walking outdoors was the best activity for freeing up the flow of ideas. This was followed by walking indoors and then being pushed around in a wheelchair outside. Sitting indoors came – appropriately perhaps – bottom.[3]

And while we're on the subject of puns, I did notice that the researchers in this study sprinkled their paper with them, something you don't often see in dry academic papers. Phrases such as 'putting observations on a solid footing' and 'putting your best foot forward' were used and the title is 'Give your ideas some legs', which made we wonder whether the researchers followed their own advice and took some long walks to unleash their creative writing powers.

By the way, to reassure wheelchair users, the authors note that had the people assigned to wheelchairs been allowed to push themselves, their creativity may well have been just as high as that of the walkers. What is clear from this research and other studies is that there is something about movement under our own steam that seems to free us up to think. Of course, Aristotle and the rest knew that already, but the point of research is not always to discover new things but rather to confirm our intuitions scientifically.

But it is not just enhanced creativity (and, of course, improved fitness) that we get from walking. If we walk with another person, the evidence suggests we experience increased levels of empathy and become better at cooperating. As we walk side-by-side we begin to synchronise our movements without even realising it. Automatically we pause the conversation to cross a busy road or because something we pass grabs our attention. Then through unspoken rules we return to conversation, as though we'd never broken off from it. If a group of people is instructed to walk in synchrony, there is evidence that they even become more willing to make sacrifices for the group. For this reason it has been suggested that conflict negotiations should take place while the warring parties are out on a shared walk.[4] Instead of confronting each other across the conference table, which accentuates fixed positions, the negotiators would be alongside each other, looking out on the world. I doubt this has been trialled in real peace talks, but it sounds like an idea worth testing.

Picture men and women in suits embarking grave-faced on hikes together, becoming inspired to find creative compromises as they stroll along Alpine paths. Wouldn't it be wonderful if delegates could descend into a valley one late afternoon, exhausted and exhilarated, and say, 'Hey, we've solved the Syrian civil war!'

Of course, there is always the chance that the peace hike passes in stony silence. I'm quite a chatty walker. I'm quite a chatty person. But even for me, sometimes walking – even alongside someone else – lends itself perfectly to the restfulness of not having a conversation. The French philosophy professor and writer Frédéric Gros describes walking with another person as a 'shared solitude'.[5] You can speak if you choose to, but no one has to fill the silence because the silence is already filled with walking. Solitude side-by-side perhaps. It reminds me of porch-sitting, an idea from counselling where people sometimes feel more able to discuss personal issues when they are sitting beside rather than opposite someone. Likewise, some parents find that the easiest time to talk to their teenager is when they're driving and the adolescent is in the passenger seat. You can talk without having to face each other. The talk doesn't have that element of staged confrontation.

With walking there's an added element. Because you are slightly removed from your everyday world, just as you are given permission to think, you are given permission to discuss the issues once removed from the humdrum and quotidian – such as your relationship, or the future, or the meaning of life, or even what happens after death. The point is, walking frees us not just to think, but to think deeply. Is that restful? Well, sometimes it is in thinking about the most profound questions that we find the deepest peace.

Rest from Exhaustion?

Walking has all sorts of benefits, but when it comes to rest there is still the paradox that true rest surely means stopping, whereas walking is all about forward momentum. This raises a broader question: when we talk about rest, is it the mind or the body that we are trying to rest? Can exhausting one free the other to rest? Or is true rest about getting the right relationship between the two?

Steve Fowler is a now a poet, but he used to be a cage fighter. He's so gentle that you wouldn't guess it when you meet him. But he is still very fit and strong. Nowadays he throws punches not at opponents but at punch bags in a gym, pummelling and pummelling until he is shattered. He has even made films of 'exhaustion performances' where he has punched and kicked for several hours, continuing when he is clearly shattered. But this, he insists, is how he achieves restfulness.

He told me that he often feels extremely fidgety and that exercising to the point of exhaustion is the fastest way for him to reach a rested state where he is no longer restless. And afterwards he's not only more creative when it comes to his poetry but is sure that he's become a nicer person. He also mentioned something to me which might get to the heart of why extreme exertion can be restful. He finds it is the most direct way of taking 'himself out of himself'.

The activity Steve Fowler is describing is of course far more energetic than walking, but he's not alone. In addition to the 38 per cent of people who chose walking as restful, another 16 per cent chose exercise of some kind and 8 per cent said that even running is restful. Running is surely the opposite of rest: not sitting but standing; not still, but moving; not breathing slowly, but fast; not resting your muscles, but activating them. Yet many do count it as rest, and even find it essential as a route to restfulness.

I will come back to walking soon, but I wonder whether there's something we can learn from the runners. One foot in front of the other. One foot in front of the other. One foot in front of the other. A senior executive who's an endurance runner in his spare time once told me if you keep repeating this mantra you can keep going for mile after mile after mile. Far further than you might think possible. One foot in front of the other. If you just keep swinging your legs, he said, there's no stopping you. He used the phrase to motivate himself to run all night across rocky sand dunes in Morocco when he took part in the Marathon de Sables. The name implies one marathon – 26 miles, 385 yards – but, in fact, it involves completing six marathons in a row. Those who drop out halfway through (the lightweights) are termed 'abandoned' and have to wear green armbands to mark them out at the cluster points. Despite the embarrassment, they might at least be glad of the chance to rest, I thought, but no, he tells me, they're beyond gutted. And I suppose if you feel as upset as that about anything, you're not in a restful state.

New research could shed some light on why extreme exercise could be considered restful. Neuroscientists have discovered that the brains of elite distance runners have different patterns of connections from those of more sedentary people. Even while these runners are at rest, lying in a brain scanner, doing nothing in particular, there is an increase in coordinated activity in the areas related to working memory and executive function . . . and reduced activity in the default mode network – the brain's chatter. This work is at a preliminary stage, but it echoes the neural patterns found in the brains of experienced, regular meditators. The more frequently the athletes took part in endurance events, the stronger the effect. It was as if running was having a meditative effect on the brain. The bodily exertion was allowing the brain to rest, allowing the brain's chatter to quieten down. And this effect even lasted after the running had stopped. Perhaps something less extreme happens with walking too. Frédéric Gros has called it the 'western form of meditation'.

Still, you have to wonder how much the restfulness of exercise is connected with the joy of stopping. I run regularly (although I'm not sure the endurance runner would even call it running), and although I miss it if I can't go, the best bit probably is getting home at the end and resting in a self-satisfied kind of way. Stopping is one of the joys of walking too. Rousseau said, 'I like to walk at my ease, and to stop when I like.' If you're walking alone you don't even have to consult anyone else. You pause when you please and take in the views of countryside and bask in the warm glow of your achievement. You might find somewhere out of the wind to shelter, under a rocky outcrop perhaps. The jam sandwich squashed at the bottom of your rucksack, that you wouldn't choose to eat under any other circumstances, now tastes good. When you eventually get home and can rest properly, the weariness you feel is somehow a delicious kind of tiredness, not the kind of stiff fatigue you feel after too many hours working at your desk, not the aching muscles you get after overdoing it at the gym, but a satisfying feeling that now, at last, you really can . . . rest.

The question remains as to whether more expert exercisers do enjoy every moment of their sixth marathon or are they mainly looking forward to finishing? The only way to find out is to ask them and hope that they answer you honestly, which is exactly what one team of researchers did with a group of marathon runners. First, these runners were trained to give a running commentary on their own thoughts. The process went something like this:

Imagine I asked you to name twenty animals and to talk through your thought processes. Try it out. It's quite fun and quite interesting. Here's mine: dog, cat, mouse, how about some big animals? Lion, tiger, elephant, whale, dolphin, porpoise, and while we're in the water, seal and walrus. Some small wild animals – fox, stoat, badger, rabbit, hare, deer – is that enough yet? No, need some more – beaver, otter. There must be some more African animals I've not had – leopard, cheetah, lion. Have I had that? Maybe I have. Monkeys. Haven't had those. Chimpanzees, gorillas, lemurs. Must be enough by now. Thinking of wildlife films for some ideas – flying frogs, crocodiles, alligators, snakes. Surely that's twenty. Lizards. Hard to stop now.

Once the runners had practised this sort of exercise they set out running and recorded their commentary on the thoughts that came to them. We can't be entirely certain the runners were being honest all the time, but still the results were interesting.

When I run I am constantly distracted from the act of running itself. Sometimes, that is because I am listening to podcasts or music. At other times, I'm distracted by things I see in the street. But the serious marathon runners were different: 72 per cent of their thoughts concerned their pace, their distance, their pain and discomfort and how they must keep going. Just 28 per cent of their thoughts focused on the landscape, the weather or the traffic. Here are some examples they gave of the self-talk they did in order to motivate themselves: 'Don't go to negative town! No negative town. Starting over, not a big deal,' said a runner called Laurie. And when running up a steep hill, 'Mental – it's mental,' said Bill.[6] There's not much here to suggest that they were finding the experience restful, but maybe that came later. Concentrating on your running is probably the key to success if you're entering competitions, but if you want exercise to escape from everything else, and in order to free your mind to rest and refresh you, then letting the mind wander is probably the better course.

A Rest from Sitting Down

Walks distract our minds and tire out our bodies, leaving us feeling more rested, but there is another way to view walking, particularly brief walking – as a rest from sitting down. Office workers now tend to spend up to 75 per cent of their time sitting at their desks, much of that is unavoidable – it is not as if they can just go off for a hike for a few hours during office hours. But the good news is that they don't need to. Even micro-bouts of walking have been shown to make a difference to well-being, if not to fitness levels.

In one study people had to sit working at a computer for six hours, only leaving the desk when they needed 'to void', as the researchers put it in the paper. (How's that for a euphemism that is somehow more disgusting than just spelling it out.) At the start of the day half of these same people walked moderately fast on a treadmill for thirty minutes. The others in the study did the same amount of walking, but in five-minute intervals every hour. Which group do you think felt more rested and energetic at the end of the day? The answer is: those who did the walking in tiny bursts. Both groups felt they had more energy immediately after their walk, but for the people doing the micro-bouts the effects lasted all day. When they were ready to go home, they were not only in a better mood, but felt less hungry than the people who did the single, longer walk. So to get the restful benefits from walking you don't need to live in the foothills of a mountain and take long hikes every afternoon. You don't even need to take a long walk through the city. Simply getting up from your desk and having a quick wander around the building can refresh, restore and rest you.

Assuming you can stop for a lunchbreak, which of these two options do you think would help you to achieve restfulness: a fifteen-minute walk in the local park or fifteen minutes spent doing relaxation exercises? Finnish research found that the answer was either, but that they worked in different ways.[7] After both activities people felt less tired and more able to concentrate in the afternoon than usual. The relaxation worked best when people felt they had switched off from work, while the walking was most effective when people enjoyed the excursion. The lesson here is that if you're choosing an activity to refresh you, it either needs to be something that stops you thinking about work or something you simply enjoy for its own sake.

Plenty of research has found that exercise improves our mood and that it might even help to prevent negative moods by making us more resistant to stress. These kinds of studies have tended to focus on more energetic exercise than walking, but recently researchers scoured the best studies from around the globe in the hope of working out the ideal intensity of exercise for improving mood. Is walking just as good as running? And how long do you need to spend doing it? The good news is that ten to thirty minutes is enough to a make a difference. Neither running nor walking stood out ahead of the other, so maybe the key is to choose the activity you are most likely to actually do. The researchers did find, incidentally, that the greatest improvement in mood came from activities such as weightlifting, which are distracting and not too unpleasant, while achievements are easy to measure, leading you to feel good about having done well. Which to my mind begs the question: *weightlifting?*

A study in 2018 of more than a million people in the USA found that walking was linked with a 17 per cent lower rate of mental health difficulties.[8] The researchers took a snapshot in time, so we can't be certain that walking prevents or reduces problems; it's possible that people who are already in distress can't face going for a walk. With any cross-sectional study like this we have to be careful about causation. Did walking protect against mental illness or do people who are ill do less walking? But another 2018 study overcame this methodological issue by following 34,000 people for a decade. This time researchers found that if people had not had depression previously, regular exercise did protect against them experiencing it in the future. Of course, it didn't prevent every case of depression, but the figures from this study show that if everyone had exercised for an hour a week, 12 per cent of cases of depression could have been prevented. Again, the good news here is that walking is just as good as running, in terms of mental health, which means people who are not particularly physically fit can see the benefits.

But take care if you're thinking of asking someone with depression whether they've tried exercising. Although GPs sometimes prescribe exercise for patients with depression, often with success, I know people with depression who hate that people constantly ask them whether they've thought about taking up running. Running is not for everyone, even if it is beneficial. And while most of us have to do some walking, not everyone enjoys it. A theme of this book is that there are different paths to restfulness and we should find the way that suits us best. That said, there is also good evidence that people sleep better at night on the days when they've exercised.

Now, there is one other curious element in the relationship between rest and exercise that I need to mention. In the Rest Test we found that the people who do more exercise also believe that they get more rest. And they're right. In the preceding twenty-four hours they reported spending a greater number of hours resting in general than people who exercised less. The reason is simple when you think about it. As well as finding the exercise itself restful, people who exercise tend to reward themselves with sedentary rest afterwards. A double whammy.

Counting Every Step

Back when I was converted to the joys of walking on that hike in Chile, there was no such thing as a Fitbit or a step-counting app. Cereal packets sometimes gave away pedometers, but not many people used them. If I'd had the app then that I have now, barely a quarter of the way through the walk bright green confetti would have been flowing down the screen of my phone, congratulating me on reaching

10,000 steps. Would it have given me a boost? Perhaps. But perhaps not in the best way.

The rise of the Fitbit shows just how many people today are not only keen to walk, but to measure their walking, to quantify it, to visualise it on a graph and then receive the equivalent of primary school gold stars for their achievements. I am one of those people. But maybe if I want walking to be restful, I should rethink that.

This is the age of 'the quantified self', where people are using technology to track everything from their moods to the number of times they pee. In terms of fitness, it's surely a good thing if we find ways of encouraging ourselves to move more. After all, Public Health England released figures in 2017 estimating that four out of ten middle-aged people don't even manage a brisk ten-minute walk each month.[9]

But is counting steps the best way to persuade yourself to walk more? And is there a risk that quantifying a walk might rob it of its restfulness? When researchers in the US compared two groups of people trying to lose weight, one with a step counter and one without, they found that those counting steps ended up losing fewer, rather than more, pounds.[10] Then in a British experiment thirteen- and fourteen-year-olds were armed with Fitbits for eight weeks. At first, the teenagers liked the novelty of the gadget and enjoyed competing against each other, but soon they were bored and complained the 10,000-steps-a-day goal was unfair because it was too high.[11]

Maybe they were just looking for excuses. But they have a point. I've long wondered where this magic figure of 10,000 comes from, apart from being a nice round number. It turns out that it all goes back to the Tokyo Olympics in 1964.

Shortly before the games began a company started marketing a pedometer called the Manpo-Kei. In Japanese, *man* means 10,000, *po* means steps and *kei* means meter, so it was the '10,000-step-meter'. It was a huge marketing success and ever since then the number has stuck. Later on, studies were conducted into the health benefits that came from doing 5,000 versus 10,000 steps and not surprisingly the latter led to higher fitness levels. But we shouldn't make the mistake of thinking that a whole range of goals has been extensively tested, with 10,000 coming out on top. For all we know there might be a point where the extra benefit of doing more steps starts to wear off: 9,000 might be the optimum number or it could be 11,000. Brand new research has just found that for women in their seventies, the benefits of walking in terms of living longer seem to plateau at around 7,500. It was the jump from 2,700 steps to more than 4,000 that had the biggest impact on health.[12] Then there's the question of what the optimum number is in psychological terms. For someone regularly doing a fifth of that number, 10,000 will seem a high and almost impossible target, which might discourage them from even trying, while people who reach the goal easily might be tempted to stop at the magic 10,000 when they could be doing more.

The upside of step counters is that they show you how easy it is for a couple of days to pass by without you walking much at all, even if you consider yourself to be busy and active. If you are someone who finds walking restful, maybe you should rethink the Fitbit as a Restbit, to tell you whether you've devoted enough time to that all-important rest. But beware the pedometer taking the pleasure out of walking. Jordan Etkin, a psychologist at

Duke University in the USA, found that people who tracked their steps walked further but enjoyed the walk less, even when they had chosen to wear the pedometer. They said tracking their steps made walking feel more like work and, crucially, their happiness levels at the end of the day were lower.[13] If you think back to the study where people walked for fifteen minutes in their lunchbreak, the effectiveness of walking in refreshing them depended on how much they enjoyed the walk. So, if counting steps reduces the intrinsic pleasure of walking, it might also spoil its restful effects.

If you use a step counter you should also remember that it's a blunt instrument which ignores your age or the speed at which you're moving. As I mentioned at the start of this section, my counter rewards me with more digital green confetti for walking 10,000 steps than for running 9,000, when of course the running does more for my fitness. The answer is to use the step counter as a guide, but make up your own rules, since only you know what other activities you might have done. And if you're really determined to reach your goal every day but don't want to ruin your rest, there are ways of cheating of course – put it on your dog, attach it to a metronome or rent a walker to stride around the park for you. Meanwhile, you can be lazing in a hammock.

More seriously, there are strategies for fitting more walking into your every day life without being spurred on by a step counter. Try getting off the bus one stop earlier than usual or walking in the street parallel to your normal route, which means walking slightly further but keeps it interesting. If you do get bored with the same streets, look up. The tops of buildings, particularly in roads lined with shops, are more varied than you might think. Likewise, if you're in the countryside don't only look around at head height. My naturalist father is excellent at spotting the wildlife I fail to notice, and I've noticed that he does it by constantly scanning at ground level and way up into the trees and sky, as well as at eye level. The more you see, the more distracting and restful your walk can become. And remember that what we're trying to do here is get enough rest, so it's important not to make yourself feel guilty for not walking constantly. Or always pushing yourself further. And if you don't feel like going out for a walk, but feel you really should, try motivating yourself by reframing your walk as going for a rest.

Throughout this book I've talked about how we need a balance between rest and activity each day. And I wonder whether walking is a special way of resting because of its inherent internal balance. It lets us off working, but while we do it we're not exactly doing nothing, so can obtain some peace without feeling guilty. We have permission to think, but we also have distractions.

DOING NOTHING IN PARTICULAR

Bartleby

'I would prefer not to,' is the answer Bartleby the scrivener gives when he is asked to examine a legal document by his boss. 'I would prefer not to,' is his response when he is asked to bring copies of papers for proofreading. A request to run an errand to the post office elicits the same response: 'I would prefer not to.'

Bartleby is a fictional legal clerk working on Wall Street in the 1850s who appears in a short story by Herman Melville. He has been called the most radically lazy person in nineteenth-century literature,[1] though Oblomov, the eponymous hero of Ivan Goncharov's novel, might dispute that. (Could he be bothered, though?) Much of the humour in 'Bartleby, the Scrivener' comes from Bartleby's boss finding himself helpless in his attempts to counter his clerk's passive resistance. And infuriatingly for our unnamed narrator, and for us, Bartleby never gives any further explanation for his inactivity. He just prefers it to the alternative. Soon he is doing no work at all, simply staring at the wall all day. Even when he is sacked, given his final pay packet and asked to leave, naturally he says: 'I would prefer not to,' and doesn't. Eventually the lawyer is driven to move offices in order to escape from Bartleby.

Bartleby is a virtuoso at doing nothing, a master of the art. But does his doing nothing equate to resting? Oblomov is more of an idler. He wouldn't dream of going into an office; he can't be bothered to get out of bed. By contrast, Bartleby has to be quite focused and determined. He shows that to do no work at all is actually quite hard work. Doing just enough to keep his boss off his back would have been easier.

So, keeping the example of Bartleby in mind is useful when we consider the restfulness of doing nothing. Of course, in a sense, doing nothing is rest in its purest form. What could be more restful? It is no surprise then that in the Rest Test 'doing nothing in particular' proved popular, coming in at number five in the top ten. But dig a little deeper, and we find that while doing nothing is a popular way to rest it isn't something that most people find easy.

In our survey 10 per cent of people told us they find rest of any kind so difficult that it makes them feel guilty. How hard must it be for these people to do nothing? In Bartleby's case doing nothing was difficult because of the demands of his employer, but often the only one stopping us from doing nothing is ourselves. Even watching a trashy TV programme can feel preferable to sitting on the sofa not doing anything at all. At least you're doing *something* – if someone asks the next day what you did last night, it is socially acceptable to say you watched a bit of telly. Or maybe listened to music. Or you might even answer 'nothing much', meaning you pottered about. But to actually confess to 'sitting and doing nothing'? How comfortable would you feel about admitting that?

To the modern mind, Bartleby's fondness for just sitting there staring at the wall comes across as bizarre. It disturbs and troubles us. This is no route to restfulness. It is why the 'in particular' part of our desire to 'do nothing' is important. In fact, we are always doing something, if not physically then mentally. And more than that, to achieve even the illusion of doing nothing generally requires quite a lot of focus and discipline, and these days even a brand name and a guidebook and a guru. This doing nothing business can get tiring. But that's not to say we shouldn't try to do less. In this chapter, I will be showing the benefits of not exactly doing nothing but of almost doing so. As ever, it is a question of balance. Not all or nothing, and not simply a mid-point between the two, but because most of us need more rest, a gentle tilt towards the latter.

When Rest Can Kill

We have a love/hate relationship with the absence of activity. When we're busy it's what we yearn for, but as soon as we're free to idle we tend not to. Instead, we fill up this free time with other activities. We don't have to do anything perhaps, but still we do. Working people often dream of retirement. Yet when the time to retire gets closer they often dread the prospect. All those hours and nothing in particular to do. Yet doing nothing in particular can turn out to be quite time consuming. Once it's happened, retired people often say they 'don't know where time goes', that 'the days just fill themselves'. Increasingly, people who are retired have only retired from formal work. In many ways – book clubs, ramblers, pilates, University of the Third Age courses, cruises – they are as busy as people of working age. But even those who claim they 'do nothing' are often closer to doing 'nothing much' or 'nothing in particular' than 'nothing at all'. They are happily pottering – reading the paper, sorting things out, going to the shops, making lunch, mending things, tidying up, watching *Pointless* perhaps, thinking about supper and, before they know it, the day is done.

Yet it does seem there is a part in all of us that does still yearn to do nothing at all. It is why many of us have a sneaking affection for the sloth. Oh, to slow right down and hang upside down from a tree all day. The sloths have turned the hammock habit into a way of life. In fact, their name slanders these animals; they're not lazy as such. Or rather, they are lazy for a purpose. The less energy they expend, the less food they need, so it makes sense for them to stay still. Plus they digest their food very slowly. Perhaps it's more accurate to say that they aren't doing nothing as such; they're digesting. A 1970s study observed that it took fifty days from the moment the sloth finished eating a meal to that food leaving its body (or voiding, as some researchers like to put it, as we learned in Chapter 6). But sloths are rather particular about their toilet. Despite their general lack of physical activity, they make the effort to come down from the tree and do their business neatly on the ground. It troubles conservationists that sloths are fastidious in this way because it leaves them prone to attack by the increasing number of dogs that run wild in the country. Up in the trees, the stationary habit of sloths disguises them from predators. And indeed from tourists keen to see them on jungle walks.

Perhaps sloths are helping to change the meaning of a word which traditionally has such bad connotations that it makes it into the Seven Deadly Sins. Thomas Aquinas, the medieval theologian, in his *Summa Theologiae*, outlines the problem. Sloth, he says, is 'sluggishness of the mind which neglects to begin good' and that makes sloth 'evil in its effect' as it stops us doing God's work. And it isn't just the Christian tradition that takes a dim view of doing nothing. Hippocrates said 'Idleness and a lack of occupation tend – nay are dragged – towards evil.'

This is probably a bit much for most of us these days. But even if we don't see doing nothing as evil or a sin, we feel it is bad. It must be – because we all know that effort is good. Effort leads to achievement and success. Doing nothing does not. Activity leads to fitness and long life. Doing nothing does not. Sedentary lifestyles are bad. Sitting is the new smoking, say the headlines. I'm even writing this at a standing desk, not daring to do something that has been compared with puffing away on a cigarette. In Scandinavia many workplaces have standing desks as standard fixtures. They are becoming more common in the UK. Soon standing will be the new sitting.

As for lazing in bed? Don't even think about it. Or not beyond the odd lie-in. Spending extended periods in bed is so bad for our health that it's been used as a proxy for space flight in order to estimate the damage that weightlessness can have on the body. Complete bed rest might sound nice but it leads to reductions in calcium absorption, body weight, muscle mass and muscle strength, as well as alterations in

117

bone density, bone stiffness and circadian rhythms.[2] Even people recovering from major operations or severe illness are made to get out of bed as soon as possible. Lying down for long periods can literally kill you. Even for the more vertical of us, if we don't move about enough we are in trouble. There's good evidence that a sedentary life raises your risk of obesity, type 2 diabetes, heart disease, stroke and cancer.

With all these health warnings flying about, you could be forgiven for thinking that there is nothing to be said health-wise for sitting and doing nothing in particular. But again it's all about balance and rhythm. Moments of rest where you do nothing are fine as long as that is not *all* you do all day. I'll go further than that. It's not only okay, but good for you. As we'll discover, taking a break matters.

Owl and Proud

Moral judgements about rest are at their most severe when it comes to doing nothing. We have invented phrases which make doing nothing sound more carefree and casual – chilling, loafing around, vegging out – but whatever we call it in the modern age, we still fear that idleness is wrong. We strongly associate doing nothing with laziness and fear that the only way it can take us is down.

Imagine staying in bed for an hour after you've woken up staring at the ceiling, looking out of the window if you can, letting your mind wander where it will. There's nothing wrong with starting the day this way, yet as a society we can't help but view the larks, people who are up bright and early and allegedly raring to go, as more energetic, more virtuous – as *better*. They are admiring the dawn light, probably after making healthy fresh juices to set them up for their pre-work swim. The owls on the other hand are slobs, layabouts, slackers. While the larks are making the most of the morning the owls are snoring away, fast asleep – or worse perhaps, awake but lying in bed, doing nothing.

You might have guessed by now that I am an owl. Or to put it more scientifically, because it doesn't sound so bad, and reminds us that there is a genetic basis for not liking early mornings, I have a late chronotype. Though having sought to justify myself through science I wonder why I feel the need to do so. I should be owl and proud.

Between 5 and 10 per cent of the population are at the extreme ends of the early/late spectrum. These are the people who nod off at the dining table even though it isn't yet eight-thirty in the evening (a friend of mine is like this), the people who stumble into work at a minute before ten o'clock in the morning (I'm like this), still bleary-eyed and sleepy. Most people are more towards the middle. But wherever you lie on the spectrum, you are not necessarily lazy. Try telling that to the larks, though.

If only I would force myself to get up early every day, I'd soon get used it, they insist. You're missing the best part of the day, they tell me. You will feel better for it, they say. Yet no one – not even fellow owls – preaches the virtues of late nights to larks, and it would be considered perverse to suggest that the early birds are lazy because they go to bed at 9 p.m., and just lie there and sleep, while us late types are still up and active. No, owls are forever considered the lazy ones, like teenagers. (At last research showing that teenagers' body clocks are set later is becoming well-known enough for fewer teenagers to be hounded out of bed early at weekends by their parents, although still only 1 per cent of schools start the day after 9 a.m.[3] – I say this with feeling, remembering my own adolescence.) These days I can lie in, if I want to. At worst, my husband comes over all self-righteous and opens the blinds at the ungodly hour of 9 a.m. This is at the weekend, I should add. Though why am I being defensive again? What's wrong with still being in bed at nine in the morning on a week day?

The fact is, though, I am always up and out of bed by, well, no later than 8.45 a.m. Monday to Friday. But I never, ever, agree to a breakfast meeting. I'll happily meet someone after work, but if they want to meet before work, it is always no. Yet, for some reason I daren't just say, sorry I'll be resting at that time. Instead I'll say early mornings aren't going to work for me, hoping they'll assume I'm doing the school run or an actual run, not the truth, that I'll still be lying in bed. Of course I could force myself to get up earlier, and sometimes I have no option because of flights or needing to do radio interviews with people in different time zones. But it's a myth that you get used to it. It feels unnatural. It feels unhealthy. I have not been made in a way to like early mornings. And research backs me up. Parents with late chronotypes forced into early starts by babies crying, toddlers jumping onto the bed, older kids needing to be taken to school, return to their old ways as soon as they can – even if they have to wait for years or decades. In the end, they revert to chronotype.

Busyness as Status Symbol

Our freedom to rest, and in particular to do nothing, is of course dictated to a large extent by the demands of work. Many of us see rest as the opposite of work or busyness. But this is not the case with everyone, or indeed everywhere. While most people in the UK and the USA told us they considered rest to be the opposite of work, 57 per cent of the respondents to the Rest Test living in India had a different view. These Indian respondents were perhaps among those people who love their job, who feel so good about their work that they find it restful, leaving them feeling energised rather than exhausted at the end of the day. And depending on how conventional and strict your workplace is, there are restful moments at work.

Despite the evidence that it is good for us and increases productivity, few workplaces outside trendy ad firms and tech companies cater for power naps, or provide crash pads. And putting your feet up on the desk or having a snooze (or even a think) at your work station is still generally frowned upon. But most of us have opportunities to relax and kick back at work, and even to have some fun. I can remember when I was little being truly shocked when my father came home from work with a broken finger. It wasn't that I was horrified by the injury, it was how he inflicted it on himself. For it turned out to have occurred during a desk-leaping contest. I had no idea that adults behaved like this. Now I am older than my father was then I know differently, of course. Whatever their job, most people succeed in making it more fun if they possibly can – like newspaper journalists challenging each other to write stories where the first letter of each paragraph in a larger, bolder font, spells out 'The editor is a xxxx . . .' Fill in the gap as you choose.

It is probably best not to know how some other professions, doctors for example, rebel against the strictures of their profession as a way of relaxing at work. But we do know that work is not sheer grind all the time, that restful moments pop up in the middle of the day, just as work surfaces during leisure time (that work email that pops up and spoils your weekend).

For centuries, a good proxy for a person's wealth was the number of hours they had to work. Simply put, the fewer you did, the richer you were. The economist Thorstein Veblen coined the phrase 'the leisure class', a class that were noted not for conspicuous hard work but for conspicuous consumption and conspicuous leisure. Classic members of this class were wealthy industrialists and, in countries like Russia, moneyed landowners, like Oblomov.

To some extent, this picture still holds true, with the cleaner in a City office block working several shifts to make enough to live on, and with no prospect of ever retiring, while the trader in the same building earns so much he (and mostly they still are hes not shes) can retire at forty to play golf. But you can see the catch here: for, whatever you think about City traders, they are known for working long hours, and for working hard. Manically, dangerously so. Why do they do it? To get filthy rich of course, but it's more than that. Today we have another way of viewing long working hours and busyness – it makes us look important.

At Columbia Business School Silvia Bellezza asked people to assess fake Facebook posts written by a fictional woman called Sally Fisher.[4] One version of Sally said things like, 'Enjoying a long lunchbreak' and at 5 p.m. on a Friday she posted, 'Done with work!' In the other version, the busy Sally Fisher posted 'Quick ten-minute lunch' and at 5 p.m. on Friday she posted 'Still working!' This study gave participants no opportunity to comment on the dullness of Sally's social media posts, but people were asked to assess her social status. You will not be surprised to learn that they rated the busy Sally as higher in status, more in demand, and put her on a top rung of a pictorial ladder of economic wealth. If she's too busy to stop for a proper lunch, they reasoned, she must be important. Lazy Sally languished low on the ladder.

Silvia Bellezza says that just as we often value products according to their scarcity, so the same is true of people's skills. High demand equals scarcity, equals higher value. Therefore, the busy person is more valued in our society. Bellezza also found that we tend to believe that busy people do things quicker, are better at multitasking and have more meaningful jobs. It is no surprise, then, that boasting about busyness is endemic on social media. Bellezza's team looked at so-called 'humblebrags' through which people (sometimes very famous people) post comments on social media to show off how brilliant they are. As 12 per cent involved comments about how these people were so busy and so hard working, we can conclude that the days when the rich and famous mainly want to be known for doing very little are gone.

But perhaps this is not true everywhere in the world. Bellezza wondered whether the American culture of enterprise, with its almost sacred belief that anyone can succeed if they work hard enough, meant that busyness as a badge of status is a peculiarly American characteristic. In other words, is the basis of the American dream somehow singularly American? To test this hypothesis, she gave a group of Americans and a group of Italians the story of a thirty-five-year-old man (named Geoff for the Americans and Giovanni for the Italians) who worked very long hours. Meanwhile different groups of Americans and Italians had a version of Geoff/Giovanni who barely worked at all. As she predicted, the participants in the USA tended to ascribe the hard worker a higher status than the man who had a more leisurely time, while the Italians assumed the hard worker had been forced into long hours through necessity, and the other man must be so rich and successful that he didn't need to work much. So, the *dolce vita* survives in Italy, which for me is one more reason to love Italy.

Sadly, here in the UK attitudes are closer to the American view than they are to the more sophisticated sensibilities of our European neighbours. But whatever your attitude to busyness as a sign of status, it is clear that the leisure society we were promised has not come to pass. Who thinks that John Maynard Keynes' prediction that a fifteen-hour working week will be standard by 2030 will come true? After all, when the Wellcome Trust, which funded the Rest Test, announced in January 2019 that it was 'considering' moving all its 800 head office staff to a four-day week, this was considered such an unusual policy that it made the main news bulletins. Of course if the workload isn't reduced the unintended consequence might be that in order to fit the work in people have to work very hard with no breaks at all for the four days. Who knows until they try it!

The good news is that surveys of how we use our time do show that on average we have more free time than in the

1950s. Yet it often doesn't feel like that. We seem to be busier than ever, perhaps because of a blurring of the boundaries between work and leisure time, with some sections of society feeling they are always on call, even if their employment does not demand it. It is not even that our spare time gets interrupted by work that often – just that it's a constant possibility. We reflexively check our phones for new messages, even when the chance of anything urgent that demands our attention coming up is remote to say the least. And this leads us to replying quickly to work emails at midnight on a Saturday or first thing on a Sunday instead of switching off and leaving it until Monday morning. Even if we don't reply, that work is now occupying our minds.

This is not just a first-world problem. In many low-income countries the boundaries between work and leisure are fluid – or nearly non-existent – for millions. The woman who tends a small stall selling fruit on a remote road in Bangladesh might spend much of the day 'not working', resting, snoozing even. But she cannot clock off, and at any moment the arrival of a customer can disrupt that rest. Now in high-tech countries texts and emails do the same thing. There's equity of a sort in this, but hardly of the most beneficial type. Rich or poor, high- or low-income country, we find it hard to switch off from work, even when we're not actually working.

Taking a Break

In what some are now calling 'the attention economy', companies compete for a moment of our attention, and as we constantly check our phones we grant them that attention.

Is this work or leisure? It is an extension of the notion of being constantly on call. We might not be working as such, but we find ourselves reading a gas bill or confirming a purchase online when there is no need to do that now. Even replying to a party invitation or thinking about where we might go on holiday starts to count as admin, as we are being bombarded by information or constantly being reminded that this is a task on our to-do list. It's all encroaching on our supposed leisure time, making those 'doing nothing' moments even rarer.

If we want to show real commitment to a project – even a voluntary one or a leisure activity – we often say we 'won't rest until' a task is done, somehow viewing a break as an optional extra, even though we all know breaks are essential. And this is not just a modern phenomenon. The historian Mike Greaney points out that religious teaching – at least in the West – has for centuries emphasised the importance of the work ethic, terrifying people with tales of punishment in the next life if they dare to be indolent in this one. But few of us believe in eternal damnation now, and we know that priests preaching the evils of laziness were in league with lords of the manor, or later with mill owners, who wanted to sweat the workers so that they could grow rich from their labours. Now we are freer to embrace our lazier inclinations. Or we would be if it weren't for the demands of the attention economy. To counteract its pressures, Greaney calls on us to be intentionally lazy. If we want to avoid 'being defined as creatures of the attention economy, then we cannot afford not to be lazy'.[5]

Hear, hear. But we are still a long way from that stage. For the moment, rest is for wimps. Particularly in the USA, with its famously short vacations: an average of ten days' annual leave for those new to a job, rising to a still measly fifteen days' holiday for employees in their fifth year at a company. Despite this paucity of paid leave, endless polls (funnily enough, always sponsored by holiday companies) reveal that many people in the USA don't even take all their allotted leave.

Shockingly, only 74 per cent of employees in the US are entitled to any paid leave.[6] As someone who loves holidays, and who would struggle to live and work in the USA because holiday entitlement is so low, I'm both aghast and intrigued by these facts. Employees in the USA know that they get far less paid holiday than in comparable high-income countries, so why is there no big movement for change? You would think a campaign to get something nearer the European average, twenty-five days, say, would be hugely popular and almost impossible for business and politicians to resist. But no, even a campaign to mandate a minimum number of days of paid leave didn't generate much support.

When hotels.com started the Vacation Equality Project, demanding that all companies grant paid leave, they needed just 100,000 signatures on a petition to require the White House to respond. After two weeks, how many people had signed up? Only 13,000.[7]

For if lack of leave isn't a pressing issue in the USA, it should be. Life expectancy is lower there than in many other high-income countries, despite the high proportion of GDP spent on healthcare. And as we'll see, holidays could be a factor in making us live longer.

You'll have to bear with me while I explain the best evidence for this assertion. If you want to prove something

127

in epidemiology, you need a large sample of people and you need to track them over a long period. This is what Professor Timo Strandberg did in his seminal Helsinki Businessmen Trial.

Back in the late 1970s, a sample of more than a thousand businessmen were recruited who were all at a higher-than-average risk of developing heart disease and had been born in the 1920s and 1930s. For a five-year period half of them were required to visit the researchers every four months to be given copious health promotion advice. They were warned against smoking and told plenty about the benefits of a healthy diet and plenty of exercise. The other half of the sample got no such advice.

Over the following forty years some of the men, from both groups, died. That was to be expected. But on average, which group members would you expect to have lived longer? The healthy lifestyle group, of course.

But that's not what happened. In fact, the health promotion advice group on average died younger. As you can imagine, this was a startling and worrying finding for the health promotion industry. Health advice is supposed to help people live longer, but it seemed to be having the opposite effect. Strandberg concluded that pressure to live more healthily was causing some men in the healthy lifestyle group acute stress.[8] Interesting as this is, this is not why I have included this study here.

First the bad news: this is where the evidence from this study doesn't back up the idea that plenty of holiday time extends your life. For among the control group – that is the businessmen who didn't get healthy lifestyle advice – the amount of holiday they took made no apparent difference to their longevity. But among the ones who were encouraged to live healthily, longer holidays did make a difference – a big difference. Those who took less than three weeks holiday a year were 37 per cent more likely to die before 2004, when the men's ages ranged between seventy and eighty-five, compared with those who took three weeks or more.

I'll grant you that it is not the clearest evidence. Studies can be frustrating in this way. But perhaps the holidays *were* helping the people who most needed them. And there is another study on the impact of holidays on life expectancy, this time published in 2000. It involved 9,000 middle-aged men at risk of coronary heart disease, and even in just nine years it was apparent that those who didn't take holidays were at higher risk of dying.[9] Both these studies back up to some extent what we all surely feel intuitively: that a holiday is good for us. To what extent holidays involve doing nothing is another matter, of course. Some of us pack quite a lot of activity into our annual breaks, while others spend the time resting by the pool. But whether it is a real rest or a change that is as good as a rest, as the old saying goes, holidays refresh and restore and keep us healthy. Strandberg certainly seems to think so.

In 2018, when he presented this research at a medical conference for the first time, after slides packed with graphs and data, he ended his presentation with a photograph of the sun setting over water. This, he told conference delegates, was the view from his sauna on vacation.

So, whatever your work, try to take as much holiday as you can. Holiday are good for us.

And so are breaks.

Do feel free to go and make yourself a cup of tea at this

point. Even though we know that reading is another thing that is restful, it does no harm to take a break from the page now and again.

Depending on where you live in the world, it might be tea, it might be coffee, it might be *mate* or something else, but usually there is a drink that people will stop to consume several times a day, often inviting others to join them. A teabreak gives us permission to pause, punctuates the day and helps us to keep going. The most effective breaks involve a change of situation and a change of scenery – moving to somewhere different, outside even, and doing something different – or doing nothing in particular. Instinctively, we all like to take a break and there is copious evidence that we perform better after we've had one

Breaks allow us to recover both physically and mentally, replenishing our resources ready to go again. Athletes are careful not to overtrain. They take recovery seriously and don't exercise all day every day. Rest is scheduled, particularly after an injury. But most of us don't tend to do that. We take breaks, but rather haphazardly, often working through them – even at lunchtime – if we are busy. Who outside the world of sport schedules downtime? Perhaps we should.

We all know from experience that breaks matter, but the busiest days when we are most likely to benefit are, of course, the same days when deadlines make it feel impossible to stop. So we press on. But a break needn't be lengthy to have an impact. A micro-break could involve simply leaning back in your chair in the office with your eyes closed for a few seconds, pausing to join in with some banter, or a purer form of doing nothing maybe – staring out of the window. Anything that doesn't count as work or chores constitutes a micro-break. Studies have shown that without even realising it we all use these micro-breaks as a strategy to reinvigorate ourselves. And it works. An hour after a micro-break energy levels are still higher than they were before.

Research from South Korea provides us with some tips on what works best. Office workers kept diaries from lunch-time onwards for ten days. First they noted down how they were feeling and their expectations for the afternoon's work. Later they recorded any momentary breaks they took during the afternoon and lastly, how they felt at the end of the day.[10] Those who had taken micro-breaks generally finished the day in a better mood, but some activities were more effective than others. Staring out of the window, stretching, having a hot drink, or listening to music worked better than reading or going online. And it was on the most demanding days of all that these tiny breaks had the greatest impact on people's moods.

Not every workplace allows such autonomy, of course. A boss might not delight in walking into the office only to see half the staff chatting, others away making coffee and the rest staring out of the window, but the more enlightened and informed employers are coming to realise that these moments of downtime are essential not just for individual employees but for the company's bottom line. Higher productivity doesn't come from constant grind, but from greater concentration and creativity – and breaks help with that.

There's even an oft-cited study demonstrating that judges make harsher parole decisions as the time since they've had a break gets longer.[11] A re-analysis of this study suggests an alternative reason for the findings, that the decisions not to release are faster to deal with and so judges might juggle the timetable and squeeze them into the end of sessions.[12] No one can know for sure, but there is enough evidence from elsewhere to suggest that we do make our best decisions and achieve more when we are sufficiently rested. Take exams, for instance. In a Danish study of more than two million test scores, school pupils did better if they happened to take the test after one of the two daily break times.[13]

School pupils can't choose when to take a break of course, and often neither can adults, but when we can we're not very good at choosing the best moments to do it. German researchers found that instead of taking a break when we're tired and struggling, most of us tend to wait until we have finished and then take a break as a reward.[14] Now maybe we know ourselves well and are trying to control our procrastinatory tendencies, so we plough on. But virtuous as it is to wait until the task is done before we stop, we are missing out on the benefits of doing nothing. A two-minute break halfway through a task could make all the difference to both the quality of the work and the way you feel.

And if you don't have two minutes to spare, a 2019 study found that even a ten-second pause helped people do better at a task where participants had to learn to tap a series of four finger sequences.[15]

Rest needs to be taken seriously. If you can't even take micro-breaks at work, stress can build up. Research conducted in Germany and the Netherlands found that agreeing strongly with statements such as, 'When I get home after work, I want to be left in peace for a while,' and, 'I have difficulties in showing interest in other people immediately after I get home from work,' served as an early warning sign for bouts of prolonged fatigue and lower well-being. If these statements apply to you, you really need to be finding a way to incorporate more breaks into your working day. Or if you really can't do that, then you might need to rest more when you get home. And in this instance, a change is not as good as a rest. A real rest is what you need. Research shows that the most effective activities for promoting recovery from a stressful day are low-effort things like lying on the sofa rather than house-work or childcare.[16] This is one of those 'No shit, Sherlock' results that won't surprise anyone, but it is a reminder that sometimes we really do need to do nothing.

Progressive Relaxation

The idea that deep, do-nothing relaxation is beneficial came long before the twenty-first century wellness movement began. We tend to associate the 1930s with austerity and hard work, but a psychiatrist in Chicago, one of the cities hit hardest by the Great Depression, was an early scientific advocate of the serious benefits of doing nothing.

Edmund Jacobson made his name developing the technique of progressive relaxation. You might well have tried it out for yourself in the hope of getting to sleep at night. I've mentioned this technique earlier in the book. It's often referred to as a 'body scan', and can appear in classes in everything from yoga to mindfulness. First you lie down flat. Then starting either at your toes or at the top of your head, you scan your way up or down your body. You clench and then relax each set of muscles in turn. The idea is that then your whole body begins to feel more relaxed, along with your mind.

Jacobson's interest in relaxation stemmed from his fascination with the opposite – the startle reflex. As a ten-year-old growing up at the end of the nineteenth century, he was horrified by a fire that took place in a hotel owned by his father. Three people were killed, including a man he knew, who, it was said, had clung onto a fifth-floor windowsill for as long as his fingertips could hold on, before falling to his death. As Jacobson described his reaction in an article he wrote near the end of his life, 'I was appalled by the nervously excited state of various individuals following the fire.'[17] He became so fascinated by the reaction he saw in his parents and others to this traumatic event that he chose to investigate the subject at university, beginning with an examination of the startle reflex. This involved inviting participants into his lab and shocking them with loud bangs, while monitoring their reactions.

Jacobson discovered that if he taught people to relax their muscles before the surprise noise, he could blunt their startle response. He saw how the same exercises could be applied to other situations and so began his development of the technique of progressive relaxation, which he published in 1924. Looking back, he recalled that he was somewhat sceptical about what he was doing – healthily so: 'Thirty years ago as I went from room to room trying to get individuals with different maladies to relax, I recall saying to myself, "What kind of nonsense is this that you are practising?"'[18] Yet his data demonstrated that his techniques did work. Gradually, Jacobson grew in confidence and felt sure he was on to something important. Indeed, his technique was so successful, he claimed, that it allowed his wife to give birth without pain relief, or apparently without even crying out.

The historian Ayesha Nathoo points out that Jacobson was anxious that his work was seen by colleagues to fall within the scientific discipline of medicine. He demanded dedication from his patients, insisting that in contrast to the bedrest often prescribed at the time, muscular relaxation was a skill to be learned, requiring one or two hours of practice at home each day in addition to weekly lessons.[19] His techniques involved serious rest, physiologically measured and thoroughly taught.

But as well as being taken seriously by medical researchers, Jacobson wanted to reach the general public. It led him to write a popular book with the less than relaxing exhortatory title: *You Must Relax!*

With sufficient training, Jacobson said, anybody could enjoy 'modern civilisation without burning the candle at both ends', and he remains one of the most important figures in the discipline of relaxation. Yet how exactly does this equate to doing nothing? The point is this: despite the detailed technical instructions and the necessity to maintain concentration throughout, significant amounts of time during progressive relaxation are spent doing nothing. Indeed, one way of looking at Jacobson and others who have followed him is as clever 'reframers'. We are more comfortable with the idea of doing nothing if we do it via a medically tested technique. Learning and practising how to do nothing makes it feel, ironically, like doing something. And that's a lot easier for us.

Boredom Good and Boredom Bad

Literally sitting doing nothing is more challenging. Can you actually bear to do it? 'All of humanity's problems stem from man's inability to sit quietly in a room alone,' wrote the French philosopher Pascal roughly 350 years ago. This quote could have featured in the I Want to be Alone chapter, or even in the Daydreaming chapter, since Pascal goes on to say that we fear taking away distractions because then we will have to face up to the truths of the thoughts left behind. Or the quotation might have fitted into the first chapter on Mindfulness, a practice which requires us to be still and to notice, to accept our thoughts, even if they seem self-critical. This leads me to wonder whether Pascal gets closer than anyone to the fundamental difficulty we have with resting. It's not just that we find it hard to find the time, or hard not to be distracted, but that we actually *fear* it.

Imagine you're asked to sit in an empty room on your own for fifteen minutes. What would you do? Reach for your phone perhaps? No, the researchers have locked it away for the duration of the experiment. Open a book or news-paper? No, you're not allowed those either. Get out a pen and paper and make a to-do list? No, likewise. Wander around the room? Do some press-ups? No, the rules state that you must remain in the chair. Fold your arms and take the opportunity for a nap? No, that's the other rule. You must stay awake. So really the only entertainment left is your own mind. A series of psychological experiments conducted in empty rooms was published in 2014. And Pascal was right. People didn't like the situation at all.[20]

Of the eleven variations of the experiment, one in particular gained worldwide publicity. Participants were led one at a time into a bare room with all distractions removed and electrodes were fitted to their ankles. They were shown how to press a computer key which would deliver an electric shock. Then they were left alone wearing the electrodes for fifteen minutes and told they could 'think about whatever you want to'. Oh, and they had the added option of giving themselves more shocks if they chose to.

And here's the shocking thing, the thing that made this experiment so notorious: one participant shocked himself 190 times. Just one masochist? No, 71 per cent of the men gave themselves at least one electric shock, and even though the women were less inclined to inflict pain on themselves, a quarter did self-administer a shock. It appears that people hated spending fifteen minutes with their own thoughts so much that they preferred to endure pain rather than do nothing.

There is one caveat. The numbers in this study are small. I also wonder whether curiosity comes into it too. Would the shock hurt as much a second time? We're obeying the same impulse as we do when we touch a plate the waiter has just warned us is hot; we want to discover things. Not that long ago when I was camping I touched the sides of an iron ring around a fire pit with all ten fingers because I had an irresistible urge to find out how hot it was. The answer was very hot indeed; I burnt all my fingertips, which hurt a lot. Our desire for control plays a part in this experiment too. Almost all the participants' choices had been removed. The one thing they had power over was the choice of whether to shock themselves again, so why not exercise that option and feel a little more in charge? Nonetheless, the finding from this famous experiment is intriguing, and highlights more than any other study how difficult we find it to do nothing, particularly if it is enforced.

Just as solitude becomes loneliness once it's no longer optional, doing nothing is only restful when we choose it for ourselves. Enforced rest can result in excruciating boredom, something that was discovered by many patients in the nineteenth century. This was when the American doctor Silas Weir Mitchell invented 'the rest cure', believing that a combination of 'entire rest and excessive feeding' would improve the condition of the emotionally exhausted. It was described as 'the greatest advance of which practical medicine can boast in the last quarter of the century', but its use in oppressing women in particular by confining them to bed, force-feeding them if they refused to eat copious amounts of food, and forbidding them from reading, sewing or in some cases turning over in bed without the doctor's permission, has been well-documented. Charlotte Perkins Gilman based her short story 'The Yellow Wallpaper' on her experiences of the rest cure when she had postnatal depression. Although she admits that she embellished some details for the story,[21] of the real experience of doing nothing all day she wrote, 'the mental agony grew so unbearable that I would sit blankly moving my head from side to side'. When she emerged from her rest cure, Dr Mitchell advised her to have only two hours' 'intellectual life' a day and to 'never touch a pen, brush or pencil for as long as you live'. Luckily for literature she took no notice.

The results of the Rest Test would suggest that there is still a limit to the amount of rest we can enjoy before it becomes stultifying. Well-being scores rose along with the numbers of hours of rest people had enjoyed the previous day, but began to dip if people had rested for more than six hours. There seems to be an optimal amount of rest that we can bear before it tips into tedium.

For most people, however, there is little chance that they will find themselves feeling bored for long. In a study conducted in the USA in 2017, nearly 4,000 adults spent a week using an app which buzzed every thirty minutes during waking hours to ask them what they were doing and how they felt.[22] This gave the researchers more than a million observations of individual moments in time and the opportunity to discover how people really feel at those times when they do nothing. The results showed people recorded feeling bored on fewer than 6 per cent of the occasions when they were not doing anything.

This sounds like a positive finding. Boredom is deadly, right? In fact, it has a positive side. It can prompt us to seek out something new. This kind of human curiosity (as well as enticing us to touch hot plates and give ourselves electric shocks) has, after all, been key to the success of the human race.

It is why doing nothing, which is the state in which we

are most likely to experience boredom, can be the state in which we generate new ideas. As we saw when I discussed daydreaming, the mind wanders and begins to make new connections between different thoughts until eventually, if we're lucky, we think of something new. Plenty of the world's most creative figures have put doing nothing to good use. Leonardo Da Vinci used to instruct his pupils to stare emptily at a wall until faces and movement seemed to rise from the mottles and damp patches. I wonder whether Virginia Woolf knew this when she wrote her short story 'The Mark on the Wall', noting the meanderings of the mind as someone gazes upon a mysterious dark blotch on the plaster.

The psychologist Sandi Mann demonstrated the impact of boredom on creativity by setting people the dullest task she could think of – copying numbers out of the phonebook. After this mind-numbing activity, the same people were asked to come up with as many uses as they could for a plastic cup (lollipop moulds, plant pots, chandeliers, whatever they could think of). This is a test of what's known as divergent creativity, like the test used in the Stanford University walking research. The results from this study showed that people who were forced to do the boring phonebook task first came up with significantly more uses for the plastic cup than another group who went straight to the cup task.[23] More broadly, doing nothing allows us – or forces us – to introspect, to work out what we want from life and how we can find meaning in it. And according to Sandi Mann, it is meaning rather than fun, that is the antidote to boredom at the existential level. So being a bit bored for a while can open our minds to the avoidance of boredom in the long run.

If doing nothing still feels too indulgent, remember that

it can even improve your memory. Over the last two decades it's become clear from research that if we learn some information and then have a good night's sleep, we are more likely to remember it the next day. Sleep and possibly dreaming consolidate our memories, embedding them more firmly in our minds. We also know, as I've said, that taking breaks now and then helps us work or study more effectively. Recently, studies have cleverly combined these two ideas, but using rest rather than sleep.

People experiencing amnesia as a result of a stroke were given lists of fifteen words to memorise. These people then spent the next ten minutes working on other mental exercises before recalling as many of the words as they could. Due to their amnesia, the average score was just 14 per cent. But if instead of doing mental exercises the amnesiacs spent that ten minutes before the recall test sitting in a darkened room, their score rose to an impressive 49 per cent.[24] The technique was later found by Michaela Dewar at Heriot-Watt University to be effective for people in the middle stages of Alzheimer's disease. And with healthy people the positive effect remained a week later.

The fragility of the creation of new memories is such that they are more likely to be embedded in our minds if we rest and do nothing immediately after acquiring them.[25] Dewar's most recent finding is even more favourable to advocates of doing nothing.

Here's a puzzle for you. Which well-known phrase or saying is represented by this sequence of letters: AWTEW. Or how about this: ABITHIWTITB. (The answers, should you need them, are in this endnote.[26])

But if you're confident you are right anyway, how did you

141

come to your answer and how long did it take? When the solution came to you, whether quickly or after a long struggle, it probably dropped into place quite suddenly. This is known within psychological research as insight – the eureka moment.

One way to stimulate eureka moments – people who get stuck on crossword clues favour it, I've noticed – is to leave the puzzle for a few hours. When you get back to it, the solution to that clue will often come to you easily almost as though your brain has been subconsciously incubating the idea while you've been consciously doing something else. The question is what is the best thing to do in the meantime? Dewar's research suggests the answer is – nothing. When people had a go at a puzzle followed by a ten-minute break in which they did nothing, they were more likely to find the answer when they returned to the puzzle than people who'd been given a simple spot-the-difference game to play for ten minutes.

How to Do (Almost) Nothing

The philosophers Seneca and Socrates both worried about people with a wanderlust, fearful that they travel to escape, but then inevitably take themselves with them. Socrates wrote: 'Why do you wonder that globe-trotting does not help you, seeing that you always take yourself with you? The reason which set you wandering is ever at your heels.' It's true that your worries don't just disappear because you're away from home. Your mind is not suddenly at peace. Doubts remain because you are still you, whichever country you have landed in. You can climb a volcano before dawn to watch the sun rise above its lip, but however unique and otherworldly this might feel, you still have your own world in your head. Seneca and Socrates were correct, but although we do take ourselves with us when we go away, we don't take all our stuff. This has an often-neglected advantage. It gives us greater permission to do nothing.

In a foreign hotel room, all we have with us is a single suitcase and perhaps a backpack. There's only so much putting away and folding up we can do. At home we are surrounded by things to do. The pile of ironed clothes waiting to return to their hangers, the broken plate that needs gluing, the hooks ready to go up on the wall, the item that needs to go back to the shop. Some things aren't even visible, but still demand your attention. The nagging feeling that you ought to switch energy suppliers in case you're overpaying, that you should check what's going on with your pension fund. This is known as 'lifemin', and lifemin is one of the curses of living. But on holiday you are largely free of it. For once, it is fine to spend ages in the bath, then lie on the bed reading, or looking at the view or doing nothing. At home the only circumstance in which you would ever come in from work and lie on the bed doing nothing is if you were ill.

I have wondered whether it might be possible to recreate this holiday-doing-nothing-window at home. It's not going to work a lot of the time. Things do need to get done. There are meals to cook and children to put to bed. But is there a way of occasionally building this kind of rest into our busy schedules? Perhaps if you're going out on a Saturday night you could give yourself permission to spend a delicious two hours beforehand, partly getting ready, but also lying on the bed?

The problem, as ever, is all those things around you that you should really be doing. Moving directly from these to doing nothing at all is just too big a leap. Perhaps this is why doing nothing is so hard to do at home, and why so many people who took part in the Rest Test found some sort of activity more restful than doing nothing. At least if you're watching TV or reading a book, you feel as if you're doing *something*, allowing you to ignore everything else that needs to be done with less of a feeling of guilt.

Let's face it, we can't wish away to-do lists or indeed ever complete all the tasks on them. As soon as you've done everything you need to do on that first list, another list of things has piled up. That's life, and there's no getting away from it. Maybe millennials are on to something by giving it a name: adulting. It is reassuring, perhaps, that this never-ending activity is something you've opted into by virtue of growing up. So acceptance that being an adult in the modern world involves doing a lot and always will is the first step. But still, we have to find a way to stop ourselves being overwhelmed. We need to find ways of getting away from the pressure to do do do. It doesn't have to involve a holiday. There are places closer to home where you can still escape your to-do list and get closer to doing nothing. I wonder if this is why so many people find train journeys restful. Travelling can, of course, be tiring, but at least for a defined length of time the demands are put to one side. People might be able to reach us by phone or email, but going into a tunnel will soon put pay to that. A daily commute where you have to negotiate new timetables, put up with strikes and delays, and travel in carriages so crowded you have to beg people to move down so that you can perch on the edge of the step and duck as the doors shut, is never going to be relaxing. But when you're on a long journey with plenty of space, being transported through the countryside effortlessly, restfulness can be yours.

Of course, for some of us, a train's movement is so soporific that staying awake is difficult. I sleep so well on trains that if I can't get to sleep at night I sometimes try imagining that I'm on a train. The British physicist Sir Alfred Yarrow was a man who felt the same way. In 1927 he arranged for the National Physical Laboratory to make him a bed which copied the motions of a train, rocking eighty times a minute but with enough irregularity to avoid inducing nausea. A lab in Zurich is working on something similar, experimenting with a series of different rocking motions, but the motor is so loud that it has to be kept in another room, so there are challenges.[27] But as we have established, it's a cheat to count sleeping as doing nothing.

This quest for a way of doing nothing might remind some people of the so-called slow movement, which started with a campaign to return to slow food in Italy after protests against the opening of a branch of a McDonald's fast food joint next to the Spanish Steps in Rome. The preface 'slow' has since been applied to everything from fashion to postgraduate study. Slow fashion encourages people to buy new clothes only when they need them, rather than because hemlines change, while the slow grad student movement in the USA urges students to do less, to put a moratorium on 'I'm so busy' status talk, and to put some time aside to 'be' rather than to do. Thinking, daydreaming, dozing, playing with a pet and going for a walk in nature are all permitted.

It's instructive that most of the slow grad recommendations for 'being' in fact involve some doing. We're back almost to where we started in this chapter. Doing anything, however inconsequential, seems to be key to this, as it allows us to rest without the guilt. Knitting or flicking through a magazine feels more acceptable than deliberately staring into space. So, why fight it? Why not go with the flow? Don't even try to do nothing, it's too hard, instead do something small. Pottering, you might call it.

In 1958 a book was published with the title *How to Do Nothing with Nobody All Alone by Yourself.*[28] It was aimed at children because the author Robert Paul Smith believed that in doing things alone they could learn about themselves. The book contains abundant ways in which they might entertain themselves with things found around the house, or in the case of broken umbrellas (which he turns into kites), in the street. Spending time sitting thinking is praised, but really it's a book about playing by yourself. There are plenty of things I'd quite like to try, if only I felt I could justify the time. For example, you can find a pencil with hexagonal sides (I'm thinking one of those black and red striped ones would look good). Then using a pen knife you whittle away a little square half a centimetre long on one edge of the pencil, before moving down a bit and across to the next edge, where you chip away at another square, until a hundred or so whittled squares later you have a pencil covered in a chequerboard pattern. Pointless, but attractive, and I'd imagine strangely satisfying.

You may consider this cheating because it's not, strictly speaking, doing nothing; it's decorating something. But depending on your temperament it might be the closest you can get to sitting in a chair staring into space. Maybe this is why people – and I mean adults – like jigsaws and more recently colouring books. I also wonder whether this is why crafts such as knitting (or in my case, crochet) remain so popular. Once you've practised enough to be able to do it without thinking, your hands might be busy, but your mind can wander wherever it likes. Once again you have given yourself permission to rest. And if it's not doing nothing, it almost is.

Even so, I still believe more of us, more of the time, should try to aim for pure nothing-doing. It's good for us. As Albert Camus said, 'Idleness is only fatal to the mediocre.' It's probably not an activity to schedule, because we know that enforced inactivity leads to boredom. But what we can do is wait until the opportunity to do nothing presents itself to us spontaneously and then embrace it. There's no need to take it to Bartleby the scrivener extremes, but if you are drawn to something you see out of the window while you're working, don't fight it. Gaze at it for a moment and then return to work. And when work gets too much, maybe make yourself a cup of tea, but instead of bringing it straight back to your desk, sit or stand somewhere else and pause for a few minutes while you drink it. Allow yourself a break. Allow yourself to rest. Do nothing, even if it is just for a moment or two. Or if that's too difficult, do nothing in particular. Or almost nothing.

4

LISTENING TO MUSIC

Once a month on a Friday night a group of middle-aged men meet up in a house in Peckham in southeast London. They all have beards, but then so do most men in Peckham. They do a variety of jobs – teaching, photography, one is a comedy critic. They gather for one activity, an activity they approach with some seriousness. Yet when they meet in the pub beforehand they seem to dawdle. It's clear they have met with a purpose in mind, but no one is hurrying to get to this month's appointed house. Then one starts chivvying the others along. At the house they find spots in the living room where they can relax, the quickest bagsying the sofa and the armchairs, the others settling down on the floor, leaning against the wall. It's time to begin. It's time to listen. A record is about to be played. Only one man, this month's 'chooser', knows what it is. He heads over to a silver and black turntable atop a fifties-era sideboard. He places the stylus onto the record and the music begins.

This is Vinyl Club. It's the ageing music fan's equivalent of a book club, where friends rotate around each other's homes each month, taking turns to discuss a chosen book. But the rules of Vinyl Club are stricter than in most book clubs, which in my experience involve as much gossip and wine drinking as literary criticism.

Once the music has started no one speaks. All talking is forbidden until the listening is done, or more accurately half done. Only when the A side of the album has finished do the men have their first opportunity to make their feelings known about their host's choice of music. The reason, the club members tell me, is that without this rule, no one would listen properly to the music. They'd all start reminiscing about their teenage years when they first saw Led Zeppelin or the Sex Pistols or David Bowie or whoever. And as fun as that is – they get to it in time – the point is to immerse themselves in the music and experience its redemptive powers.

It is indisputable that music affects us psychologically, so in this chapter rather than ask what makes music special, I want to discover what the evidence can tell us about how we can make the most of music to achieve restfulness. Brand new research from the Anna Freud Centre shows that listening to music is one of the most common self-care strategies used by people under twenty-five. The Vinyl Club shows that people double that age, and older, find it therapeutic too.

Mozart, Blur or Whatever Takes Your Fancy

Obvious answer alert: if you want music to feel restful, choose music you like. Musical taste varies far more than preferences for different kinds of landscapes, for example, where the majority of us say we prefer the seaside or mountains. And with music our level of antipathy to certain musical genres is much stronger too, so much so that several underground stations in London have succeeded in deterring large groups of young people from hanging around stations in areas known for drug-dealing simply by playing classical music loudly. The loitering groups find the music intolerable and soon go else-where. Of course, it's hard on the law-abiding young people (and older people) who might also happen to hate this kind of music – personally I like a bit of Vivaldi at full volume – but it has been extraordinarily effective.

It's often argued that classical music is the zenith of musical achievement. In his book *Instrumental* the concert pianist James Rhodes writes of how composers such as Rachmaninov and Bach helped him survive extreme abuse, breakdown and addiction. This is how he describes listening to a favourite recording of Schubert's *Sonata No. 20* by the German pianist Alexander Lonquich.

'The music floats into your ears and simply takes over your mind. I know it sounds pretentious . . . but I first listened to it after a piano lesson in Verona . . . and openly wept at the genius on display. It was a genuine reminder of everything that is great about the world . . . Lonquich's sound, his stag-gering technique, his ability to make the entire sonata seep into every cell of your body and make you stare open-mouthed in wonderment is the rarest of feats.'[1]

Given how classical music at its sublime best can elicit such responses, it is hardly surprising that claims have been made that it has a profound impact on our brains. The most famous claim of all concerns Mozart. Indeed, you have probably heard of the Mozart effect, the idea that if you listen to his music you will become more intelligent. Dozens of books and CDs for babies, toddlers, children, adults and even 'moms-to-be' promise to help you harness the power of Mozart's music to enhance brain power. But when it comes to hard scientific evidence that listening to Mozart can make you cleverer, the picture is more mixed.

The phrase 'the Mozart effect' was coined in 1991 but became better known after a study published two years later. Mozart was undoubtedly a genius, so the suggestion that if we listen to his brilliant music a little of his intelligence might rub off on us seemed plausible, as well as attractive. Soon thousands of parents were playing *Eine Kleine Nachtmusik* and *The Magic Flute* to their infants. By 1998 Zell Miller, the Governor of the state of Georgia in the USA, was asking that money be set aside in the state budget to allow every new born baby to receive a free Mozart CD in the post.[2]

Governor Miller's scheme did not extend to animals, but perhaps it should have done. Sergio Della Salla, the psychologist and author of *Mind Myths*, told me of his visit to a mozzarella farm in Italy where the farmer proudly explained that three times a day he played Mozart to his buffalos in the belief that this encouraged them to produce better milk. Who knows who else was having a go – goldfish breeders and orchid growers perhaps?

For the Mozart effect to have taken off to this extent, you might well assume that the original researchers must have discovered something pretty definitive back in 1993. They hadn't. And they didn't even claim that they had. Their scientific paper consists of a mere single page describing their experiment. And nowhere in it do they use the phrase 'the Mozart effect'. The next surprise is that the original research didn't even involve children. As with many a psychological study, the participants were undergraduate students.[3]

Here's what the original research team actually did and what they actually found. On three occasions, thirty-six students were given a series of mental tasks to complete. Before each task, they sat listening to one of three randomly assigned options: ten minutes of silence, ten minutes of a relaxation tape or ten minutes of Mozart's *Sonata for Two Pianos in D Major*. Then the researchers compared the scores of the students on the various tasks to see whether the music made a difference.

There was one particular task at which the students who listened to Mozart did indeed excel. It involved looking at folded up pieces of paper with patterns cut into them, and then predicting what those patterns would look like when the paper was unfolded. It's harder than it sounds, and Mozart did make a difference. But this enhanced ability lasted for, wait for it, a whole fifteen minutes. It's hardly a lifetime of superintelligence, is it?

Having said that, from a neuroscientific perspective it is still intriguing that music could make us better at something so specific. One hypothesis is that the intricacy of the music might lead to patterns of cortical firing in the brain similar to those associated with solving spatial puzzles. Over the years further research has followed and a meta-analysis gathering together and re-analysing sixteen more studies has confirmed that listening to Mozart does lead to a temporary improvement in the ability to mentally manipulate shapes.[4]

So listening to Mozart can enhance one very specific and – let's face it – not very useful task, but if you like listening to Mozart anyway, then I guess an improvement in your skills at mental shape manipulation is a bonus. But what if you don't like listening to Mozart? Well, don't fret. A few years after the meta-analysis was published, it began to emerge that there was nothing special about Mozart's music per se. In 2006 another experiment took place. This time it involved children and this time there weren't just thirty-six participants, but an impressive 8,000. The children listened to one of three ten-minute excerpts of audio: Mozart's *String Quintet in D Major*, a discussion about the experiment or a medley of three songs – Blur's 'Country House', Mark Morrison's 'Return of the Mack' and PJ and Duncan's 'Stepping Stone'. Once again music did improve the children's ability to predict unfolded paper shapes, but this time it wasn't a Mozart effect so much as a Blur boost. The children who listened to Mozart did well, but with the medley of pop music they did even better, perhaps because they preferred it.[5]

In 2010 a larger meta-analysis confirmed that listening to music only results in a small improvement in spatial skills, and that other types of music work just as well as Mozart. The authors of this study even named their paper 'Mozart effect–Schmozart effect'.[6] One study found that hearing a passage from a Stephen King novel read out loud improved your spatial skills just as much, provided you enjoyed it. This suggests that what matters is not the precise notes you hear but how much you engage with whatever you are listening to.[7] To do better at predictive origami all you need is a little cognitive arousal – the chance for your mind to get a little more active.

The story of the Mozart effect is a cautionary tale about believing everything you hear about the benefits of music.

But it has taken us away from the main subject, because of course we're not so much in search of music that makes the mind more active but more rested. So is there good evidence about the kind of music which is best for that?

Here we can learn something from a brand new study of the music people select in order to get to sleep at night. This practice is more common under the age of twenty-seven, perhaps because younger people are more likely to have their phones at their bedside, with access to all the music you could ever imagine, or because they're less likely to be living with long-term partners. Now it's true that the people in this research were looking to sleep rather than to rest, but 96 per cent of those who used music to help them doze off said the reason they thought it worked was that the music relaxed them, and many also reported that it cleared their minds, distracted them, or calmed their racing thoughts. These are all the same things we look for in order to feel rested. The people selected a range of genres, with 32 per cent choosing classical music and less than 1 per cent house. Bach was mentioned most, followed by Ed Sheeran, and then our old friend Mozart.[8] The key was that they selected the music themselves, which might call into question the useful-ness of the hundreds of allegedly calming/relaxing/sleep-inducing playlists available now. Unless you like all music, it's not going to work.

More than 600 people took part in that piece of research. When conclusions are based on studies with far, far fewer participants than that, I'm generally cautious, but depending on the design there are times when the tiny studies can be the most instructive. One of my favourite pieces of research on music and relaxation involved just eight Finnish teenagers, each of whom talked in depth for more than three hours about the way they listen to music, giving us a rich source for understanding more about how people actually use music in real life.[9] One of the key findings was that when it came to relaxing, again it didn't seem to matter what type of music they listened to. But, and here's where it gets interesting, the teenagers who were best at using music successfully to improve their moods liked a wider variety of music.

It seems that having an eclectic musical taste might help us to relax better because, after all, we have a wide range of moods too. Sometimes some serious Bach does the trick, at other times some schmaltzy Barry Manilow. It might be grime that's perfect for you. I always think the guests on *Desert Island Discs* who sound most sorted in life are those who choose a range of styles, from Beyoncé to Beethoven. The Finnish study seems to back this up.

So variety is good, but how about volume, how about tempo?

Loud or Low? Fast or Slow?

Imagine you've kindly given up your time to take part in a psychology experiment. You find yourself in a room with another volunteer and you're both given some unusually tricky anagrams to solve. The other person seems to get through them very quickly, making this very clear by saying 'Haven't you finished yet?', adding that anyone with brains can solve anagrams easily. Then this rude person starts wondering out loud how you managed to get into university if you're this slow, before saying you probably got low grades at school. Then to top it all they have the nerve to start criticising your fashion sense.

By now you are probably wondering who this rude person is and feeling more than slightly annoyed. That, of course, is the idea. And to ensure that you definitely do get cross, this so-called study participant, who is, in fact, of course part of the research team, has been given the freedom to deviate from their script to follow up on whichever topic of discussion seems to wind you up the most.[10] They then niggle away at you until you're thoroughly fed up.

You might be relieved to learn that, these days, it is hard to get permission to do a study like this one. It took place back in 1976, under the leadership of the psychologist Vladimir Konečni, not long before ethical regulations were brought into psychology in the wake of the notorious Stanley Milgram experiments, where people were tricked into thinking they were giving people fatally strong electric shocks. I'll let you decide how bad it is to wind people up for the sake of an experiment, but for our purposes if we want to discover the impact of music on mood, we are left relying on some studies that date back a few decades.

After bombarding them with so-called ego-thwarting remarks, the next step for Konečni was to give the participants in his experiment the choice between listening to various kinds of music, some of it loud and complex, some of it quiet and simple. What music would they choose to calm them down and recover from the insults? The results were striking. Seventy-nine per cent chose the simpler and quieter music. By contrast, a control group who were given the anagrams to solve without distraction from a rude person were split down the middle in their musical preferences.

The lesson from Konečni's 1976 study is clear: generally speaking, as you would imagine, when you are feeling stressed and yearn to relax, put on some easy listening. It doesn't have to be Nat King Cole or a chill-out compilation, it could be some Mozart, but nothing too complicated. Personally, I like Stockhausen, but not when I'm feeling tense and het up. My husband likes the German prog rock band Can, whose music is notoriously complicated and cerebral. But it is not music he unwinds to. It is common sense really. If we're in a good mood we can afford to experiment with different levels of complexity in music, but if we're in a bad mood we need to reduce the level of arousal in our brains and simpler music is best for that.

It's not just when we feel upset that we prefer certain types of music. The same thing happens when our bodies are tired. The music psychologists Adrian North and David Hargreaves conducted an experiment where they divided volunteers into two groups.[11] One group had the easy job of lying down on a quilt and relaxing for seven minutes. The other group cycled on exercise bikes for the same amount of time. Meanwhile each person could choose between a fast and loud or a slow and quiet version of a tune 'loosely labelled as pop music'. Everyone could decide how long to listen for and could swap between the tracks if they chose to.

The findings of this first part of the study probably won't surprise you: people matched the music to their activity – fast and loud for the cyclists, and quiet and slow for the relaxing-on-a-quilt people. But then the experiment was repeated with a new set of guinea pigs, this time with one crucial difference in the procedure. They could choose which music they would like to listen to *after*, rather than during, the activity. It transformed the results. Under these conditions, the quilt people showed no real preference, but the exercisers much preferred slow music. Clearly, after a vigorous workout on a bike most of the cyclists were tired and wanted to relax, and so chose music to help them do that, while the people who had been relaxing already either wanted to stay relaxed or were ready to liven themselves up a bit and chose different music accordingly.

Mood Music

Deliberately using music in an attempt to transform your mood is not unusual. People with depression sometimes decide to create what is known as a 'happy box', filled with items which might help them when they're feeling low. Into the box they put anything that might remind them that however they are feeling now, they won't always feel like this, and that there are people in the world who value and love them. The box might contain a few holiday photos, a card from a friend that made them laugh, a favourite pair of socks, some hand cream that smells nice, a piece of chocolate, a note congratulating them on a past achievement, even some bubble wrap, purely for the pleasure of popping. And there's one item you find in most happy boxes – a CD or a playlist of music that makes the owner feel happier.

We might adapt this idea and create 'rest boxes' filled with things that might help us calm down or relax – perhaps a scented candle, or a favourite book, and almost certainly some music – or maybe we already try to make our living rooms and bedrooms shrines to relaxation with these kinds of objects.

There are some general rules that research has generated on the effects of different music on our moods.[12] Not surprisingly, excitement is best stimulated by loud, fast music in a major key, and it's more effective if it has uneven rhythms; loud, fast music with flowing rhythms and a higher pitch is more likely to lead to happiness; and slow, low-pitched music in a minor key with a firm rhythm and dissonant harmony induces sadness. But the most relevant finding for us is that slow music in a major key with flowing rhythms and consonant harmony is the most likely to produce a feeling of tranquility. Again, most of us could guess that, and all the various studies are doing is confirming our intuitions. We also have to remember that these are generalisations, and won't apply to everyone in every circumstance. Moreover, in practice, when we feel in need of rest, we're probably unlikely to sit scrolling through playlists or survey our record collections in search of a piece of music that exactly conforms to the 'slow in a major key with flowing rhythms and consonant harmony' template. What we do is find a piece of music that is more or less of this type, which has worked for us before, and which – crucially – we like.

The psychologist Tabitha Trahan, who conducted the study investigating the kinds of music people use to help them get to sleep, emphasises that if we were trying to name 'the perfect sleep song' it would need to obey certain psycho-acoustic guidelines, but then somehow also be tailored to an individual's preferences. The same would apply to finding 'the perfect rest song'. The evidence tells us that the music which proves the most analgesic and anxiolytic (lovely word there, meaning 'anxiety reducing') should be selected by no one but us.

The best studies on mood and music employ a technique known as experience sampling – where people are asked to note down their activities and moods in real time as they happen. In Sweden the psychologist Patrik Juslin gave a set of students a palmtop device to carry with them wherever they went.[13] It paged them at random times between 9 a.m. and 11 p.m. each day. As soon as they heard the signal the students were required to complete a questionnaire on the palmtop which asked them whether they were listening to music, what else they were doing at that moment in time and which emotions they were experiencing. The dedicated students kept this up for a fortnight.

On 64 per cent of the occasions where music happened to be playing at the moment of the beep, the students were convinced it was affecting their mood, and those of us in search of rest will be glad to learn that the most common emotion people said they felt when listening was calm. Moreover, people in this study felt calmest when they consciously listened to music for relaxation.

The Finnish teenagers have much to teach us about trying to use music to help us rest. Some of them said that music simultaneously made them feel relaxed *and* provided them with energy, reviving them, getting them ready to go out. Sometimes this was very deliberate. Alice said that to give herself energy, 'I sung Killers songs with all my heart. I hope the neighbours weren't at home.' If we feel in need of rest perhaps we should start with something peaceful and traditionally relaxing, then move on to something more energetic as we begin to feel refreshed. We could even create a 'resting playlist' which takes us from deep relaxation to restoration, with every song one of our favourites, of course. The next question is when to listen to it.

If your day has been mildly – but not acutely – stressful, and you are looking to rest, then several studies suggest the best time to listen to music is in the evening. Of course, for many of us, this or the journey home from work will be the first opportunity we get. If you work in a restaurant or shop, background music might be playing all day, but if you don't get to choose it, then it might induce stress rather than relieve it. In these cases, getting home in the evening and putting on some music you really like could certainly help you to de-stress and make you feel more relaxed. And I am sure it was this conscious listening – listening through choice – to which respondents to the Rest Test were referring when they chose listening to music as one of their top ten.

But your motivation for putting on some music at the end of the day could make a difference to its effectiveness. A German study suggests using music to block out thoughts could be counterproductive. In this study, researchers not only measured students' subjective stress levels after listening to music in everyday life, but asked them to collect saliva samples in test tubes and store them in their freezers.[14] Later the saliva was tested for one hormone and one enzyme. If people listened to music specifically to help them relax then the stress hormone cortisol was indeed reduced, but on the other hand, when people listened because they were looking for distraction from their thoughts, the opposite was true.

When I was in my early twenties I found classical music concerts quite hard work. I would marvel at how other members of the audience seemed so rapt and attentive. They barely moved. They never appeared at all restless. I assumed they were concentrating hard on every bar of music and on every sweep of the cellist's bow. I was nothing like as focused, I thought. My mind would wander far from the music making in front of me, and I'd struggle to bring it back to the concert.

But then my partner, who loves concerts, told me there was nothing wrong with my mind wandering. Indeed, part of the point of concerts, he said, was that the music set your mind free. Sitting still, and with few other distractions, you could float away, coming back to more intent listening and looking at times, but then floating away again. That was a great moment for me, and I now find concerts much more relaxing. Ironically, I suspect I actually concentrate more too, as I don't feel under pressure to do so.

At the last Prom I went to at the Royal Albert Hall the man next to me took it a step further by reading a novel on an e-reader throughout. I was distracted by wondering what he was reading, but he was completely absorbed. Patrick Summers, the music director of the Houston Grand Opera, tells a story of how during *Parsifal* at the Royal Opera House, Covent Garden, a woman in front of him in the stalls texted throughout the entire performance. 'Ushers tried to stop her. She refused. Her fellow patrons tried to admonish her. She refused. Everyone finally gave up and put what attention we could back to Wagner.'[15]

Clearly Patrick was appalled by this behaviour, and given how distracting smartphones can be to others this woman was being discourteous to her fellow operagoers. But for all we know, the combination of the lush music of Wagner and the pleasure of texting friends (perhaps to say she was listening to Wagner at Covent Garden) was her perfect way to relax.

Alone or With Others?

We know from research that listening to music in the presence of other people can amplify the emotions induced by that music. I'm sure the men in Vinyl Club would agree, and I certainly do. I've never liked watching Glastonbury festival on TV because it makes me feel left out. People in the live audience are clearly having an experience that's much more intense and pleasurable than mine.

When the music is happy, as it generally is at Glastonbury, then contagion is fine. It is why people log on to the Glastonbury website within seconds of the tickets being made available. It is why people are willing to pay hundreds of pounds to camp in a muddy swamp for four days. They want to be part of the collective joy and emotion of the festival. They want to be part of something that people like me, reluctantly watching at home, don't experience in anything like the same way.

But what about when the music is sad and depressing? For decades parents have worried about teenagers sitting in rooms together listening to music they, the parents, consider depressing, particularly if the teenagers are part of certain subcultures such as goths or emos. Are those parents right to be concerned? I had a bit of a goth phase myself. I spent a fair amount of time listening to The Sisters of Mercy and The Mission with fellow fans. And I'm tempted to say it never did me any harm. But such habits have now become a serious topic of research among psychologists. There is a good reason for this. We know that rumination – which is different from everyday worrying – when a person obsessively ponders the same events over and over again, focusing only on their feelings of distress and their possible causes, rather than any solutions, is associated with depression and even an increased risk of suicide.

The Australian psychologist Sandra Garrido set out to investigate whether hours spent listening to sad music in a group could lead to a kind of group rumination, or whether those hours together have the opposite effect, providing shared support and companionship. For her research Garrido recruited people living in Australia, the UK and the USA via mental health and depression websites. Roughly half were experiencing mild to severe depression at the time; the rest might well have experienced mental health problems in the past but were not feeling depressed at the time of the study. They all filled in questionnaires, indicating the extent to which they agreed or disagreed with items, such as 'Listening to music reminds me about the sad things in my life' or 'The music I listen to when sad gives me a reason to be sad', as well as statements about listening to music in a group, such as 'Sometimes when I am with my friends we listen to the same songs over and over again', or 'My friends and I like to talk about how the music we listen to is like our own lives'. Each participant was also asked to name a song they might listen to when they're sad. This gave the researchers a list of songs to use for some in-depth analysis of miserable lyrics.

The findings are striking and worrying.[16] The depressed

people did indeed listen to more songs with negative lyrics. They also tended to listen more often with their friends than alone, compared with people who weren't depressed at the time of the study, and were more likely to ruminate while the music was playing. Unfortunately while most other people said listening to sad music made them feel better, the depressed people said it made them feel worse. So listening to sad music if you have depression – and in particular listening to it in a group – would appear to be a bad idea. But the implications of this study are, in fact, more nuanced. For this research found that people with anxiety did benefit from listening to music in groups, perhaps because bonding with the other people in the group helped them to cope with their anxious feelings.

What about those of us who are lucky enough not to experience overwhelming anxiety or depression? Does listening to music in a group or on our own make much difference to our mood? And, specifically, is a group experience more restful? Or is listening alone better for that? In the Swedish study mentioned above, people felt calmest after listening to music alone, followed by listening with a partner. Likewise, the Finnish teenagers were clear that if they wanted to relax after a stressful day and then feel refreshed, then listening to music alone was more effective. It allowed them to get away from other people, to reflect on their day and to find solace.

These studies would suggest that, for relaxation, listening to recorded music at home is best. Yet, this is hardly the optimal way to experience music. Serious musicians would certainly subscribe to the idea that music is at its most powerful when listened to without distraction. Patrick

Summers, the music director of the Houston Grand Opera, who we met earlier in this chapter, certainly falls into the category of serious musician and in his recent book *The Spirit of This Place: How Music Illuminates the Human Spirit* [17] he makes a typically bold claim: 'I believe that the art of listening is perhaps the most important on Earth; and the arts, particularly serious music, teach us to listen closely, with intent, with intelligence, with pliability.'

However, Patrick is certainly not suggesting that the best listening is done on your own. As you would expect of an artist of his standing, he thinks the best way to experience music is to play it, followed by hearing it live, followed – in a distant third – by listening to a recording.

There is a lot in this, I'm sure. And I know that my most profound musical experiences, including feeling utterly soothed and relaxed, have come when I have been totally immersed in the experience of listening to music in a concert hall. But there is only so much time we can spend going to gigs, and although it is a curse in some ways, we are also lucky to live in an age when we can listen to music – pretty much everything ever recorded – instantly, anytime and anywhere.

So if you want to listen to music to help you rest, what seems to be significant is less whether you do it on your own or with other people, and more whether you choose the right circumstances and the right music. And by the right music, I mean – let me stress again – the sort of music you prefer.

David Byrne of Talking Heads would surely agree with this rule. He ends his bestselling book *How Music Works* with a section in which he says he likes music that is liberated from 'the prison of melody, rigid structure and harmony' but also music that adheres to these guidelines. He refuses to privilege one genre of music over another.

But it is another observation of Byrne's that I am going to end this chapter with. Earlier in his book, he makes the point that the world is now 'awash' with music. 'We used to have to pay for music or make it ourselves; playing, hearing, and experiencing it was exceptional, a rare and special experience. Now hearing it is ubiquitous, and silence is the rarity that we pay for and savor.'[18] Perhaps in this world of noise, the sound which can feel most restful of all is silence.

3

I WANT TO BE ALONE

I've never lived alone. I lived with my parents until I went to university, then I shared a house with friends, then I moved in with my partner. As a result, if I am alone at home for a few days I enjoy the novelty of having the house to myself. I relish the peace and quiet. But only briefly. I'm soon out in the front garden dead-heading or watering the plants, not only because they need it but because I know my neighbours or even strangers will stop to chat.

The extraordinary thing about spending time on your own, is the way time stretches. The days seem to dawdle by and the evenings can feel endless. Having written a book on the psychology of time perception, I know all too well how and why time can warp, but it still surprises me whenever it happens.

And there's a paradox here. Why is it that there seem to be so many more hours in the day when I'm on my own, yet I get less done? I have a lie-in and stay up late, I muck about on my phone and watch more TV than normal. I eat more randomly and rarely clear up any mess I've made until the following day at least. There is no one else to consult or consider, leading to a disconcerting combination of more freedom and a lack of purpose.

Yet there's undoubtedly something special, even magical, about being on my own. And I certainly feel more rested. When my husband returns from whatever trip he's been on, I am always pleased to see him, but it feels as if normal life has returned too. And normal life, for me, tends to be full and busy and sociable.

Humans have evolved to be social beings and cooperation has been key to our survival and success as a species. Our ancestors who lived on the edge of early societies quickly found themselves in danger, picked off by wild animals or left behind when a hostile tribe attacked. And with the development of larger societies and sophisticated economies, the need to cooperate, to trust each other and build relationships has become more important, not less. The notion that human beings have thrived through selfishness has been demolished by an endless line of anthropologists, sociologists and economists.

In their recent book *The Inner Level,* a sequel to the hugely successful *The Spirit Level,* the renowned academics Richard Wilkinson and Kate Pickett draw extensively on evidence from these fields and from evolutionary neuroscience to come to the following conclusion: 'Clearly, the human brain is, in a very real sense, a social organ. Its growth and development have been driven by the requirements of social life. This is the case because the quality of our relationships with each other has always been crucial to survival, well-being and reproductive success.'[1]

It is for these reasons that we have evolved to find being on our own difficult, even painful. That pain is important and serves an evolutionary purpose. The social neuroscientist John Cacioppo argued that the hurt caused by loneliness is positive in that it acts as a signal to us to look for new friends or to find a way of improving our existing relationships. It prompts us to maintain our connections with other people. He likens feelings of loneliness to thirst. If you are thirsty you look for water. If you are lonely you look for other people. For many thousands of years humans have stayed safe and lived better by living in cooperative groups, so it makes sense to have a survival mechanism which drives us to connect with others.[2]

But despite these evolutionary and social factors, and despite the recent high-profile interest in tackling loneliness, and the misery and stress it can undoubtedly cause, some people, in fact many people, long to be alone and can't really rest until they find solitude. Sartre famously said, 'Hell is other people,' and the Rest Test certainly seems to suggest that if we are looking for heavenly peace we find it on our own. All of the top five activities in the survey are frequently carried out alone, while seeing friends and family or socialising didn't even make it into the top ten. Some individuals even selected spending time alone as the most restful activity of all, especially women under the age of thirty.

You may be thinking, 'Oh well, that all depends on how sociable people are; introverts might yearn for solitude, but surely not the extroverts?'

Yet when we examined personality factors in the Rest Test we found that even the extroverts rated time spent alone as more restful than time spent with other people, though it's true that they were less drawn to solitude than natural introverts.

We all crave some solitude, but not too much and only at certain times. We can all relate to the pleasure Wordsworth took in wandering 'lonely as a cloud', and the 'bliss of solitude' he experiences when he thinks back on seeing those daffodils in the wild while lying on his couch 'in pensive mood'. But it is noteworthy that he describes the dancing daffodils as 'a jocund company', and of course as often as the poet was walking the peaks and fells of the Lake District alone, he was striding out with his friend Coleridge and his sister Dorothy. As ever, balance and choice are important factors in our attitude towards being on our own. To quote another great writer, this time the Nobel Prize-winning French novelist Colette: there are days when solitude is 'a heady wine' and others when it's 'a bitter tonic'.[3]

Lonely v. Alone

Today, because more of us than ever before live in urban areas, surrounded by people, and because modern communication links us together 24/7, it can feel as if we are almost never on our own. But, in fact, this is a false impression. On average we spend about 29 per cent of waking time alone.[4] It is worth pausing to digest this fact.

A lot of that time we are not really appreciating that we are alone. We're sat in front of a screen doing some boring work task or we're travelling home on our own, but in a packed train, tube or bus. We do not see this as quality 'me time' and it is mostly not very restful. The study in which people were beeped at random throughout the day and asked each time to take swabs of their saliva for testing, revealed that levels of the stress hormone cortisol were, on average, higher at the moments in the day when they were alone. And, not surprisingly, cortisol levels were higher still in people who were not just in a circumstantially solitary state but also *felt* sad and lonely.[5]

The psychologists Christopher Long and James Averill have found that if you are alone it is important to recall that you have many meaningful connections with other people if you want to avoid slipping into actual loneliness.[6] And the eminent historian of solitude Barbara Taylor told me she asks her students to think about who is with them in their heads when they're alone and most, on considering the question carefully, answer 'with people they most love' or a few say 'with God'.

If you feel you lack meaningful relationships with people who really understand you – or you don't have faith in a higher being who might serve the same purpose – then loneliness can strike whether or not you're alone. Isolation can of course contribute to feelings of loneliness, but it's often the quality of relationships that you have in your life – not the immediate fact of being with people – that determines whether you feel lonely.

Quantity is a factor too. Loneliness is also driven by a person's sense that there is a mismatch between the number of close friendships they'd like to have and the number they actually do have.

Researchers at Iowa State University found that among college students, as the number of close friends they have approaches the number they think ideal, so feelings of loneliness decrease.[7] It doesn't matter how high or low that number is – that's a subjective judgement – but if a person *feels* there is a deficit of quality relationships in their lives, then they tend towards loneliness. The Iowa researchers also discovered something which surprised even them. When the number of friends students have exceeds the number they desire, the students begin to feel lonelier again. Perhaps they find having an excess of friends a burden, or perhaps although they consider these friends to be close friends, they aren't close enough. Or maybe – and this is most interesting for our purposes – these students have so many friends that they feel they aren't getting enough time alone.

In a survey on loneliness we asked people: what is the opposite of loneliness? A third were unable to answer the question, but of those who could, contentment with social relationships was the most common answer, followed by happiness and friendship. Then afterwards a musician I know called Sean O'Hagan stopped me in the street to say he'd heard the radio programmes I'd presented on loneliness and had been thinking about this question ever since. He summed it up nicely: 'The opposite of loneliness is wanting some time alone.'

Perhaps he's right. Perhaps the true sign of not feeling lonely is longing for solitude.

Losing Yourself When You're Alone

Being alone has an impact on our sense of self. This impact can be positive or negative, depending on the degree of solitude. Let's think for a moment of the most extreme situation of aloneness – the appalling punishment, solitary confinement.

Some prisoners who have experienced it say that initially,

when they first move into a cell on their own, it's a relief to get some peace from other inmates, some time to daydream, some time to rest. But what begins with the mind wandering can end with the mind ruined. As one man, Tabir, who'd been held in isolation for many months as a political prisoner in North Africa, told me, 'No one knows that you are there, so you are nothing. You are zero.'

Tabir's cell had no bed or toilet, just a small, high window. The long days passed in silence until the sun set. Then the noises began: the screams of fellow prisoners undergoing torture. As appalling as it sounds, he found these cries comforting in a way, as they reminded him that he was still in a world shared with other people.[8]

Craig Haney, a professor of psychology at the University of California, Santa Cruz, has studied the impact of solitary confinement on the inmates of the California supermax jail Pelican Bay State Prison, where more than a thousand inmates are locked up alone. Some have spent more than a decade in solitary confinement. And you will not be surprised to learn that this is a situation that is far from restful.

Each prisoner reacts differently, with some experiencing a terror, known as isolation panic, the moment the door is locked behind them. Others find that they can cope at first, but gradually lose hope and become depressed. As times goes on, the lack of stimulation takes its toll on prisoners' cognitive abilities and they can begin to experience memory lapses. Haney has also seen instances where people permanently lose any sense of who they are: 'I've seen it happen – an extreme case of somebody's identity becoming so badly damaged and essentially destroyed that it is impossible for them to reconstruct it.'

In everyday life, we constantly use our interactions with people to establish and reconfigure our own identities, so a complete lack of contact with others can lead some prisoners to wonder whether they still exist. The modernist author David Markson explores this idea in his brilliant novel *Wittgenstein's Mistress,* in which the sole protagonist, Kate, is revealed to be the only person left alive in the world. Kate's interior monologue constantly and inconclusively comes back to questions of the meaning of existence and whether, if you are the only person who exists, you do, in fact, exist. Though, in a nod to the Lonely v. Alone debate we explored above, Markson also has his heroine muse that 'she had paradoxically been practically as alone before all this happened as she was now, incidentally'.[9]

In an attempt to hang on to some sense of his own self, Tabir spent the nights talking or singing to himself. Sometimes he picked fights with the guards solely to experience some human interaction by prompting a procedure known as 'cell extraction'. If he disobeyed an order, by refusing to hand over an empty food tray, for example, then a group of armed guards came to the cell to restrain him. Although some physical pain was usually involved, the event at least brought him into contact with fellow human beings. Throughout his incarceration, Tabir, like the Auschwitz survivor Viktor Frankl before him, was determined that whatever the guards did to him, they would never 'conquer his mind'. 'Whatever you do,' he told me, 'don't give up fighting. Smile and be happy – and don't be afraid of anybody.' Tabir did eventually manage to escape his captors during a hospital stay, then travelled to the UK and sought asylum.

While extreme isolation causes a loss of identity that is very serious, if we choose to spend a short amount of time alone, a much milder, and this time beneficial, kind of loss of self can take place. The advantage of choosing to spend time alone is that you have no identity thrust on you by others. You are free to let your mind wander to examine who you really are and what you really think, free from the influence of others. Some people speak of achieving a new understanding of themselves. This makes sense of the common desire to get away from it all at the times of your life when you have the most important decisions to make.

A study of eighteen- to twenty-five-year-olds in the USA found that spending time alone was associated with greater creativity.[10] This makes sense if you consider the benefits of daydreaming discussed earlier. Daydreaming can foster creativity, but is harder to do with others present, so time alone gives the mind the chance to wander. Solitude also helps us to deal with our emotions, by giving us the chance to reflect on what's been happening in our lives and to explore our memories from the past. Then hopefully we can make the best decisions about the future.

This has led to calls for leaders in business, who are forever in meetings, answering emails or at the mercy of their door-always-open policies, to spend more time alone in order to help them come to the right ethical decisions.[11] In the late 1950s and early 1960s the then Prime Minister Harold Macmillan famously found time each day to spend an hour alone reading Jane Austen or Anthony Trollope. I somehow doubt any recent prime minister has had that opportunity.

In these cases, being on your own is an opportunity to lose yourself, to refresh your thinking, without being endlessly distracted by other people. It is not a state in which we would want to exist all the time or for very long, but in small doses it is undoubtedly good for our well-being and can help us to feel rested.

Solitary or Lonely?

What really matters is how much control you have over the time you spend on your own. Choosing to spend some time alone is very different from having no choice about it. However sociable you are, you will certainly enjoy some time on your own if you can choose when and how; and however introverted you are, you will find enforced solitude leaves you feeling lonely.

The problem of loneliness has attracted a great deal of media coverage recently. The UK even has a Minister for Loneliness, charged with working across government departments to address the issue. At Radio 4, I instigated the BBC Loneliness Experiment, a collaboration with three psychologists from British universities and the Wellcome Collection, in which we asked listeners to complete a survey.[12] Even though it was a lengthy process to answer the questions, typically taking thirty to forty minutes, 55,000 people from around the world took part. We were staggered at the response. It shows how seriously people are engaging with this topic.

Some people talk of an epidemic of loneliness, and it is true that the total number of lonely people is rising.

But that is simply because there are more people in the world now. When it comes to proportions, the picture is more mixed. The first image that tends to spring to mind when we think of a lonely person is of someone elderly, stuck in their home, seeing no one from week to week and spending Christmas day alone. This is the reality for a lot of older people, but Christina Victor from Brunel University has examined data in the UK going back to 1948, and found that the proportion of older people experiencing chronic loneliness has remained steady for seventy years, with 6 to 13 per cent saying they feel lonely all or most of the time.[13]

Moreover, in our survey, mirroring the findings of several others, a higher percentage of younger people than older people said they often felt lonely, with middle-aged people falling in between. As I say, this isn't the image we tend to hold in mind of loneliness or isolation, and in fact 84 per cent of people in the survey believed they would or might feel lonely in old age. But they also said that, looking back, the loneliest time of their lives was when they were young.

Perhaps the explanation is that we find solitude difficult to cope with when we're young and start to both cope with it better and even desire it more as we mature. It is possible too that we appreciate the restfulness of being alone more as we get older. And it might be linked with our growing ability to regulate our emotions. One of the best things about ageing is that we get better at comforting ourselves when things go wrong. Just as babies gradually (and to the huge relief of their exhausted parents) learn to self-soothe and to get themselves back to sleep when they wake up, so as children we gradually learn how to improve a bad mood by distracting ourselves or trying to put things into perspective.

Our ability to regulate our emotions continues to improve after we reach adulthood. With years of experience comes the insight that we won't always feel this way and that there are steps we can take to make ourselves feel better. I wonder whether these skills have a particular relevance to loneliness. Perhaps we simply become more accustomed to dealing with an unpleasant feeling and learn that most of the time it is temporary. Or perhaps we take steps to mitigate it, seeking out new friendships or finding ways to reinvigorate older ones.

However we mitigate loneliness, it is important that we do. Chronic loneliness is associated with poor physical health. Reviews of the research have found that people who say they are chronically lonely have a third higher risk of heart disease and stroke,[14] higher blood pressure[15] and a lower life expectancy.[16] These are serious outcomes, but many of the studies are cross-sectional, taking a snapshot in time, so we can't be certain of the direction of causality. It is possible that unhappy isolation leads to more illness, possibly by increasing inflammation in the body. But it could also happen the other way around. The poor health could come first, leading people to become isolated and lonely because their illness prevents them from going out. Or maybe lonely people show up in the statistics as less healthy because their loneliness has robbed them of the motivation to look after their health. And of course it could work both ways.

Although it's hard to disentangle exactly what's happening

here, research can definitely tell us something that anyone who's ever felt lonely can tell you: loneliness has a significant effect on well-being. There is good evidence that it can lead to sadness and affect the quality of our sleep.[17] It can also result in a vicious cycle in which people feel so lonely that they withdraw from social situations and become acutely sensitive to any signs of rejection, which in turn makes them feel even lonelier. Research has shown that if a person feels lonely, then a year later they are more likely than others to have symptoms of depression.[18]

We tend to think of loneliness as a modern phenomenon resulting from the ills of modern life, in which we live in atomised social units and disconnected communities, but the historian Barbara Taylor, who studies the history of both loneliness and solitude, points out that the unpleasant emotion of loneliness has been described since antiquity, even if the word 'loneliness' wasn't always used. Before the seventeenth century the word lonely was seldom applied to people and used more often to describe something set apart, such as a single tree or building or – back to Wordsworth – a cloud. Over the centuries the word loneliness was gradually used more and more, as the idea grew of the modern world as an alienating place.

While loneliness was on the whole viewed negatively, the valence of solitude has, as Barbara Taylor admits, presented more of a challenge for the historian because it has had many meanings over the centuries, sometimes negative and sometimes positive. Before the eighteenth century solitude often referred to life in the country. The rich would talk of 'retiring into solitude'. This meant going to their country estate, but they weren't alone there. As well as their staff, they took their families and often close friends too. In antiquity there was a sense that only through solitude could a mind seek the truth. This was fine for philosophers, because like the gods, they could survive alone, but it would be dangerous for the less-educated.[19] This fits in with a view that Barbara Taylor has found at times throughout history, of solitude as unnatural and even immoral: 'They were misanthropes, they were egoists, they bore no sense of responsibility to the common man.' One of the fears was that time spent alone would lead to 'unbridled creativity'. Petrarch, Montaigne and Wordsworth, writing in the four-teenth, sixteenth and eighteenth centuries respectively, all saw the benefits of solitude, but also discussed the pain and anxiety it could cause.

We can see echoes of this in modern Japan today, where the word for solitude and loneliness is the same – *kodoku*. It's a state viewed so positively that there are hundreds of books on the topic, some bestsellers with titles like *The Power of Loneliness* and *Loneliness is Beautiful*. Twice as many men as women live alone and the numbers are rising. Junko Okamoto, a writer from Tokyo who goes into companies to help prepare people for retirement, is trying to raise awareness of the downsides of solitude. She's concerned that its glorification hides the fact that some people really are painfully lonely.

For a country famous for its collectivist culture, social capital is weak in Japan, and with a hierarchical system at work and respect centred on seniority, it can be difficult to make strong friendships in the workplace. With long hours before retirement there's little time for hobbies or friends outside work. So retirement can come as a shock.

Perhaps these books celebrating solitude bring some comfort, suggesting it is a state to revere, rather than fear, but Okamoto is still worried that plenty are not living alone by choice. She feels she's a lone voice, ironically. When she tries to emphasise the downside of loneliness in the media the comments she receives tell her to leave people in peace, to leave them to their resting perhaps.

This ambivalence towards solitude is nothing new. The great German novelist Thomas Mann said 'Solitude gives birth to the original in us, to beauty unfamiliar and perilous – to poetry. But also, it gives birth to the opposite: to the perverse, the illicit, the absurd.'[20] Those who have read the work of two other great writers drawn to solitude, Emily Dickinson and Samuel Beckett, will see what Mann was getting at.

We want to be alone, but we also fear being alone. And we're suspicious of other people who want solitude. It's rare to invite someone out and for them to decline by saying they want to spend the evening alone. Instead an excuse is needed, because why would you prefer to spend time alone than with friends? 'Sorry, I'm washing my hair' has become a joke euphemism among women who don't want to go out with someone on a date. Perhaps it also signals that it is okay to be alone.

The desire for solitude has often been pathologised, with people who like spending time alone viewed as 'self-indulgent, dangerous rebels who risk losing their minds'.[21] 'Loner' tends to be an insult, not a compliment, implying that a person is a bit weird, if not a downright sociopath or worse. Think how often the phrase 'a bit of a loner' seems to be used to describe paedophiles and serial killers.

In William Trevor's prize-winning novel *Felicia's Journey*, the gloriously sinister Mr Hilditch, who preys on vulnerable young women, is portrayed as living on his own in his late mother's house, opening a tin of pilchards for his supper and then making a cup of Ovaltine before going up to bed. The solitary life is made to sound spine-chilling.[22] Spending some time alone tends to be seen as benign, but choosing a largely solitary life is viewed as eccentric, a risk to health and sanity. We are often wary of those who prefer their own company to ours.

Achieving a Balance

If you are looking for solitude in order to get some rest in the modern age, the question is the same as it always has been, even if we phrase it differently: how to achieve me time that doesn't become lonesome time?

First, it's important to remember that not everyone finds solitude restful. Even though it scored highly in the Rest Test, some people do find time on their own leads them to ruminate on what's going wrong in their lives, making them feel sad or depressed. It's clear from Christopher Long and James Averill's research that solitude is not equally nourishing for everyone. Those who don't like it are more likely to distract themselves from the lack of company by watching TV or phoning people – anything to get a human connection. Some feel anxious and disconnected.

Not surprisingly introverts are more enthusiastic about spending time alone.[23] The people who have the best moods when they're alone tend to have lower than average moods when they're with other people, while the people who are happy when they're with others can feel sadder when alone. But don't forget that when it comes to rest, rather than fun, in the Rest Test most extroverts still chose solitary activities as the most restful.

Relishing time alone is something we gradually learn to do as children and it might start earlier than that. Even babies look away from faces when they are feeling over-stimulated. Donald Winnicott is a psychologist whose work can comfort parents because he wrote about the idea of not being a perfect mother, but a 'good enough mother'. (Writing in 1970, he did only refer to mothers.) Winnicott also emphasised the importance of children gradually learning to enjoy short amounts of time alone. The development of this ability was, he said, a major achievement in their development. He called solitude in childhood 'a most precious possession'.

A study of seven- to twelve-year-olds in Greece demonstrated that even before they've left primary school, children understand that solitude can be useful. The older the Greek children were, the more benefits of solitude they could list, including peace, quiet, relaxation, reflection, concentration, problem solving, planning ahead, daydreaming, freedom from criticism and a reduction in anxiety, tension and anger. Two thirds of the children acknowledged that it is a human desire to want to be alone sometimes.[24]

Adolescents in the USA and Europe spend on average a quarter of their time alone, which when you take into account the time they spend at school or with friends is more time than they spend with their families.[25] And the older they get, the more they value this time alone. This finding mirrored research in Flanders in Belgium. Teenagers were followed for several years and the study found that their fear of spending time alone steadily diminished as they got closer to the age of eighteen and became more independent. The girls were the first to begin to view solitude positively, with the boys soon catching up.[26]

There might even be a sweet spot for the amount of time alone that benefits teenagers. This was illustrated by research conducted with a group of ten- to fifteen-year-olds in four suburbs of Chicago.[27] They were beeped seven times a day and asked to immediately fill in a questionnaire about the company they were in at that very moment, along with information on how they felt and whether or not this company was their choice. Those who liked spending some time alone were better adjusted psychologically in the view of their parents and their teachers. But they needed to spend just the right amount of time by themselves. Too much or too little was associated with more negative moods.

So where did the Goldilocks zone lie? The ideal was spending 25 to 45 per cent of non-class time alone. Which, looking back to the beginning of this chapter, is – happily – about the average amount of time all of us spend on our own anyway, suggesting that as adults we are intuitively quite good at seeking out the right amount of solitude.

Solitude can, of course, mean different things in different places. At school students are expected to be sociable, both in the classroom and outside it. Those children who prefer to be alone during breaks at school or to read a book are seen as loners and a bit strange. The 'normal' thing to do is to play together or chat together. But, of course, not everyone at school who is on their own during school breaks wants to be. Children can be cruel about shunning others. And the very sociable nature of the school environment can magnify the loneliness felt by pupils who don't have many friends. In response to the BBC Loneliness Experiment a young woman in her twenties, who is blind, wrote a heart-breaking blog about the loneliness of lunchtimes when she was at school, in which she included a list of the tips which had helped her to find people to talk to. They included holding doors open so that she could start a conversation or thinking of topics in advance that might allow her to have a chat with teachers during the break. If she knew someone had new kittens, she asked about those. Teachers, after all, couldn't just ignore her, and even a brief conversation made a difference

Fortunately, by the time we enter adulthood and the workplace, in many situations there's no requirement to socialise during breaks. (Although even this depends on where you live: employers in Japan and increasingly in Californian tech companies might expect it.) But where people do have the choice about how to spend their breaks, as we have found throughout this chapter, the key to enjoying being on your own, and finding it restful, is choice. The same, of course, is true of being with others.

A Restful Solitude

It is important to understand just how much our appreciation of time alone as restful rather than painful depends on the nature and strength of our relationships. The psychotherapist Jonathan Detrixhe has looked at attitudes to solitude through the lens of psychological research on attachment.[28] Toddlers who feel securely attached to their parents see them as a base from which they can safely explore. At this young age, children generally want their parents physically close by, even if they find it fun to run off sometimes. But as they mature, children become accustomed to spending time away from their parents and even on their own. By the time we become adults, we generally don't live with our parents and may see them rarely. Our key relationship may be with a partner, or we may live alone. Either way, the chances are that we are much less likely to feel lonely when we're alone if we have a strong human attachment to someone. The person or persons to whom we have that attachment don't need to be physically present all the time, but we need to know we can turn to them.

Abraham Maslow is the psychologist who was famous for his hierarchy of needs, often drawn as a pyramid with basic things like food and shelter, which are essential for survival, at the bottom of the pyramid and the higher needs such as love and esteem stacked up above. The happiest people of all get right to the top of the pyramid, where they achieve 'self-actualisation'. They have realised their full potential, becoming everything that they could be. It sounds like a great state to be in.

Unfortunately, according to Maslow, only 2 per cent of people get there. Now, Maslow's methods have been criticised for their lack of rigour. He made subjective decisions about who was and wasn't self-actualised, declaring that Einstein, Beethoven, Eleanor Roosevelt and, funnily enough, he himself all were. He found that he, Albert, Ludwig and Eleanor were all creative, spontaneous, concerned for others, witty, tolerant of uncertainty and good at accepting themselves. They also enjoyed 'peak experiences' daily – those moments where everything feels fantastic, where they felt completely in the moment and nothing else concerned them.

The reason I'm mentioning all this is that Maslow found that these lucky self-actualisers were more likely than the rest of us to seek time alone. This finding would appear to back up what we have found throughout this chapter, that solitude is most enjoyed and most valuable when it is voluntary and is part of a well-rounded and satisfied life.

In order to feel truly rested we need to get away from other people, to escape their chatter, and hopefully the chatter of our own minds too. In the right quantities, time spent alone can allow us to retreat and to tend to our emotions, hopefully leaving us feeling renewed. It can also give us the opportunity to think more deeply, to discover ourselves, and perhaps to stimulate creativity and new ideas.

Maybe we should try to schedule some solitude, but we shouldn't pressurise ourselves to achieve any of its potential benefits. If the appeal of solitude is a withdrawal from the pressures imposed upon us, the last thing we want to do is to impose different pressures on ourselves. Being alone gives us all the chance to spend some time without others judging us – without having to keep up a social face.

Social media can be wonderful for alleviating loneliness by allowing people to connect, but the new 'always on' culture of social media can also make it harder to avoid outside pressures. Somehow we have to ensure that we don't allow social media to rob us of the benefits of solitude, or it might stop feeling so restful. After all, can we even call

being alone genuine solitude if we are constantly commu-
nicating with others?

I end this chapter with a question: where is the best place
to spend time alone? If you ask people where they most
commonly spend time by themselves, the answer is at home,
but if you ask a slightly different question, where people
would most *like* to spend their time alone, you get a rather
different answer – out in nature.[29] It is to nature that we
turn in the next chapter.

2

SPENDING TIME IN NATURE

A t first sight it looks like a large lamp post, painted green. But there's no lamp at the top. Just a four-metre high, cast-iron pillar standing in a grassy clearing in the middle of woodland. What is it and why is it here?

Back in the middle of the nineteenth century, the post was driven into the peat until only the top of it was visible above the ground at what was thought to be the lowest point in the area, and indeed in Britain, at the edge of Whittlesea Mere, a huge fen in Cambridgeshire. The mere was due to be drained to provide more space for farming, and the pillar – the brain child of William Wells of Holmewood Hall, a nearby stately home – was designed to measure the shrinking and sinking of the land as the water was drained from the bog.

Quite quickly, the marker post began to emerge as the ground subsided – a process that has continued over the decades.

By 1957, the post stood so high and was so unsteady that it needed to be held aloft by steel guy ropes radiating out from the top of the pillar like taut maypole ribbons. Before it was drained, Whittlesea Mere was the largest lake in lowland England. Writing in 1697, Celia Fiennes, who spent almost twenty years travelling the country on horseback, described it as '3 mile broad and six mile long. In the midst is a little island where a great store of Wildfowle breed . . . when you enter the mouth of the Mer it looks formidable and its [sic] often very dangerous by reason of sudden winds that will rise like Hurricanes.'[1] Despite these hurricanes, the mere was a place of recreation, with yachting and regattas. In the harder winters, people flocked to the fen for skating and ice fairs.

This was all lost when the needs of agriculture led to the draining. But some 150 years on, in 2001, the process was put into reverse when the Great Fen project was started. It will take half a century to complete and will see thousands of acres of redundant farmland reflooded to join two of Britain's earliest nature reserves. The Great Fen will provide a habitat for creatures which have not been present in the area for centuries, such as the bluethroat, the common crane and even the European bison. Butterflies, such as the purple emperor and silver-washed fritillary, have already been attracted to the restored wetlands.

But the restoration of the ecology and biodiversity of this area of eastern England is only part of the plan. A large reason why the project has attracted millions of pounds of funding is because it will give people living nearby the opportunity to spend time out in nature.

This part of Britain is flat. On a grey day you could even call it bleak. It is not traditionally picturesque English countryside. But it is peaceful and has its own charm, particularly now that reflooding of the area is taking effect. There's a reason I know this area and have a special affection for it. I grew up not that far away, and my father was one of the people who put the Great Fen conservation scheme together.

Soon after it started, he brought me to see the project, which he knows won't end until long after he's dead, and which I might not live to see in all its glory. We sat on the top of a ridge, surveying the narrow waterways criss-crossing the bright green land stretching in every direction, mentally time-travelling back to imagine how it might have looked a century ago and forward to how it might look in a century's time, after the flooding is complete. There are more beautiful, and certainly more spectacular views of nature in Britain, but it was a poignant experience and one that induced a feeling of great calm and contemplation.

With an ornithologist for a father, my sister and I spent much of our childhood on walks in the countryside. Looking back, I feel we were lucky, of course – but at the time we used to moan about the length of these walks and the fact that we were told not just the species of every bird, but its sex and whether it was a first, second or third year, information that my sister and I didn't feel we needed. We couldn't wait to get home and put on the telly.

On the upside, when the teacher asked us to bring in items for the nature table at school it was an easy task. All we had to do was to be brave enough to plunge our hands into the pockets of my dad's battered khaki jacket and we would be able to pull out an abandoned robin's nest or regurgitated owl pellets or otter spraints (otter poo, if you're wondering).

Now that I live in a city and the chance to get out into the countryside is rarer, I miss it. When I do go on a country walk, I relish the experience, and I find myself peering into cottage windows on sunny afternoons and feeling disappointed when I see people watching TV. Why aren't they out enjoying nature? Isn't that a whole point of living in a rural area? If I lived in a place like this, I would be out walking all the time, I think.

Except, of course, that I probably wouldn't. I look back on my childhood and how I preferred watching the motorcycle cops' series *CHiPs* to walking with my father by the river. And I notice just how often I am at home now watching the television to relax when I could be out in London enjoying the hundreds of plays and concerts and other cultural events that take place every evening . . . Just as I like knowing that at about 7.30 p.m. curtains are simultaneously rising all over the West End even if I'm not there to witness them, so I am sure it's nice to know that wonderful landscapes are available a moment's walk from your front door if you live in the countryside, even if you choose to stay indoors much of the time. In both situations, the opportunity is not going away. You can always do it some other day. Perhaps it's like good health. You value it most when it's taken away.

For the city dweller like me, spending time in nature is one of the classic means of escape from everyday life, a great way to rest and relax. Often, being out in the countryside involves walking and we've already seen how that can feel restful, despite the physical exertion it requires. But there are ways to enjoy nature without walking.

Nature Bathing

Throughout this book we've heard how hard many of us find it to do nothing. While practices like mindfulness work for some, for others such disciplines and techniques are irksome. This is why being out in nature is so valued, I think. Sitting silently at the summit of a hill surveying the dales around you (even if you drove there) doesn't involve you doing anything, or anything much, but somehow it is the opposite of vegging out on your sofa. In the same way, watching the water flow by while lying on a riverbank somehow feels more purposeful than lying in bed. There can be idleness in being out in the countryside, but it is excusable idleness. We are *doing* something, even if it is just being in a natural place. There is meaning in it.

Take a moment to think about where your favourite place is. You can choose anywhere at all, indoors or out. Don't read on until you've decided on one place.

Did you select a room in your home or perhaps a cherished café or pub? Or did you choose somewhere out in nature? Your answer might depend on your mood (although of course in this book I've skewed your answer by posing this question in a chapter where I've already got you thinking about nature).

In a Finnish study people living in two cities were asked to mark their favourite and least favourite local places on a map, while also completing a questionnaire to assess their current mood. Transport hubs didn't fare well, coming out as overwhelmingly unpopular places. But when it came to locations that people really liked, the answers depended on their mood. Those feeling positive were more likely to choose a residential location such as their living room, while the people in a low mood were much more likely to choose somewhere out in nature.[2]

From toddlerhood onwards, we learn to regulate our emotions, at times consciously choosing an activity which we know will make us feel better, such as leaving the room and going for a walk when we're angry or playing happy music when we feel sad. Sometimes we aren't even conscious that we're doing it. After an especially difficult day at work you might find yourself taking a diversion through the local park on the way home without thinking about it.[3] Many of us seem to have an instinct that there's something that nature can do for us, that it is restful, especially when we don't feel so good. The surprise is that so far science has found it hard to pin down exactly what that something is.

Subjectively we know nature feels calming. In Japan spending time in the woods is considered so therapeutic that it even has its own name: forest bathing. In therapy when a client is asked to visualise a relaxing scene, they tend to be encouraged to think about a sunny day on a beach or a mountain view. Admittedly our idealised view of nature is fairly specific, not only visually but even temporally; if someone talks about moving out to the country, we picture them enjoying the great outdoors on a perfect summer's day, not plodding home up a dark country lane on a freezing evening after their train home was delayed yet again.

Some people go as far as to describe spending time in nature as a 'cure'. When the writer Richard Mabey had depression, knowing his long-term love for nature, his friends tried to encourage him to go for walks in the countryside. His psychiatrist even offered to drive him to see the red kites flying nearby. But none of this helped. When I went to visit him at his Norfolk home, he told me that this kind of 'facile nature cure' in fact had the opposite effect. 'To witness without any emotional response what had previously moved me sometimes beyond words, but hopefully into words, just made me feel worse. Worse than nothing. I felt rejected by it because I could no longer connect with what had been the most important thing in my life.'

But after moving to East Anglia and falling in love, he slowly began to recover, and nature started to have a powerful impact on him again. 'I know I was affected psychologically by its extraordinary mutability. You would gaze at a patch of saltmarsh for ten minutes and it would be completely different at the end of that time from what it was before. And that sense of change and recovery from change bedded itself quite deeply in my psyche. It was that which most profoundly affected me – to be part of a living system that wasn't that dreadful, static, stuck-in-the-mud, immemorial cliché we like to imagine the countryside is, but a mercurial, mobile, adaptive system where water especially is driving everything.'[4]

Curiously, in scientific terms it's not easy to demonstrate that nature does always have a calming effect or which factors are essential if nature is to soothe you. For Richard Mabey it needed to be ever-changing, not static. Some researchers believe green vegetation is essential, others that it's all about the contrast with a busy, urban environment or that the crucial factor in a landscape's power to relax us is the absence of any signs of human intervention.

A Room With a View

In a hospital in Pennsylvania an architecture professor called Roger Ulrich conducted a famous study which kick-started this field of research. He discovered you don't even have to be out among nature in order to feel its benefits. Simply looking at it will do. In a study entitled 'View through a Window May Influence Recovery from Surgery' published in 1984 he found that patients who had undergone gall-bladder surgery needed fewer painkillers and left hospital almost a day earlier if they recovered in a hospital room overlooking trees, compared with similar patients accommodated in rooms with a view of a brick wall.⁵ More than thirty years later this study is still quoted frequently.

But when you look at the details, it does not stand up that well. Much as most of us would prefer to look out of a hospital window on to trees rather than brick walls, we can't be absolutely sure that Ulrich's famous study proved that a view of nature helps us to get well. Ulrich came to his conclusions after looking back at nine years' worth of medical notes for just twenty-three patients who stayed in each kind of room. With numbers this small we can't be certain that there were no other differences between the patients allocated to the two types of rooms, or even differences in the quality of care they received. The nurses' stations were closer to the patients with the view of the brick wall, so these patients could have been put there because they were sicker in the first place, and that could explain why they stayed in hospital for longer. Or they could have ended up taking more painkillers because the nurses were close by and more likely to respond to their requests for more drugs.

But the team did follow up almost a decade later with a rather better-designed study. This time the patients didn't even look out of a window at real nature. They looked at photographs of nature. The patients underwent heart surgery at Uppsala University Hospital in Sweden before spending their recovery time in hospital beds facing large photographs on the wall. Some faced a photo of a tree-lined stream or a forest, while others looked at an abstract painting, a white panel or a blank wall. This time the patients were assigned to different groups at random, making the results more convincing and all the more fascinating for it. Patients looking at either of the nature scenes felt less anxious and required fewer painkillers.[6]

To be clear, looking at nature isn't going to *cure* illness. But this study suggests that looking at nature allows us to rest better, which is of particular interest for readers of this book, but also for medical practitioners because rest is known to help the body to heal faster.

Over the years numerous studies have followed, but in this field they're often very small and sometimes study people who have already chosen to spend lots of time in nature, which can't tell us whether it's universally beneficial. From exercise bikes sited in fields to farms run by volunteers with mental health problems, researchers have studied different situations, hoping to demonstrate what we sense intuitively – that nature provides a restful sanctuary. Some studies have succeeded in showing this to be the case, finding that walking outdoors rather than indoors increases our sense of calmness and tranquillity. Others have found that it's walking rather than spending time in nature that makes a difference; as long as you walk, it doesn't matter where you do it. One study even found that people exercising outdoors actually felt *less* calm afterwards.[7]

But much more recently it's been shown that even taking a micro-break to look at photos of the natural world might make a difference to your mood. And when I say micro, I really do mean micro. We are talking breaks of just forty seconds. In this study, people were given a tricky computer task followed by a micro-break in which they looked either at a photo of an empty grey flat office block roof or a photo of the same roof, but this time digitally doctored to look as though it were covered in meadow. Not surprisingly people preferred the green roof. But would looking at this picture for such a short amount of time make any difference to the participants' ability to concentrate when they returned to the tricky task? At first it appeared not. Everyone returned to task, apparently refreshed by the break and doing a bit better, but after a few minutes the people who had viewed the bleak, grey roof began to flag, while the green roof people only showed a tiny dip in attention.[8]

This suggests that the power of nature to refresh us could be considerable. It would certainly suggest that if you are feeling tired at work and have the opportunity to pop out briefly and enjoy a green space nearby you should consider doing so. Don't worry if the boss shouts 'Where are you off to in office hours?' Shout back: 'I'm just popping out to improve my productivity.'

Born to Be Wild

Let's take at face value that spending time in nature has therapeutic benefits, even if not enough good research has been conducted yet to show this applies in every situation. The next question is: why does this experience feel so restful? Some researchers have suggested that we have evolved to love nature, that back in time, when all of our ancestors lived in the countryside, those who adapted to it best were more likely to survive. It is argued that we have carried this propensity to enjoy nature with us even though most of us now live in towns and cities.

Roger Ulrich, of hospital window fame, believes that nature rich in vegetation is especially attractive because that vegetation signals an unthreatening environment, rich in food. He says we prefer places that look as much as possible like the savannah.[9] I'm not convinced. True, I like nature rich in vegetation, but for me that means rolling green hills and river valleys, the classic landscape of England, where I grew up. I can't see how such a love has any link to my ancestors who lived in the savannah many thousands of years ago. And anyway, the savannah doesn't conjure up images of rich vegetation to me, but instead a kind of rather parched, brown landscape.

It has been claimed that humans even prefer the shape of the types of trees typically found in the savannah, trees with spreading crowns, rather than trees that are more rounded or conical in shape.[10] Many humans have lived and evolved for the past 40,000 years in places without these kinds of trees, living above the tree line, or in deserts or on tropical islands. Not even all of Africa was covered in savannah. But again, give me an old English oak or a weeping willow. And I quite like a bit of English garden topiary, such as can be found in perhaps my favourite garden of all, Great Dixter in East Sussex.

Another suggestion is that natural landscapes appeal because the moment you see them they appear immediately habitable, in a way that an urban view does not. I'd argue it depends what you're used to. To me a street of houses looks more habitable that a stretch of desert or a forest. I would also question whether vegetation always signals safety. In the long grass out on the savannah there may be lions lurking. Likewise waterfalls may be beautiful to admire from a boardwalk constructed to give the perfect view without getting wet, but they are lethal if you're rafting along a placid river and then find yourself suddenly swept rapidly towards the lip. Humans survived this long by cooperating and clustering together in settlements, not wandering alone in nature in search of rest, when dangerous predators were lying in wait. So if evolution did have anything to do with the places we find restful, then those places should be safe settlements, not wide open landscapes.

The difficulty with hypotheses like these from the field of evolutionary psychology is that they are hard to test. You could ask people their preferred tree shapes and check that this applies in all cultures (although a study of that kind is rarely done because it's so difficult to arrange), but even if you establish a universal preference for a certain shape of tree, you then have to speculate on how this preference would aid survival or reproduction or occur as a side-effect of some other characteristic that aids survival or reproduction. And here it's easy to insert whatever hypothesis suits you, whether it's that women are made to stay at home and look after babies or that men can't help but be violent (claims that are unfair to both men and women). In an elegant and, to be honest, quite entertaining critique of the evidence Dutch and Belgian researchers Yannick Joye and Agnes van den Berg have pointed out several flaws in the assertion that humans have evolved to feel good contemplating landscapes featuring vegetation.[11] For example, some studies have demonstrated that the calming effects of nature occur almost instantaneously, but it's hard to know why we might have developed such a response. Why might it be useful to feel instantly calm when we chance upon some vegetation? Those trees aren't going anywhere, so unlike the fight or flight response when we encounter a lion there's no need for an urgent rush.

I would concede that in the past people needed places where they could safely rest, relax and restore themselves, which some landscapes might offer more than others. But when we talk about being in nature, it's not always the case that the wilder the countryside, the more we like it. In a Swiss study, half the participants were sent on a walk through a forest that had been left to grow wild. The remaining participants walked through a managed forest, with piles of newly felled pines piled up neatly. When the participants' moods were assessed at the end of the walk, it wasn't the wild wood which made the biggest difference. In fact, those who walked in the managed forest felt significantly better than the other group. So in this study at least, tamed nature scored better than wild nature.[12]

Of course, the aesthetics of nature change over time and with culture. There is no fixed image of the most attractive kind of landscape and what is supposedly 'natural' is often more managed than we realise. The Scottish Highlands are generally regarded as one of the wildest parts of Britain, and yet they have been shaped by clearances and sheep farming and grouse shooting. For centuries, these mountains, moors and lochs were seen by most people as brutal and bleak. It is only since the Romantic Movement in the late-eighteenth century that such landscapes have come to be generally viewed as beautiful and peaceful places. At a more micro-level, one person's wonder plant is another person's weed. In parts of New Zealand my beloved agapanthus, which I tend with such care in London, is classed as an invasive nuisance.

Often implicit in evolutionary theories is the idea that because being out in nature is 'part of our human heritage' we feel more at ease there.[13] I'd challenge that claim too. If you've grown up in a city, the countryside can seem muddy, smelly, uncomfortable and even threatening. I have city friends who grew up in north London (and who still live there) who find crossing a field full of cows far more alarming than dashing across a busy dual carriageway. They are used to walking streets after dark in which people get stabbed or the wailing sound of police and ambulance sirens is a constant. What scares them is a night in a country cottage with not a sound outside but a hooting owl. They think they're bound to get murdered.

I like a walk in the English countryside or up in the Alps or even in the jungle, but I was terrified on a night 'safari' in the Amazon when, despite having a guide with a powerful torch, I kept walking into and swallowing – yes, *swallowing* – spider's webs that had been woven across the narrow paths. And I'm guessing that even the most dedicated lover of the English woodland would find that spending a night in the woods induced thoughts of the *Blair Witch Project* or Mole's night in the Wild Wood in *The Wind in the Willows*. Of course, the countryside has been for millennia the place where human beings have found food, and made their home, and felt at home, but they have also been attacked by wild beasts and other humans, and been exposed to the elements, and felt fear, fallen sick and died.

There's a small study which illustrates this rather nicely. Students were instructed to go on one of two walks alone in a country park. Half the students went across an open area where they could see far into the distance and were unlikely to get lost. The others walked in a part of the park with less visibility and more bushes and undergrowth. The students walking in the open landscape found it more restorative, while the others reported a wariness, concerned that it was full of hiding places and more dangerous.[14]

All of this is really common sense. Those people who put spending time in nature high up on their list of restful activities were influenced not, I'm guessing, by some deep element of evolutionary psychology. Rather the influence was more casually cultural. A day out in pretty, peaceful countryside is calming, particularly given that many of us spend a lot of our time in busy urban settings. But if that time in the countryside involves a cold night in a dark forest or a day of driving rain on an open moor it is not likely to qualify as restful at all.

A Break from Worrying

If nature's relaxing properties are not because of our evolutionary past, we need to look to other explanations for why its power can sometimes be so profound.

Nature seems random, but often has fractal qualities, where patterns are not only repeated, but repeated at finer and finer magnifications. Picture a coastline consisting of particular rock formations, replicated again and again, sometimes larger, sometimes smaller. Or clouds fringed with curls of different sizes. Or think of a single tree. Every leaf conforms to the same pattern. Each twig is a scaled-down version of the branches. Psychologists have discovered that the more repetition there is in a landscape, the more we enjoy the scene.[15]

One hypothesis is that this repetition allows our brains to process landscapes quickly with little mental effort, in contrast to a view of a city which requires us to identify a range of different kinds of buildings, bridges and vehicles. So instead of taxing the brain, a countryside scene gives us the space to refocus our attention, leading us to feel a bit better afterwards. This is known as restoration theory. And it works better for some than others. If you're someone who finds it hard to concentrate in a noisy office, then ten minutes spent at peace in the park during your lunchbreak could bring particular benefits.

Or does the answer lie not so much in what we can see in front of us but yet again in quietening the chattering mind, and in particular the negative chattering that can make us feel so bad? Research conducted at Stanford University gives us a clue as to what happens in the brain when we spend time in nature.

At the beginning of the study people lay in brain scanners while the researchers looked for ruminative activity, signs that the people were worrying away at negative thoughts. To complement the scan, the participants also completed a questionnaire on the extent to which they felt they were focusing on the negative. Then they were driven one at a time to the starting point of a ninety-minute walk. Each volunteer was given the route and instructed to take a number of photographs along the way of anything that interested them. In fact the photo-taking was just a ruse to divert the volunteers away from the real purpose of the study. It also served as a check, alongside GPS tracking, that the participants really did complete the walk and didn't cheat and head for the nearest café.

The first route took people on a nature trail described by the researchers as 'open California grassland with scattered oaks and native shrubs, abundant birds and occasional ground squirrel and deer'. Sounds lovely. Though, in fact, the walk was just outside the grounds of Stanford University. Now I've been there and it is a particularly lush, green campus, but the route of the walk went past towns such as Palo Alto (of Facebook fame) and Mountain View (of Google fame), and the rather less lovely Menlo Park. So there were plenty of reminders of the urban world. It's not quite what I could call a countryside walk. But still, it's quite nice.

Likewise, the urban walk was the most urban the team could find in the vicinity, but we're not talking downtown San Francisco with its panhandlers and other reminders of inner-city deprivation. The road the volunteers walked along is called El Camino Real. Admittedly it's a highway with at least three lanes of traffic in each direction, but most buildings are only one or two storeys high, so there's a big sky, and the verges are planted with hundreds of trees and vast bright blue agapanthus (so vast that they make the agapanthus in my garden look like seedlings). It is by no means a lovely road, but with the pavements well set back it's pleasant enough for me to have chosen it for many a morning run when I've stayed in motels nearby. So just as the nature walk the researchers selected wasn't entirely natural, neither was their urban walk all that urban. These might sound like flaws in the study, but curiously they could render the results even more striking.

On their return from the walk each person filled in the rumination questionnaire again before sliding back into the scanner. You might expect a ninety-minute stroll of any sort to have cleared the minds of participants, but in fact it was only the walk in nature which was followed by a drop in levels of rumination. This was backed up by the brain scan. Only those people who had taken the nature walk showed reduced activity in the subgenual prefrontal cortex,[16] the part of the brain associated with feelings of sadness, rumination and withdrawal.

There have been attempts to enhance this beneficial effect by encouraging people to think certain thoughts while they're out in nature. In 2010 the first well-being trail was opened at a hiking track in the Finnish countryside. The information signs spaced out along the trail don't give walkers information about the flora and fauna. Instead they say things like 'Breathe slowly and let your shoulders relax', or 'Feel your mood improve'. The signs have been popular and may have helped walkers to feel more relaxed. But it has proved difficult to assess how much of an extra difference the signs along the trail might have made to well-being.[17]

Another way of achieving the effect of the signs on the hiking trail is to attend an outdoor mindfulness class where you are encouraged to pay attention to all your senses, listening to the sounds of the forest, watching the light change, smelling the leaves and feeling the textures of bark and mosses, even tasting berries and mushrooms (with the right person to select them for you). No doubt this would be a restful experience for many, though it might be difficult to work out how much is added to overall restfulness by combining two already restful activities. In my experience, walking in the countryside induces 'natural' mindfulness without my needing to consciously do exercises.

Before you start making deliberate changes in the way you experience the countryside, it is worth noting the results of a study in which people were shown photographs of the rolling plateaus of Staffordshire. Those who felt the strongest connection with nature were not those who attended to the details in the picture, but the people who took the opportunity of a pause to admire nature and also to reflect on themselves, peacefully introspecting.[18]

This is key to the question of why nature can help us to put our daily worries aside. To get the most from nature we need to consider the natural world, but also consider ourselves. Our experiences in the natural world help us to set our concerns in the context of the bigger world. Even in a small local park, thousands of creatures are carrying on with their lives, regardless of the problems in ours. And that's just a park. How much more is there in the real outdoors.

In *Sightlines* the nature writer Kathleen Jamie writes of the time she was walking on a Scottish moor when she spotted a moth floating, dying, trapped in a tiny triangular pool of water between three rocks. Painstakingly and only succeeding on the second attempt, she used a teaspoon to rescue the moth. She was totally absorbed in saving one tiny life and even then was doubtful about whether the moth would survive. Then she stood up too fast, felt slightly dizzy and was struck by the vastness of the land around her.

'There was the wide moor, the loch and breezy grasses reaching for miles, all scaling up to meet me. I'd been absorbed in the miniscule, a moth's eye, a dab of lichen. Been granted a glimpse into the countless millions of tiny processes and events that form the moor. Millions. Tiny creatures, flowers, bacteria, opening, growing, dividing, creeping about their business. It's all happening out there and all you have to do, girl, is get your foot out of your eye.'[19]

The philosopher Massimo Pigliucci has used the idea of our individual insignificance, that each of us is just one of trillions of living things in the universe, to create a thera-peutic slideshow for himself. It begins with a picture of his own home, then each slide zooms further and further out, like a child addressing an envelope with their house number, street, town, region, country, continent, world, universe, and on and on to infinity (and to infinity + 1 – who knows?). He finds that sitting and simply viewing these slides reminds him that he is obsessing about things which probably don't matter very much in the great scheme of things.

Over the years I've interviewed several astronauts and each one has told me the same story – how they took books up to space to keep themselves occupied during their rest time but barely opened them. The reason? The view out of the window. They could not resist spending every spare moment looking back at the Earth.

Michael López-Alégria, who undertook three shuttle

missions, as well as living for seven months on the International Space Station, told me about that moment when the view of the Earth from space is first revealed. 'There are these incredible amounts of energy that result in very, very strong forces on your body, ending in a very abrupt stopping of the motors where it's like slamming the brakes on in a car. You've been head down looking at instruments and displays until that moment and now you finally have a chance to kind of look up. That's when you see the Earth. It's a sensation that is incredibly hard to grasp and quite emotional. It's really very impactful to see the place where the entirety of human history has occurred below you, looking a lot like it does on maps and globes, but actually being real. There is a sense of the vastness of the Earth and the population of humanity compared to the seven of us on board at the time.'

The impact that this view can have on people is known as the 'overview effect'. Annahita Nezami made the overview effect the topic of her PhD. Among the astronauts she spoke to, she detected a shift in their awareness. After seeing the Earth as a fragile ball in the void of space, nourished by a thin atmosphere, they developed an intense feeling of interconnection with other people, as well as the strong sense of a broader responsibility towards the planet. The astronauts were left with an overwhelming desire to cherish and protect it. Stephen Hawking said the message when you see the Earth from space is clear: 'One planet. One human race.'

There are those who credit photographs from space with spearheading the environmental movement. Annahita believes that these views could have therapeutic value for the rest of us back on terra firma too. Her dream is for every TV weather bulletin to end with a picture of the Earth from space, highlighting sandstorms or hurricanes, wherever they might be occurring in the world, to give us a global perspective and the sense that, although we've been watching the news focused on the place where we live, we are all connected with a wider world.

Online you can watch the Earth live from space through a series of cameras mounted on the European Space Agency's Columbus module.[20] As I look at it right now, I can see a depth of blackness because the space station is currently over the Atlantic where it's night time. But while I appear to sit stationary at my desk for the next hour and a half, the Earth will still be turning around the sun and the space station will orbit the Earth completely. The next time I look I see bare brown deserts in West Africa fringed with ridges of cloud. This view is both compelling and restful.

I wonder whether positive experiences in nature do something similar, reminding us that in the scheme of things we are small and insignificant, and allowing us to put our day-to-day concerns into perspective. When out in nature, the world can feel whole and still, giving us a chance to experience a deeper sense of reflection.[21] An activity that's fun, such as going out for a meal or to a party, can bring us hedonic happiness. But there's another type of longer lasting well-being called eudaimonic happiness. This requires more profound activities and comes from finding meaning in life and realising our true potential. Being in nature can help us to achieve this state of being by allowing us to experience a sense of our place in the world.

Nature also reminds us of time passing, while offering

hope of renewal. As we walk by a rotten tree stump or a dying bush we are confronted with death and decay, yet we also notice signs of rebirth, particularly as a long winter comes to an end and the first signs of spring start to appear. No wonder this is a particularly popular time for being in the countryside.

I remember visiting the volcano Mount St Helens in Washington State, which erupted, destroying everything around it, back in 1984. Ten years later, when I went there, the landscape still looked postapocalyptic, with thousands of straight, dead tree trunks strewn like matches across the bare, scorched-earth hillsides. Yet in the midst of this scene of devastation there was new life. Plants were shooting up. Renewal was in progress. It was a surprisingly fresh and hopeful experience.

However stuck we might feel in our current position, however impossible it might be to see a way out, one thing is certain. Time will move on. The future will keep on coming, and the past will keep on receding. Nature reminds us of this truth.

Soft Fascination

In 2017 the Wellcome Collection in London did something risky. Instead of expert curators carefully planning an exhibition over several years as usual, they decided to turn a gallery space over to the public. People were asked to bring in an object that summed up their relationship with nature.

The staff then waited and, if they were honest, worried. Here was a venue with a reputation for excellence allowing visitors to curate their own exhibition. What if it was no good? What if no one came?

The staff needn't have feared. On the appointed day, people queued up on the pavement outside on the Euston Road, one of London's most unlovely thoroughfares, with six lanes of constant thundering traffic and levels of air pollution that are among the highest in the capital. There could hardly be a place further from nature. Nonetheless the people stood queuing patiently, cradling their objects as though they were in line for the Antiques Roadshow. Except they weren't waiting to find out whether the porcelain jug they never really liked was going to make their fortune; instead, they were bringing objects of no monetary value, but which had real meaning for them. An extraordinary range of objects were delivered for the museum staff to choose from. Here are descriptions of just some of them.

A round wooden barometer, shaped like a discus or one of those giant old tape measures my grandfather had.

A bundle of 81 walking sticks all made from the dried stalks of a crop of Jersey kale grown in a garden, then cut, sanded and varnished, complete with gnarly handles.

A square of artificial turf, bright green and apparently perfect, until you look closely and see that weeds have started growing on top of it, like cress on a piece of kitchen towel. Real plants on top of fake plants.

A hand plane – a smooth oval piece of wood, the size of a large chopping board, that's pointed at one end. It helps bodysurfers to catch a wave. On the back it's engraved with a name. 'Felix'. Felix was Rosa's younger brother, and he took his own life in 2012. While Rosa awaited the inquest she wanted to attenuate the wait, so she set herself the task of going for 32 wild swims in 32 days, each in a different body of water. She says the power of the sea and of nature helped her to heal.

168 dinky toys – tiny Beetle cars lined up in a vast square grid pattern in rainbow colour order like a beautifully arranged miniature car park. Growing up in Australia, the owner, 47-year-old Stephen Hall, had collected real full-sized Volkswagen Beetle cars. Now he was collecting the dinky toys for his toddler son.

Two white cardboard coffins just 15cm long, one decorated in red felt tip pen with a picture of a crab and the words 'In loving memory of the crabs of Medway Riverside Country Park', the other with black writing bordered by a pattern of black waves 'In memory of the brave crabby crabs who fourt [sic] for their lives and hoped that they wouldn't die. R.I.P.' These crab coffins were made by two sisters who at the age of 10 and 12 were out walking their dog when they found hundreds of desiccated dead crabs on the sand. They brought some of them home in a dog poo bag and wanting to honour the crabs appropriately the girls created coffins for them. Five years later they still have the coffins and their contents. Describing their exhibit they say, 'I think we were reasonably serious.'

Faced with these diverse experiences of nature, the curators somehow found a way of grouping the objects into themes, though they were fairly vague themes, such as 'change', 'imagine', 'sustain' and 'ritual'. My conclusion from wandering the gallery, pondering these artefacts for some time, was that it's not surprising that researchers are finding it hard to pin down exactly why nature can have such an effect on us. On the one hand the people who brought these exhibits seemed to be searching for nature wherever they went, seeing it in tools and cars even. On the other, they were using nature as a metaphor to help them express their thoughts and feelings, to consider life and death and to heal themselves.

Nature's ability to leave us feeling restored does, of course, depend on the meaning we ascribe to it. We shouldn't assume that everyone likes it, or that it always provides a restful escape from work. If you're a farmer living in rural India, is the countryside your place of solace or your busy workplace? Research from Finland has confirmed that the locations people rate as most restorative fall into specific categories: places associated with childhood memories, places where people used to live, places which relate to identity or places where people feel they can contemplate the present and plan for the future. The shape of trees doesn't matter. It is all about meaning.[22]

Even our enjoyment of something as apparently pure as birdsong is affected by the memories stirred up by those sounds. In one study, researchers asked people to imagine they were finally getting the chance to sit down and take a break after a long day at work and an argument with a friend on the way home. They hear a bird singing. What memories or associations does it prompt? People were played ten-second clips from a range of fifty different birds singing. The participants all lived in England, but the researchers deliberately included birds from Australia which might be unfamiliar to them – everything from a yellow-faced honeyeater and a crimson rosetta, to the more familiar long-tailed tit and the humble chicken.

The range of associations was huge. For some it reminded them of home or spending time with their grand-mother as a child. Others daydreamed about travelling to the jungle on family adventures. Not all the associations were positive. Some were reminded of *Doctor Who* or *Twin Peaks*, and of course Alfred Hitchcock's film *The Birds* made an appearance, as did 'pigeons roosting in the gutter, crap-ping down the house'. When people were asked how restorative they considered the sounds, these associations were key. It won't surprise you to learn that if the birdsong was associated with negative memories they felt far from rested afterwards.

So the perfect landscape for restfulness has no nega-tive associations. Instead it holds what psychologists call a 'soft fascination'. In order to distract us enough from our pessimistic thoughts, yet allow us to achieve restful-ness, it needs to contain just the right amount of mystery, making it easy to take in at a glance but leave us wanting more. Garden designers are fond of the trick of creating a display with instant impact with the addition of an arch or gateway suggesting something more is hidden beyond. Nature can do the same. Think of the sea. It is distracting, yet enigmatic. There's something to watch, but also plenty to wonder about beyond the horizon or below the waves.

I've already said that this is a field plagued by small studies, but I can't make that criticism of this recent research on the types of landscape which best restore us. Kayleigh Wyles at

Surrey University analysed a sample of more than 4,000 people living in England, who provided information about their experience of being in nature during the previous week. The greatest feelings of restoration and connection with nature came from seaside experiences and officially designated sites such as nature reserves. And as for how long you need stay there for? People felt most rested if they were in nature for at least thirty minutes.[23]

Back at the Great Fen recently, sitting up on the bank on my own, I contemplated all these different psychological theories and wondered which might best explain why so many people do find spending time in nature to be a restful experience. I think the reason is not so much nature itself, or how we've evolved to view it over millennia, but how we've learned to view it during our own lifetimes.

This is nicely illustrated by a Dutch study which compared what farmers and visitors thought of various kinds of landscapes. It probably won't surprise you if I tell you that the farmers liked the cultivated farmland scenes best, ordered and safe from flooding, while the visitors preferred the meadows and the views with rough edges.[24] If we are to find nature restful, experience and meaning matter. So do our own lives, but, like those astronauts looking down on us from space, imagining millions of tiny people scurrying around like ants, or giving birth, or cheering good news, or dying, time in nature allows us to take a step back.

For me, a great place to do that is the fenlands of Cambridgeshire that are gradually being reflooded to create a more natural landscape. For all sorts of reasons this place has more meaning for me than for most. And while I went back to ponder on the sometimes baffling psychology of being in nature, I quickly realised something else. I was just sitting there, I was not worrying – about this book or anything else. My mind was momentarily quietened. I was at peace.

I

READING

I bet you remember playing this game when you were a child. You wait until someone – hopefully an adult – is sitting on a chair with one leg crossed over the other and then, quick as a flash, you slice your hand sharply into the soft part at the front of their knee. Cue childish delight and adult protest, as their foot kicks out involuntarily.

Great fun, but why am I mentioning this at the beginning of a chapter about the restfulness of reading? Well, although it might seem obvious that it is relaxing to sit and read a book, surprisingly few experiments have looked into it. One notable study dates all the way back to 1928 and was conducted by a doctor we have already met: Edmund Jacobson from the University of Chicago. He was to become famous as the man who invented progressive relaxation (which was discussed in the chapter on Doing Nothing in Particular). This, if you recall, involves systematically clenching and relaxing each muscle in your body from your toes all the way up to your forehead as a way of calming yourself down.

You might also remember that Jacobson entitled his book on the subject *You Must Relax!,* suggesting he didn't really understand how relaxation worked. In fact, he knew very well that when a doctor instructs their patient to relax, the patient tends to do the opposite and tense up. And in the context of measuring the knee reflex, which was the point of his 1928 study, the magnitude of the jerk increases if a person is tense to start with. Jacobson wanted to know which kind of activity might best allow patients to relax, blunting this involuntary reflex response.

The answer, of course, is reading.

Jacobson reached this conclusion via elaborate means. The description of the complex mechanical apparatus used in his experiment takes up more than a page of his scientific paper. Each participant sat in a Morris chair with one thigh attached to a board by leather straps. An automatic electromagnetic hammer set to administer gentle blows to the knee was held in a clamp, while a string and pulley system measured precisely the extent of the reflex reaction as the foot shot up into the air, a measurement Jacobson calls 'the amplitude of the jerk'. Meanwhile, a set of levers and rods were in place to measure whether the knee itself moved.

In his paper, Jacobson mentions drily that at the start of the experiment five of the forty participants were 'markedly nervous', which is hardly surprising given they must have thought they'd entered a torture chamber. If all the straps, hammers and pulleys weren't enough, the special soundproofed boards fixed to the walls might have added to the anxiety of the volunteers, though in fact these boards were there to prevent any distraction from outside noise, rather than to muffle the screams of participants.

The whole set-up might seem rather ludicrous, yet Jacobson's experiment yielded some interesting results. What he found was that if the hammer blows were too regular – every thirty seconds or so – the participants were not relaxed sufficiently by their reading to soften the knee jerk, but if the blows came at greater intervals, reading worked its magic and people did become calmer and calmer, as proved by progressively gentler knee reflex actions.

The study was far from perfect. For a start, the participants were instructed to read out loud, which isn't how most people generally read to themselves. More importantly, there doesn't appear to have been a control condition in which half the participants did no reading, so we can't rule out the possibility that the volunteers simply grew accustomed to the banging on their knee and became more relaxed irrespective of their reading. However the experiment *did* show that most of the participants found reading relaxing, apart from three people diagnosed with 'neuroticism' and an unlucky volunteer called J.C. who 'failed to relax' due to 'unusually tight strapping'.

But for all his study's weaknesses, Jacobson was clearly on to something. Almost ninety years later, reading emerges in the Rest Test as the activity which is more restful than any other. An impressive 58 per cent of respondents selected it. And these people also seem to have cracked how to live the good life, as they were especially likely to score high on a scale which measures whether a person is flourishing, a concept which combines self-esteem, purpose, meaning and optimism.[1]

Of course, those of a cynical disposition might wonder whether so many people ticked reading in our survey in order to appear cultured and intelligent, rather in the way sixth formers list reading as an interest on their application forms for university. The counter to this charge is that all the responses were anonymous and if respondents' chief concern had been to appear studious, then it seems unlikely that 'doing nothing' would have appeared in the top five. I'm taking people at their word when they say they find reading relaxing.

Relaxing and Arousing

In fact, there are people who find they can't relax *unless* they have a book with them.

BOOKWORMS REQUIRED

IF YOU READ A LOT OF LIGHT FICTION AND ENJOY IT VERY MUCH, PLEASE VOLUNTEER TO ADVANCE THE CAUSE OF SCIENCE

This advert was placed in South African newspapers in the 1980s by Victor Nell, a Zimbabwean clinical psychologist keen to recruit readers for a series of studies on people's reading habits. Anyone who read at least one novel a week could take part. The average volunteer in fact read four books a week, while one family of four claimed that between them they read 101 books a month.[2] As a result of attracting all these voracious readers, Nell was able to carry out one of the most detailed studies of reading that we have, so it's a study I'll refer to a lot. My favourite question in it asked people how they would cope if they arrived at a strange hotel at their favourite time of day for reading and then realised they had nothing to read. The answers were aggregated into a 'Frustration Index' in which those who scored highest went as far as to say they would feel 'desperate', 'desolate' or 'dispossessed'. So striking were the reactions that Nell suggests that these people could almost be said to be addicted to having a novel with them.

For most people, of course, the immediate absence of the latest Dan Brown or J.K. Rowling isn't going to leave them in a cold sweat or subject to a panic attack, but still, books are a big thing in most of our lives. In the UK alone book sales totalled more than £1.6 billion in 2018. This gives us some sense of the important place of books in our world.

I was surprised that reading came top in the Rest Test because remember, people weren't voting for the activity they find most enjoyable, but the most *restful*. And reading is not a passive pastime – it requires quite a bit of effort. True, unlike running, you can lie on a sofa or in a hammock while you do it, but it does demand cognitive work on many different levels.

We read the letters. We form words from them. We take meaning from those words. We relate that meaning to what we've read before. We reach into our own memories. We create images in our minds. We mentally simulate the action, the sights and the sounds of the scenes. Meanwhile we use what psychologists refer to as 'theory of mind' to inhabit the characters' minds in order to understand their motivations, to imagine their thoughts, to feel their feelings.

Curiously, reading is not only effortful cognitively, but also physically, in a way that you might not expect. One of the things Victor Nell wanted to investigate when he recruited his bookworms back in 1988 was what happens physiologically while people read. This involved another complicated experiment.

First, Nell induced boredom in his volunteers by fitting them with translucent goggles and playing ten minutes of white noise into their ears. Then he got the volunteers to take part in a series of activities: reading for thirty minutes, relaxing for five minutes with their eyes shut, looking at photographs, doing mental arithmetic, or completing puzzles like this one:

When a red apple is cut in half and halved again, how many sides will be red and how many will be white?[3]

Meanwhile Nell took numerous measurements. He placed electrodes on the faces, heads and necks of the participants to assess their muscular activity. He timed the intervals between their heartbeats. He measured their rates of breathing. All these measures helped him to gauge how the bodies of the volunteers were responding to the different activities.

So which of these sessions do you think their bodies would reveal to be the more restful: the boredom, the relaxation, the mental arithmetic and puzzles, or the reading? Bearing in mind that these bookworms had already rated the effort they had to put into reading for pleasure as close to zero, you might expect their physiology to reflect this. Reading would surely be physically effortless. In fact, the volunteers were notably more physiologically aroused during reading than when they were bored or relaxing with their eyes shut. What's more, reading was more arousing than doing tricky puzzles and on some measures more so even than doing the maths.

The conclusion we can draw from Nell's study is that, although it is relaxing, particularly for keen readers, reading is yet another restful activity which has nothing to do with switching off the brain or shutting down the body. Which invites the question: should we read before going to sleep?

A Book at Bedtime

Many people do, as they find reading helps to quieten the mind. But it is not obvious from a psychological or physiological perspective that a book before bed is a good idea.

Sleep experts often advise adopting 'sleep hygiene', which doesn't mean changing your sheets every couple of days but keeping the bedroom strictly for sleep and nothing else (in case you're wondering, they make an exception for sex). The idea is that you come to associate the bedroom solely with restful sleep. And in time this association becomes so strong that you fall asleep more easily.

As you might expect, these sleep experts tend to be very negative about the idea of watching TV in bed, let alone playing with your phone, for fear of overstimulation. But books on the whole escape their wrath. Is this just cultural snobbery at work or are they right to treat reading differently? Survey evidence seems to back up the idea that reading in bed is preferable to watching TV if your aim is a good night's sleep. A poll of 5,000 people living in Britain found that 38 per cent of those who watched TV in bed said they sleep very poorly most nights, while 39 per cent of those who read before they go to sleep said they sleep very well.[4] Many psychologists researching sleep also recommend that if you find yourself awake for a lengthy period in the middle of the night, rather than fretting about how terrible you are going to feel the following day or worrying about all the things you need to get done, you should get out of bed, sit in a chair (even if it's cold) and read a book until you feel sleepy again. If you're lucky, when you return to bed with your mind distracted and your body yearning for the cosy warmth of your duvet, you fall straight to sleep.

Yet we've seen that reading can activate the body, not just the mind – in which case, how come it allows us to relax enough to drift off to sleep? Victor Nell argues that, first, reading activates us mentally and physically. But then, when we put the book down and there is a fall in our arousal levels, it is this fall which helps to induce sleep, similar to the fall in the temperature after a hot bath that makes us doze off. It's an interesting hypothesis, but I'm not completely convinced. For a start it doesn't explain why, for instance, so many of us fall asleep *while* reading? And why doesn't the same thing happen when you read a bunch of annoying emails instead of a book just before turning out the light? There should be a drop in activation when you snap the laptop shut, but in this instance dropping straight off to sleep is rarely the result.

So it remains a bit of a mystery as to why reading, restful as it is, should be for so many of us the perfect preparation for a night's sleep. Perhaps it is something to do with memories of childhood when before lights out we were all read *to,* something that still makes me drop off, as I will explain later in this chapter.

A Lazy Pastime?

An intriguing aspect of the research on the restfulness of reading is that much of the best evidence for it has emerged almost by accident. Surprisingly few studies have specifically tested reading as a way to relax, but some have included it as a neutral task in research on other activities only to find that reading came out as equally or indeed more restful than the activity under investigation.

For example, there was an American study published in 2009 investigating yoga. I guess that the authors hoped to prove that yoga was the ultimate form of relaxation. Unfortunately for them, they chose something unusually restful to compare it with. While blood pressure and stress levels did drop after thirty minutes of yoga, these levels fell by the same amount after half an hour spent reading *Newsweek* articles.[1]

In another experiment in Australia people who regularly practised tai chi were put under stress by doing an hour of tricky mental arithmetic in a noisy room complete with insistent reminders that the time for the task was running out. At the same time another group spent an even more unpleasant hour watching a sixty-minute video about people having horrible experiences. As you'd expect, by the end of the viewing session everyone was feeling quite stressed. For the next hour they were assigned to meditate, walk briskly, read a book or practise tai chi. Again, the set-up of the experiment suggests to me the researchers were hoping to show tai chi was the ideal way to de-stress and relax. But physiological measurements revealed that the reading session and indeed the other activities were just as effective as the tai chi at reducing levels of the stress hormone cortisol and inducing a more restful mood.[6]

Of course, most readers know what researchers sometimes struggle to grasp: that reading is among the most restful activities in life. When researchers in Chicago asked adults to keep diaries listing everything they did and their motivation for doing these things, 34 per cent of those adults read books with the specific aim of relaxation in mind. On 89 per cent of the occasions when people read, they confirmed that reading involved low or no effort.[7]

In earlier centuries the idea that reading might be restful wouldn't have been a surprise. Indeed, reading was seen as lazy and self-indulgent. In eighteenth-century England, sitting down with a novel was considered 'as to drink wine'. It was a wicked vice. As well as promoting indolence and laxity, the reading of novels was thought to damage your posture and present a fire risk because, of course, at that time you needed candles in order to read on dark evenings. Mobile libraries, known as circulating libraries, were compared with brothels and gin shops. 'Reading sofas' – which sound mild enough to us – were excoriated by moralisers and social reformers.

Writing in 2008, the academic Ana Vogrinčič compares eighteenth-century attitudes to the novel with the moral panic around watching TV today. 'If novel-readers were seen as smearing books with candle-wax and causing fire, television viewers are associated with eating junk food and spilling ketchup on the carpet,' she writes.[8]

Today you could replace the novel and indeed the TV with the smartphone or tablet, of course. It seems we fear anything that is all enveloping, time consuming and fun, especially when it's new.

Even when Victor Nell conducted his research in 1988, he detected a hangover of the disapproval around reading novels, particularly more popular books or genre fiction. His avid readers admitted that almost half of what they read might be judged by their high school English teacher to be trash. The readers found it perfectly acceptable to read in bed, but at any other time of the day reading made them feel guilty. They should, they felt, be doing something more active, more useful.

Inside the Mind of the Reader

To fully understand why reading is so restful, it's worth considering what happens in our minds when we read. In some ways we have more control over books than other forms of media. You can, of course, pause live TV, rewind it or turn it off, but we tend not do that very much. Raymond Mar from the University of Toronto has found that once we commit to a film or TV programme we are very likely to see it through,[9] possibly because so much of television watching is done in the company of others.

With a book it is different. With the possible exception of the most gripping of page-turning thrillers, we are unlikely to devour a book in a single sitting. And even as we are apparently reading intently, we are constantly being distracted. We pause without even thinking about it, re-read paragraphs, turn back to earlier pages, or even drift off somewhere else completely. All this can mean

we take a while to finish a book, but it adds to the restfulness of reading.

We read a book at our pace and in our own way. This
means we can take control of the emotions we're experiencing. If a horror story gets too frightening, we can put the
book down. If the suspense in a spy thriller is all too much
we can cheat by reading the end of the story. And because
along with the author we cocreate the characters in our minds,
we can decide how scary to make the villain, or how brave
to make the hero. We can invent a street that's just like ours
and imagine the action taking place close to home if we want
to. We can make the characters look like people we know.
Or we can make it all as alien as possible. The author sets
some boundaries, but within those we have a large amount
of creative freedom ourselves.

Reading a book generally takes at least a few days or even
weeks. I'm such a slow reader of novels that my immersion
in the world of *Middlesex* by Jeffrey Eugenides has continued
over a couple of years. Yet every time I go back to it, I
experience a warm feeling of return. I am now familiar with
this other world, in which I go with the flow of events and
forget my other worries.

The fact that we can choose the speed at which we read is
an important factor. The keen South African readers recruited
by Victor Nell were invited to the lab to be observed reading
a book they were enjoying. With the help of a window and
cleverly positioned mirrors, Nell could watch as the eyes
of the readers moved across the pages. Rather surprisingly
he found that rather than racing ahead when the story was
gripping, the readers slowed down significantly to savour
the pages they enjoyed most. But more predictably, when

it came to boring bits, their eyes showed they were skim reading, not wasting time on stuff that didn't interest them. This unconscious ability to speed up and slow down the pace of our reading, to linger over and savour the good bits, or to skip over the dull passages, helps to make reading so absorbing – and thus relaxing.

As we read silently to ourselves there is evidence that we articulate those voices in our own heads as a kind of inner speech. Research has shown that even when we don't utter a sound we read words more slowly if the vowels are long, such as in the word 'cake', and we go more quickly if the vowels are short, as in the word 'cat', almost as though we are reading it out loud.[10] Meanwhile the emotions generated by the episodes in the book have an effect on our minds and even in our bodies. This has been shown by measuring heart rate and skin conductance (i.e. how much your finger-tips sweat) – and also by neuroimaging. For example, when volunteers read frightening excerpts from Harry Potter stories, researchers detected heightened responses in the empathy network in the brain.[11] This shows that in some sense what we are reading is as real to our minds and bodies as things that actually happen in our own lives. The immersion in fictional events is very deep.

When we read we reflect, we look forwards and backwards. As Philip Pullman wrote, 'the book proposes, the reader questions, the book responds, the reader considers'. To the encounter we bring our own personality, our previous experience of reading, our preconceptions and expectations, and our hopes as well as our fears.[12]

The feelings and emotions evoked by a book need not be fleeting. They can stay around for days. The novels we like best are often those that summon up an atmosphere which you can feel every time you think back on the book, even years after finishing it. In her essay 'How One Should Read a Book' Virginia Woolf wrote, 'Wait for the dust of reading to settle; for the conflict and the questioning to die down; walk, talk, pull the dead petals from a rose, or fall asleep. Then suddenly without our willing it, for it is thus that Nature undertakes these transitions, the book will return, but differently. It will float to the top of the mind as a whole.'[13]

So far, we've mainly been discussing reading fiction, but of course plenty of people read non-fiction and research shows it can bring people just as much pleasure and relaxation.[14] In the Rest Test we didn't ask people what they were reading. It might have been printed or digital, fiction, non-fiction, magazines, newspapers or, who knows, annual reports. And, of course, reading is not generally a question of either/or, fact or fiction. In the South African study, for example, the participants who read the most fiction also read the most newspapers.

Personally I'm a big fan of reading newspapers in bed. I can't bear not to know what's going on in the world. The papers pile up on the floor beside my bedside table until I eventually have such a heap I have no choice but to clear out the oldest ones. Even so it is a wrench to throw away that month-old supplement or even the news section from weeks ago.

I tell my husband – who is not a fan of my newspaper pile, referring to it as a 'rat's nest' – that at least I don't go as far as one friend who saves all the newspapers for months and takes them on holiday in a big holdall. He then reads each yellowed newspaper by the pool before throwing it away, then returns home with an empty holdall flattened at the bottom of his suitcase, ready for the next accretion of newspapers.

There is one disadvantage to reading the papers in detail of course: news is, let's face it, mainly bad news and can paint a grim picture of the world. At Southampton University Associate Professor Denise Baden has found that, not surprisingly, negative news can make us feel sad and anxious,[15] as well as, disappointingly – and more interestingly – making us feel less rather than more motivated to do anything about the issues that depress us. People often say they want to read more positive news stories and it's something both newspapers and broadcasters have tried at various times, but in reality the stories people choose to read, watch and listen to are generally the negative ones. Despite what we might say, alongside our skateboarding dogs, we do want some earthquakes and political scandals. And there is one positive to be had from reading a negative story; like seeing the Earth from space, other people's misfortune does put our own difficulties into perspective.

Escaping Ourselves

Both non-fiction and fiction take us into other people's worlds, worlds which become so vivid that the experience of reading and the contents of the book itself become entwined. Books you read on holiday can feel as though they're set in the place where you're reading them as much as in the invented location in the novel.

In large part, reading feels restful despite the effort involved because it allows us to escape our own worlds. We can leave our own problems behind, but also to an extent our own minds. The author Rose Tremain hopes that by writing fiction she might make what she refers to as a tiny contribution to people's mental health. She says, 'You can pick up one of my books and think: oh well, for the next half an hour, I'm all right.'[16]

The American psychologist Mihaly Csikszentmihalyi referred to the trance-like state induced by reading as 'flow'. Others call it ludic reading, from the Latin *ludo*, meaning 'I play'. A ludic reader in the South African study commented, 'I did not choose to be born, and I cannot say (in all honesty) that I get 100 per cent enjoyment from life. So, for the few hours a day I read 'trash', I escape the cares of those around me, as well as escaping my own cares and distractions.' And a member of Victor Nell's hundred-books-a-month family remarked that reading is a kind of disease which means that on the one hand life passes him by, but on the other he is allowed to escape into a wider world.

Of course, if you are hoping for distraction not every book will suffice. In a study where people suffering from chronic pain read short stories or poems in a group, it was the most challenging and thought-provoking literature which the participants found best distracted them from their agonies. The more intriguing and puzzling the story, such as those by Anton Chekhov, D.H. Lawrence and Raymond Carver, the more absorbed they felt, and the less they noticed their pain.[17]

Nell divided his ludic readers into two types: those who read to escape from their world, who blotted out all thoughts of what was going in their lives; and those who did the opposite, who wanted to heighten their own consciousness and used reading about the lives of others as a way of reflecting on their own.

Mindless Reading

In an extraordinary neuroscientific study on reading, researchers at the University of Southern California used software to distil twenty million personal stories posted on blogs worldwide into just forty tales. These are, as it were, the forty essential human stories. The researchers wanted to see how the brains of people reading these stories responded. How differently would individual human brains respond to the same story? The answer was not very. Whether people were reading a story in English or Farsi or Mandarin Chinese, and irrespective of the different alphabets and layout of the pages, the brain response was remarkably similar if the story was the same, suggesting that the way we process particular stories in the brain is universal.[18] Even more remarkably, the researchers found that by looking at the brain scans they were able to guess which of the forty stories an individual lying in the scanner was reading. The scanner was almost reading the mind while the mind read the book.

But the main point of this research is that it revealed that the brain is not resting nor completely focused while we read. Reading engages a number of areas of the brain, including those that are part of the default mode network – that same network that is activated when we supposedly think of nothing, but in fact our minds are wandering.

Neuroscientists used to think that this network couldn't be activated while people did a specific task, unless, that is, they really weren't concentrating. But the University of Southern California study and other research suggests that while we read, the network is busy finding meaning in the stories and making sense of that meaning in relation to our own memories of the past, our thoughts about the future and our relationships with others. So although we are supposedly deep in someone else's world, we can't help but view that world in relation to our own.

Research from the Princeton University psychologist Diana Tamir backs this up. She asked people to lie in a brain scanner reading excerpts from everything from fiction such as Edgar Rice Burroughs' *Tarzan of the Apes* and Thomas Hardy's *Tess of the d'Urbervilles*, and non-fiction ranging from Rebecca Skloot's *The Immortal Life of Henrietta Lacks* and Patti Polk's less well-known *Collecting Rocks, Gems and Minerals: Identification, Values and Lapidary Uses*. Some of these books sound more stimulating than others to me, but Tamir and her associates found that reading any of these books led to activity in the default mode network, though in different areas depending on what the participants were reading.[19] What was clear was that even when we are reading about agate, jasper and sedimentary deposits, which let's face it most of us don't find terribly exciting, we still bring a world of experience and thoughts into that reading.

Maybe the fact that we don't always pay strict attention to the book in front of us is part of the joy of reading. Psychologists call it mindless reading, and I'm sure you are familiar with the concept if not the terminology. How often do you catch yourself staring at the middle of a page and not actually reading but thinking about something else? And how often do you find after you've read a few pages you can't remember a word of them because you've been busy planning what to do to the garden this coming summer or where you might go on holiday.

Reading can facilitate mind wandering, providing the perfect jumping-off point for a daydream – stimulating us to fly away from our current surroundings, not necessarily to the location in the story, but to a special place in our own memories or even to somewhere we've never been. Of course it's always hard to know what goes on in other people's minds. But research on mindless reading suggests we all think much the same way.

Interestingly, some researchers have found our eyes continue moving across the lines of a page, but our minds are elsewhere most often when we're reading something easy. But others have found this happens when we're reading something more difficult.[20] Either way there are tell-tale signs which indicate to scientists that mindless reading is taking place. For a start, people blink more frequently – but there's a second clue, aptly derived from an experiment involving Sherlock Holmes. The psychologist Jonathan Smallwood asked people to read Conan Doyle's story 'The Red-Headed League' and found that if people were really concentrating on the text they would slow down slightly when they reached a long, unfamiliar word, but if their minds were elsewhere they happily glided on past these more obscure words.[21]

The novelist and psychologist Charles Fernyhough, who we met in the chapter on daydreaming, loves reading books as well as writing them. Yet he admits to being a highly distractible reader. But that, he says, is one of reasons he enjoys reading so much. He wonders whether there is something special about that moment of breaking concentration mid-read that offers us some kind of direct line to the resting state where the mind can roam free. Is reading a shortcut to helping the mind wander?

You might assume that authors want us to concentrate on the sentences they've spent so many hours crafting, but some, such as Virginia Woolf, are happy for us to drift off. She wrote that letting our minds wander when we read allows us to exercise our own creative powers. 'Is there not an open window on the right hand of the bookcase? How delightful to stop reading and look out! How stimulating the scene is, in its unconsciousness, its irrelevance, its perpetual movement – the colts galloping round the field, the woman filling her pail at the well, the donkey throwing back his head and emitting his long, acrid moan.'

So this gives us two chief ways in which reading is restful. Sometimes it distracts us from our own worries and at other times it does the opposite. Rather than taking us away from our own world, it allows us to reflect on our own lives as our minds wander. Yet again we see this conflict at the heart of rest. It distracts us but also brings us face to face with ourselves, allowing us to mentally time travel back into our own pasts and forward into our own futures. We can both use it to block our own self-awareness or to enhance it.

With some of the restful activities I cover in this book we are looking to declutter our minds, to clear our heads, to be in the moment. But perhaps it's OK to clutter it too. Maybe adding new thoughts, other people's stories and other people's perspectives on the world, can prove just as restful.

And there is a third aspect of reading which provides us with the other reason why reading can help us to feel truly rested.

The Company of a Good Book

The top five restful activities are all largely done alone; for many, getting away from other people is an essential element of rest. But this is where reading is special. It not only allows us to escape other people, but simultaneously provides us with company, company that as well as being more interesting is more restful than real people, company you can ignore whenever you choose to, without giving any explanation. This kind of companionship can be so powerful that it can even protect against feelings of loneliness caused by isolation. In the chapter on being alone, the question 'Who are you with when you're alone?' was posed. Sometimes the answer is with a character in a book. The great American novelist John Steinbeck said, 'We spend all our lives trying to be less lonesome. One of our ancient methods is to tell a story, betting the listener to say – and to feel – "yes, that's the way it is, or at least that's the way I feel it. You're not as alone as you thought."'[22]

Two nursing lecturers in the USA who spent many years working with older people noticed that those who enjoyed reading for pleasure rarely seemed to be lonely. The characters in books were their company. One of their patients was an eighty-six-year-old woman with a heart condition which made it impossible for her to leave her flat. When the lecturers asked her how she felt about being housebound and alone, she pointed to her books and said, 'I'm not alone. I have the whole world right here with me.'[23] The lecturers' subsequent research found other older people agreed. Those who read the most, regardless of whether they read newspapers or books, felt less lonely on average.

Copious research has investigated how reading novels might improve our levels of empathy, even making us better people because of the journeys we've taken into other people's minds. Unlike in the eighteenth century, reading now tends to be seen as a good thing, but I believe its value as an aid to rest has been neglected. So if you want to read to rest, does it matter what you read?

What to Read to Relax

Sometimes people choose specific books with therapeutic benefits in mind. This is officially known as bibliotherapy. The word is used rather broadly, but can mean everything from reading *Jane Eyre* to ease the pain of a broken heart to the prescription of practical manuals on beating anxiety or depression. Although the prescription of novels tends to get more publicity and may well work, it's the latter kind of bibliotherapy that has been systematically tested and found to be effective.

If rest is your desire, what can the evidence tell us about what kind of book to read? You may remember that the ludic readers admitted that half of what they read would be described by their English teacher as trash. So should you try to impress your English teacher? Or not?

The precise book you choose is down to personal taste,

but the key is to choose any book which might put you into Csikszentmihalyi's state of flow. It is a state so all-encompassing that you don't even detect time passing. It's not a case of time going fast because you're having fun. It's as though you are experiencing something that is happening out of time. According to his Theory of Optimal Experience, when you are involved in the right activity for you, nothing else matters. For an activity to promote a state of flow various conditions are required: it involves some effort, but it is within your capacities and it gives you some kind of immediate reward.

For some people, reading is the one activity which fulfils these conditions. And, indeed, Csikszentmihalyi found that of all the things that put people into a state of flow, reading was the one the greatest number of people reported.[24] But back to the question: how much effort should we put into the task?

It might seem obvious to say the least possible, but then let's consider other activities which lead to flow, such as gardening or painting. Or even more strenuously, rock climbing. People who do these things are certainly expending considerable effort, yet they report having among the best optimal experiences.[25]

This is why I believe it's a mistake to assume that if you want to rest a book needs to be easy. People talk of airport novels, the perfect chick lit or dude lit to take on holiday. But perhaps these are exactly the type of books *not* to take away with you. In everyday life, when you tend to read only at bedtime, you might find you can only concentrate for a few pages on a more challenging book before giving in to exhaustion and going to sleep. On holiday, by contrast, you might have hours to spare during the day when you are wide awake. This might be your one chance in the year to become deeply immersed in something more complex. And the more absorbed you become, the more likely you are to reach that state of flow. And the more likely you are to reach a state of flow, the more likely you are to feel rested.

So finally tackling *A Brief History of Time* or *Ulysses* or *À La Recherche du Temps Perdu* while on the sunbed by the pool could be the way to ultimate relaxation. Why not give them a try!

When people select books for themselves, some start novels one at a time and spend any reading time on that single book, while others of us let them pile up in little dust-gathering towers beside the bed, with maybe a dozen on the go at once, some of which we will no doubt never finish. If you are the latter type (I am; as well as the pile of newspapers by my bed, there's a pile of books) and provided you can remember what's happening in the plot, you have a choice at any given moment of picking up a book which somehow chimes or contrasts with your mood.

Research has found that when people feel miserable they tend to choose something uplifting in the hope of feeling better, while people in a good mood tend not to want to disrupt it.[26] Yet this would suggest that everyone chooses happy books, either to improve a negative mood or maintain a positive one, and of course we know this is not what happens in real life. Thrillers full of misery and violence are consistently popular, and just as people enjoy weepy films they like sad books too. Witness the success of the poetic novel *Grief Is the Thing with Feathers* by Max Porter, which is a read that's both quite complex and heartbreakingly sad.

Spoiler Alert

Some people find a novel even more relaxing if they already know the end. You may think you hate a spoiler, but curiously, spoilers not only allow us to process the book more fluently as we read, but on average people report enjoying a book *more* rather than less if they know what happens

Most research on spoilers uses short stories, in which people have invested less than when reading a whole novel, so I'm not entirely convinced that people don't mind them. That said, some people deliberately read the last page of a novel and then relish reading from the start to see how the story unfolds to reach its climax. And, of course, many people love re-reading favourite novels in which the storyline, the atmosphere and the characters are all very familiar.

However, other people definitely can't stand knowing what's going to happen in a book. At the extreme end of the spectrum, a Russian engineer was accused of stabbing a colleague with whom he was spending a long dark winter holed up in an Antarctic research station. Some reports claimed that the reason for the stabbing was that the colleague persistently gave away the endings of the only books they had at the research station. Now it may not be true – some reports refuted this motive – but even the fact that it has a ring of truth about it shows how strongly we can feel about NOT KNOWING THE ENDING UNTIL WE GET TO THE END.

A lot depends on the type of literature we are reading. Knowing (spoiler alert) that *Romeo and Juliet* are both going to die doesn't stop you from longing every time that someone will intervene before it's too late, whereas learning before the end the identity of the killer in a whodunit is a rather different matter. Also, in Shakespeare the plot is hardly the only reason to read the play. A large part of the pleasure is in the beauty of the language and the complex psychology of the characters.

Of course, some novels are deliberately constructed so that the ending comes first and the rest of the book is spent tracing how it came to pass. But even in these cases, unless you've read the book before, the slow reveal is still a large part of the pleasure. Research has shown that the more fiction people read for simple enjoyment, the more they want to enjoy an unspoiled story. In contrast people who don't revel as much in engaging with the thoughts and emotions within a book didn't mind knowing the plot.[27]

For some of the South African bookworms, re-reading books was even more enjoyable than reading them for the first time, despite knowing the ending. One stated that there are so few really pleasurable books in the world that he reads his favourite books as fast as possible in the hope of forgetting the plot and enjoying them all over again, as many as ten times.

Reading Aloud

Before leaving the topic of reading, I want to return to being read to, which is very special. Many years ago I visited a scheme on an estate in a deprived part of Oxford where mothers were being encouraged to read out loud to their very small babies. At the start the mothers were sceptical, believing that until the babies could talk there was no point in reading to them because they wouldn't understand. But soon they saw how much the babies loved the attention and how hearing their mothers' words seemed to soothe them. There's now good evidence that even reading to tiny three-month-olds can improve children's literacy later on, possibly simply by getting them accustomed to spending time looking at books.[28]

These days it's not only children who are listening as someone else reads. There's a new trend for shared reading groups – like a book club except that instead of the reading taking place before everyone meets up, one person reads the book aloud while everyone listens. The group shares in the experience, moment by moment. In some ways it's more like going to the theatre or the cinema.

In most groups an experienced facilitator or actor does the reading out loud. In others the group members take it in turns. Either way I trust it's not like in our school English classes where we trudged laboriously through *King of the Castle*, then *Brighton Rock*, *Oliver Twist* and *Macbeth*, by rotating around the room, each of us reading a paragraph in a monotone without daring to risk looking stupid by putting any expression whatsoever into our performance.

I find that being read to is slightly too restful. I've resisted discussing sleep much in this book, but for me listening to someone reading is where rest tips over into sleep. For many years now my husband has read to me in bed. Initially when we were backpacking and had more time, I would read out loud too. These days it's always his turn. If he doesn't read, it can take me ages to get to sleep, but if he does it's as though he turns off a switch in my head. He tells me that within a page I'm asleep, deeply asleep.

He's surprised that I'm able to drop off when he's putting so much effort into 'doing all the voices', yet I do. The next night he has to fill me in on what happened. I've 'read' dozens of books in this way, from George Elliot's *Middlemarch* to Graham Greene's *The Quiet American* and – most recently – Tracey Thorn's memoir of growing up in Hertfordshire, *Another Planet*. Something about someone else doing the reading instantly stills my racing mind and sends me to sleep. My husband must continue reading for a while after I'm asleep, mind. Otherwise I wake up again. But it's as though a magic sleeping potion has been poured into my ear.

Of course, some people turn to technology to provide this service, with audiobooks gaining in popularity and even sleep apps providing soothing stories designed to be soporific, which are specially constructed so that anything interesting only happens at the beginning. The narrators read slowly in calming tones, keeping everything on a level. They don't do all the voices. These apps are getting hundreds of thousands of downloads, with some authors finding they can earn more from deliberately writing novels that lull people to sleep than writing them with the idea of gripping their readers.

So read to yourself or find someone to read to you. Read mindfully or mindlessly. It's up to you. Reading allows us to rest by changing the nature of our mind wandering. It seems to take us away from rumination, from the repeated thought patterns about what's wrong. And even if we do daydream while we read at least it helps us to daydream afresh. While if you want to rest, but don't want to feel alone, a novel allows you to do just that.

And if that hasn't convinced you to do more reading,

there's another benefit of reading that you might not have heard of. More than 3,000 people were asked how much time they spent reading books, magazines or newspapers during the previous week. Forty-one per cent read no books at all. Others were keen readers. The sample was followed for a decade and during that time just over a quarter of the people died, but the good news for the bookworms was that they lived an average of almost two years longer than the people who only read newspapers and magazines. Health, wealth and education at the start of the study were all taken into account, and still the difference persisted.[29] It is surprising that a sedentary activity might have such a positive impact on health, but perhaps reading is a more special way of resting than we realise.

THE PERFECT PRESCRIPTION
FOR REST

B y now I hope I have convinced you that rest matters. We need to start taking it more seriously. Like sleep, rest is not a luxury. If we are to live well and flourish, rest is essential.

Exactly how you rest best will be down to your preferences and choices. But taking into account the findings of the dozens of scientific studies covered in this book, here's my step-by-step guide to how to maximise your chances of resting well.

1) MAKE SURE YOU REST ENOUGH

Just as you might take note of the number of hours of sleep you get each night to ensure you're not sleep-deprived, so you should start to count how many hours of rest you get.

Think back to yesterday. Did you have sufficient time to recharge your mental and physical batteries? Were you able to pause and reflect? Did you have the opportunity to think and not just do? But did you also have the chance to switch off?

The people with the highest levels of well-being in the Rest Test were resting for between five and six hours a day. This sounds like a lot and you may be thinking that there is no way you could ever do that, but it is likely that you are already getting more rest than you think.

Surveys of time use show that on average men in the UK have a hefty six hours and nine minutes to spend on leisure activities each day, while women have a decent five hours and twenty-nine minutes.[1] These are of course averages and some people, especially parents of young children or those caring for relatives, will almost certainly have far less free time than this. You also need to remember that these figures are averaged across the week, so some people in the survey might have had one or two hours free on weekday evenings, but had a lot of spare time at the weekend.

It's not the case that the more rest you get, the better. In the Rest Test although people who told us they had zero hours of rest each day had considerably lower well-being scores than those who rested for longer, scores also dipped among those who had more than six hours rest a day. Perhaps these were people who had experienced enforced rest due to illness or employment. This fits in with other research which has found that those on long-term sick leave are the least likely to enjoy their leisure time, while the one advantage of having little available leisure time is that when you do get it, you enjoy it more.[2] And echoing our Rest Test results, the time use researcher Jonathan Gershuny has found that the enjoyment of leisure activity rises to a peak as the amount of free time a person has increases, but then drops again if they have too much time on their hands.[3]

Don't worry if the optimum rest time of five hours a day sounds unreachable. There are more ways of carving rest out of your busy schedule than you might think. And, of course, five hours of rest doesn't mean you need to somehow set aside that amount of time to do nothing. For some people cooking meals or going for a run at the weekend is relaxing and enjoyable, and they might count it as part of their rest time. As we've seen throughout this book, rest is anything that a particular person *counts* as rest.

And we shouldn't get too bogged down in the precise number of hours of rest you need. If you *feel* you are getting enough rest you are probably right, even if it is quite a bit less than five hours a day on average.

2) PICK THE RIGHT INGREDIENTS FOR REST

To get top quality rest you need to work out which are essential elements of life that contribute most to you achieving a sense of restfulness. The restful activities I have covered in this book provided us with the ingredients for a decent rest.

- taking a break from other people
- resting your mind as well as your body
- exerting your body in order to rest your mind
- being distracted from your worries
- allowing your mind to wander
- giving yourself permission not to achieve anything in particular

Of course, some of these restful ingredients will appeal to you more than others. To create the perfect recipe for rest ask yourself which you value and which you don't. Choose as many as you want. For example, only 15 per cent of people found exercise restful, but for this minority of individuals it is an essential ingredient.

The next step is to think about which combination of activities provides you with the ingredients to create your personal recipe for rest. Of course, it may be that the restful dish you cook up is not one that featured in the top ten as chosen by other people. That doesn't matter.

In the USA, researchers concluded that the key to why students found their weekends restful was that Saturdays and Sundays were the only days of the week when they felt they had control over their own time.[4] As long as the students didn't have to work, it didn't matter what they were doing at the weekend. The days could be action packed. The point was they were doing what they wanted to do and that made them feel relaxed. This is instructive. As we have seen over the preceding chapters, a lot of different things can be categorised as rest. The key to the students feeling rested was for them to indulge in a combination of activities – some straightforwardly relaxing, others distracting enough to allow them to detach psychologically from their work.

The important thing is to take the time to consider why an activity might or might not feel restful for you. What will best replenish your energy levels when you feel worn out? What will truly distract you both from your own burdensome thoughts and from the demands of other people? What allows you to slow down or stop without making you feel guilty or feeling that others are judging you?

It's also important to consider the timing. Different restful activities will work better in different situations. If you are physically exhausted, then it is fine to flop in front of the television. But if your mind is weary with work and worry, taking a walk outside might improve your mood more.

3) GIVE YOURSELF PERMISSION TO REST

Once you've chosen your ideal restful ingredients and somehow carved out the time to put them into practice, there is another step you need to take. You need to give yourself permission to rest. How often do you push on when you're tired instead of allowing yourself a break? And remember that getting up early isn't morally better. It either suits you or it doesn't. If you can arrange to start your day with a rest, otherwise known as a lie-in, then do.

4) WHEN YOU FEEL STRESSED PRESCRIBE YOURSELF FIFTEEN MINUTES OF YOUR FAVOURITE RESTFUL ACTIVITY

Is there an activity which can make a quick difference when you're pressed for time? One which instantly transports you away from your worries and calms your mind? It might be mindfulness. It might be music. It might be reading. It might not feature in the Rest Test top ten.

I used to feel guilty about spending fifteen minutes pottering in the garden after lunch on a weekday when really I should be getting back to work. But as a result of researching rest, I've reframed that time in my tiny greenhouse or in the flower beds as an activity that improves my well-being. I now say that I am 'prescribing' myself fifteen minutes of gardening for my mental health, and I definitely feel better for it. It helps me to concentrate and work more intensely when I am back at my desk.

5) KEEP AN EYE OUT FOR RESTING WHEN YOU DON'T REALISE IT

Given that many of us are genuinely busy a lot of the time, it's important to notice those moments when you are in fact getting some rest.

The time use studies I have mentioned would suggest we get more rest than we realise, so a first step towards a greater sense of restfulness is to make a conscious effort to appreciate those spare moments. It is only by realising that you are resting that you can properly relish it.

Try to be a purposeful and conscious rester. Yes, potter if you want to; yes, do nothing in particular – but appreciate the satisfying, restful nature of that pottering and loafing. Note it, value it. Don't allow precious moments of rest to pass you by.

6) REFRAME YOUR WASTED TIME AS REST

If we are pressed for time, we can also exploit unexpected opportunities to rest. Think back to the study in the Doing Nothing in Particular chapter where some of the people shut in a room with nothing to do chose to give themselves electric shocks to relieve the boredom. On other occasions these same individuals might have revelled in the chance to relax for a while, but because this rest was imposed on them they didn't view it in that way. In this instance, being forced to do nothing felt like a kind of torture. Indeed, so much so that the participants in the study preferred to inflict some real pain on themselves.

If you think about it, we often view opportunities to rest in this negative way, if rarely with such extreme consequences. Things that disrupt our busy schedules and leave us with nothing to do for a few moments are seen as frustrating delays, as dead time, as intensely aggravating and annoying. We end up kicking our heels when we could be just kicking back and relaxing.

So instead of feeling infuriated and stressed by a ten-minute delay to a train journey, why not rebrand this time as an opportunity to rest for a short while? Instead of filling that fifteen minutes between finishing a report and going to a meeting by answering a few emails, why not just sit quietly or go for a stroll? And how about recasting the wait in a long queue at the post office as pleasant downtime, as a chance to pause, to daydream, to recharge your batteries?

7) STOP FETISHISING BUSYNESS

By now some of you might well be shouting: 'This is all very well, it might be true for other people, but in my case, what with the long hours I work, my family commitments and all the other things I have to do, I really don't have time to rest.'

I hear you. But I still urge you to take a look at your daily schedule and to consider how you view your overwhelming, never-ending to-do list. We should be aware that it's common for people to overestimate the total number of hours they work. Whenever I put this question to audiences at live events, most people in the room say they work forty-five to fifty hours a week, well over the actual average working hours of people in full-time employment: thirty-nine a week. But then if you ask the same people to take the previous week as a specific example, they tend to find that they have worked fewer hours than they thought. It might have felt like a busy week, but although they worked extra hours on a couple of days, it wasn't every day. And maybe they did knock off early one day after all.

But still, fitting in rest can be hard. There are two ways of approaching this problem. One is to set aside a couple of hours every few days to devote to completing all the small jobs on your to-do list. When you attack them in one go, you might be surprised at how many of the tasks that have been hanging over you for days in fact only take a few minutes to finish. And crossing them off the list (whether on paper, on screen, or in your mind) can feel immensely satisfying. More-over, once you've completed a few of the smaller tasks, you will feel more energised to take on some of the bigger ones.

But, even then, you won't get everything done. Far from it. And this is where the other approach comes in. Just accept that your to-do list will never end. The goal is a chimera; its pursuit is a fool's errand. Think about it: even if, by some miracle, one evening every job on your list has been chalked off, the subsequent day will bring more jobs. However diligent and organised you might be, the unexpected will happen. And everyday stuff will happen too. Pipes will leak, people will surprise you, events will overtake you, another email will arrive in your inbox, someone will text and ask you to do something. But that's OK. Your to-do list is never-ending. You've accepted that. You will get to these new tasks as soon as you can. You won't let them stress you out. For now, you will rest.

There are dozens of time-management techniques which claim to help you to make more efficient use of both your working and leisure hours, but few have been tested empirically and cramming more tasks into a shorter time is inherently unrestful. Maybe it's true that you waste some time at work chatting and you could concentrate harder all day and leave work a little earlier, but perhaps it's having some fun with colleagues and checking Instagram every now and then that makes your job enjoyable, or bearable even.

The writer Oliver Burkeman suggests that if you constantly feel pressed for time, you should actively decide what you're going to stop doing. He suggests leaving a book group, for example. Or accepting that you'll never be a good cook and giving up attempting complicated recipes. Or ceasing to make the effort to chase that friend who is always so hard to pin down to a date. This is excellent advice, with one caveat. Choose what to give up very carefully. Don't make the mistake of forfeiting the one activity that you find restful and that allows you to cope with everything else.

Instead, give up the activity you might once have enjoyed but has now become a chore. I abandoned Spanish lessons after I found myself for what must have been the fiftieth time trying to do my homework on the tube ten minutes before the class. Much as I wanted to speak Spanish, much as I liked the teacher, it was one more demand on my time that I couldn't handle. And because of the pressures on my time, the lessons, though interesting, were making me stressed rather than giving me pleasure. In this case giving up was the right decision, but dropping out of a choir, say, just because it takes a bit of time and effort to get to choir practice, might be counterproductive if it's the one activity in your week which leaves you feeling truly refreshed.

8) JUST SAY 'NO'

To free up blocks of time might require some more radical surgery on your timetable. This can be painful for those of us who find ourselves compelled to overfill our diaries. But here's one tip taken from a previous book of mine that might help. (And see what I've done here to reduce my own workload a bit?)

We have a tendency to believe that in the future we will have more spare time. But all the evidence from time perception studies shows this isn't true. We won't become better organised or more disciplined versions of our current selves. Everything will continue to take longer than we predict because we will continue to be diverted by unexpected tasks or things that go wrong. Unless we make a conscious decision to cut down on the number of activities and events we commit to, we will have no more time to ourselves next year than we do this year.

So, if someone invites you to a two-day conference in six months' time, what should you do? I suggest asking yourself this question. Does the thought of fitting a two-day conference into the next fortnight fill you with dread because you are already so overcommitted? If the answer is yes, you should turn down the invitation to the conference later in the year because it's very unlikely that in a few months' time you'll be less busy than now.

Or how about this scenario? You are asked to sit on a committee next year. Have your read the papers for the meeting you are going to tomorrow? No. Well, don't join another committee then. Because if you do, you will find yourself in the same position as now, unless you plan to take steps to change your regular schedule, which – experience should tell you – you are unlikely to be able to do.

9) PUT BREAKS IN YOUR DIARY AS WELL AS APPOINTMENTS

This is a suggestion which goes with the grain of our 'to-do' list culture, our desire to be organised and to keep to a schedule. What I'm suggesting is that you schedule periods of downtime. Yes, put 'Rest' or 'Break' in your timetable, strange as it might sound.

Decide at the start of the day when to take three or four breaks. They don't have to be long. A few minutes will do. Decide what you will do during those breaks and make sure it really does qualify as a break – ideally you should be outside in the fresh air or at least in a different room in the building. It might involve going to meet a friend in another department and having a chat. Or it could mean going to the kitchen to make yourself – and maybe your colleagues – a cup of tea. If your boss looks askance, remember to tell her that all the evidence shows that taking micro-breaks is not only good for personal well-being but is an aid to workplace productivity. It's win–win.

These breaks should certainly involve getting away from your work station. Logging on to Facebook for a few minutes or watching something on YouTube might be a distraction from the report you are writing, but it's not as restful as getting up from your chair and getting away from your screen.

And try really hard not to eat your lunch at your desk. A few firms have banned it, which is a good thing, but not as good as ensuring that staff genuinely have time in their work day to take a proper lunchbreak. This would be a really great development, or rather a return to the good old days. Just think, hour long lunchbreaks and regular teabreaks. When was the last time you enjoyed either? The most enlightened firms today understand the value to their employees, and indeed their bottom line, of time away from the desk. But if, as is likely, your company has closed the canteen and sacked the tealady (or teaboy), take it upon yourself to organise for a group of you to go out for a proper lunch or to stop for fifteen minutes for tea and a biscuit.

So, schedule your breaks, but don't be afraid to break that schedule either. This is supposed to be restful after all.

10) ADD SMALL, RESTFUL MOMENTS TO YOUR LIFE

Look to see whether any of the unavoidable jobs in life could be done more restfully. We become accustomed to rushing in order to fit in as much as possible. We try to do everything with maximum efficiency. But we don't have to.

Now and then, how about having a bath instead of a shower? And to make up for your extra hot water consumption, how about sometimes ambling to the shops on foot instead of taking the car? We don't always have to make the time-efficient choice, but it has become a habit. Taking the long route through the park might waste ten minutes, but could improve our well-being for the rest of the day.

It's usually not essential that you check your emails the moment you sit down on the train. You could look out of the window into people's back gardens, wondering about their lives. Take the opportunity when you can to do all the things you weren't supposed to do at school. Daydream. Stare into space. Doodle. Consider whether doing a jigsaw or even (and I know there's a love/hate thing going on here) have a go with an adult colouring book.

11) CREATE A BOX OF REST

If you're a fan of the new concept of self-care you might like this idea. If you're not familiar with this movement, take a look at Instagram. There you will find endless self-care suggestions.

It's true that they often seem to revolve around spending money. I'm all for cherishing myself, but why must it involve luxury oils, scented candles, face rollers, bath pillows, cashmere blankets or artisan chocolates? And I'm all for the odd treat, but is it really a good idea to take an Uber to work on a rainy Monday morning, or spend every other weekend at a luxury spa?

I deserve it, apparently. Or so the people trying to sell me things keep saying. And for all my scepticism they are clearly on to something. The self-care industry is booming. It's claimed that in the USA alone it is now worth $4.2 trillion a year.

But if rampant commercialism is the downside, there is also a more positive side to self-care, a side that I like to see as a sign that the younger generation is beginning to under-stand the significance of rest better than older generations, reclaiming rest and making time for themselves to recuperate from everyday stresses.

Bloggers experiencing mental health issues now describe their own self-care routines, often giving useful advice on how to take control of the small things in life. Lists feature a lot, such as suggestions for filling the kind of happy box I mentioned in the chapter on listening to music. The idea is that the contents are personalised. Of course, a happy box isn't going to avert a serious mental health problem or replace professional help, but some people do find this kind of self-care makes them feel a little bit better when they sense they are going downhill mentally or while waiting for more serious advice or treatment.

This makes me wonder whether we might benefit from our own personalised 'box of rest'. It would contain the items that will best induce restfulness for you. Mine would contain a crochet hook and some wool, some seeds to plant, a book of short stories to dip into, a playlist of relaxing music, a card with a few stretching exercises on it and perhaps

– never forgetting that rest doesn't have to be sedentary – some running socks.

What would be in your box of rest? I've helpfully provided you with an empty one below.

12) DON'T LET YOUR SEARCH FOR REST BECOME UNRESTFUL

Rest can be employed strategically, but what we need to do is to find better ways of managing the rhythms of rest and activity, of busyness and idleness, in our lives, without letting rest become another job on our to-do list.

While heeding my call to embrace rest, to enjoy more of it and to take it seriously, don't overdo it or take it too seriously. Don't become a restaholic or a rest bore. Don't pack your schedule with rest or feel you must stick diligently to your rest breaks. Sometimes you need a rest from rest. Living well involves balance, variety and moderation. And that goes for rest too.

Assuming you have just finished this book (and not simply

skipped to the last page in search of tips), then you have done one of the most restful things you can do. The act of reading this has already set you on your way to incorporating more rest into your own life. Congratulations!

ACKNOWLEDGEMENTS

It was several years ago when I had a call from the author and psychologist Charles Fernyhough asking if I'd like to join a small group led by Felicity Callard from Durham University. They wanted to apply for a large grant to spend almost two years at Wellcome Collection in London exploring a single topic with artists, poets, historians and others. The topic they had chosen was rest. I joined the core team and – many months of work later – to my surprise we won the Wellcome Trust grant. We named our group Hubbub and invited more than forty people to collaborate with us. Some are mentioned in the book and every one of them has influenced my thoughts about rest, sometimes through a lecture or an artwork, sometimes through a single wise remark. In particular I'd like to thank here Felicity Callard, James Wilkes, Charles Ferryhough and Kimberley Staines and from the Wellcome Collection, Harriet Martin, Rosie Stanbury, Chris Hassan, Simon Chaplin and Natalie Coe, who were all hugely supportive in allowing us to be enveloped in the world of rest (harder work than it sounds).

As part of Hubbub I had the idea for the Rest Test and it's thanks to BBC Radio 4's commissioning editor Mohit Bakaya, BBC Radio Science Unit editor Deborah Cohen and

World Service Commisioning Editor, Steve Titherington, that it was launched both on Radio 4 and the world service and reached such a wide audience. Ben Alderson-Day, Giulia Poerio and Gemma Lewis worked incredibly hard to develop and analyse the test, along with others in Hubbub that I've already mentioned. Special thanks go to the producer of the Radio 4 series *Anatomy of Rest* Geraldine Fitzgerald, who takes my work and through her own hard work makes it into wonderful programmes, for which I tend to get most of the credit. She is always a good friend as well as being such a creative producer. I'm also grateful to all the people who gave up their time to be interviewed, some of whom are mentioned in the book.

Since then I have continued to think about rest, and decided to do something we hadn't done as part of Hubbub, to research in detail each of the most popular restful activities. Lorna Stewart is a very intelligent researcher and has given me invaluable help with the chapters on TV, bathing and reading. And of course if hundreds of academics hadn't taken the time to conduct experiments, then I wouldn't be able to assess that evidence here. I've mentioned those that have most influenced me in the text. When it comes to how we use our leisure time, the work of Mihaly Csikszentmihalyi and Jonathan Gershuny has been particularly influential.

The chapter on solitude draws on the BBC Loneliness Experiment, where I was lucky enough to collaborate with three very clever women: Pamela Qualter, Manuela Barreto and Christina Victor. Many academics took the time to send me papers or answer my questions, including David Vincent, Birgitta Gatersleben, Roy Raymann and Miles Richardson. Mathijs Lucassen, Charles Fernyhough, Catherine Loveday and Adam Rutherford were kind enough to read specific chapters for me and made useful comments.

Thank you to everyone at Canongate, who are wonderful publishers – both enthusiastic and efficient. Special thanks to Lucy Zhou and Andrea Joyce, and especially to my editor Simon Thorogood, who is quietly wise and astute. He and my fantastic agent Will Francis at Janklow & Nesbitt both made this book so much better, as did the meticulous, patient copy editor Octavia Reeve.

Finally thanks to my husband, Tim, who witnessed first-hand why writing a book on rest isn't always restful, but took the time to read drafts and make excellent suggestions.

NOTES

Online sources quoted below were accessed in July 2019.

A Call to Rest

1 Peterson, A.H., 'How Millennials Became the Burnout Generation'. BuzzFeed, 05 01 2019. https://www.buzzfeednews.com/article/annehelenpetersen/millennials-burnout-generation-debt-work

2 Health & Safety Executive, 'Work-related Stress, Depression or Anxiety Statistics in Great Britain, 2018'. HSE, 31 01 2018. http://www.hse.gov.uk/statistics/causdis/stress.pdf

3 National Safety Council (2017) *Fatigue in the Workplace: Causes & Consequences of Employee Fatigue.* Illinois: National Safety Council

4 Mental Health Foundation (May 2018) *Stress: Are We Coping?* London: Mental Health Foundation

5 Baines, E. & Blatchford, P. (2019) *School Break and Lunch Times and Young People's Social Lives: A Follow-up National Study, Final Report.* London: UCL Institute of Education

6 Rhea, D.J. & Rivchun, A.P. (2018) 'The LiiNK Project: Effects of Multiple Recesses and Character Curriculum on Classroom Behaviors and Listening Skills in Grades K–2 Children'. *Frontiers in Education*, 3, 9

7   Medic, G. et al (2017) 'Short- and Long-term Health Consequences of Sleep Disruption'. *Nature and Science of Sleep*, 9, 151–61

10   Mindfulness

1   If you want to try this, there's a longer description in the excellent book by Mark Williams and Danny Penman (2011) *Mindfulness*. London: Piatkus

2   From an account of Jon Kabat-Zinn's visit to Bodhitree in 1994. *Bodhitree* 25 03 2017. https://bodhitree.com/journal/from-the-archives/

3   Goleman, D. & Davidson, R.J. (2017) *The Science of Meditation: How to Change Your Brain, Mind and Body.* London: Penguin

4   See this excellent review for the state of the evidence on mindfulness. Creswell, J.D. (2017) 'Mindfulness Interventions'. *Annual Review of Psychology*, 68, 491–516

5   Again see Creswell for summaries of all these topics.

6   Creswell, J.D. (2017). 'Mindfulness Interventions'. *Annual Review of Psychology*, 68, 491–516

7   Goleman, D. & Davidson, R.J. (2017) *The Science of Meditation: How to Change Your Brain, Mind and Body.* London: Penguin

8   Baer, R.A. et al (2004). 'Assessment of Mindfulness by Self-report: The Kentucky Inventory of Mindfulness Skills'. *Assessment*, 11 (3), 191–206

9   Giluk, T.L. (2015) 'Mindfulness, Big Five Personality, and Affect: A Meta-analysis'. *Personality and Individual Differences*, 47, 805–81

10 Gawrysiak, M.J. et al (2018) 'The Many Facets of Mindfulness & the Prediction of Change Following MBSR'. *Journal of Clinical Psychology*, 74 (4), 523–35

11 Shapiro, S.L. et al (2011) 'The Moderation of Mindfulness-based Stress Reduction Effects by Trait Mindfulness: Results from a Randomised Controlled Trial'. *Journal of Clinical Psychology*, 67 (3), 267–77

12 Galante J. et al (2017) 'A Mindfulness-based Intervention to Increase Resilience to Stress in University Students (The Mindful Student Study): A Pragmatic Randomised Controlled Trial'. *The Lancet Public Health*, 3 (2) 72–81

13 Langer, E.J. (2014) *Mindfulness*. Boston: Da Capo Lifelong Books

9 Watching TV

1 Lee, B. & Lee, R.S. (1995) 'How and Why People Watch TV: Implications for the Future of Interactive Television'. *Journal of Advertising Research*, Nov/Dec

2 See Lee & Lee again.

3 Greenwood, D.N. (2008) 'Television as an Escape from Self'. *Personality and Individual Differences*, 44, 414–24

4 Pearlin, L.I. (1959) 'Social and Personal Stress and Escape in Television Viewing'. *Public Opinion Quarterly*, 23 (2), 255–9

5 Conway, J.C. & Rubin, A.M. (1991) 'Psychological Predictors of Television Viewing Motivation'. *Communication Research*, 18 (4), 443–63

6 Tichi, C. (1991) *The Electronic Hearth*. Oxford: Oxford University Press

7 Kubey, R. et al (1990) 'Television and the Quality of Family Life'. *Communication Quarterly*, 38 (4), 312–24

8 Krants-Kent, R. & Stewart, J. (2007) 'How Do Older Americans Spend Their Time?'. *Monthly Labor Review Online*, 130 (5), 8–26

9   Valkenburg, P.M. & van der Voort, T.H.A. (1994). 'Influence of TV on Daydreaming and Creative Imagination: A Review of Research'. *Psychological Bulletin*, 116 (2), 316–39

10 Tukachinsky, R. & Eyal, K. (2018) 'The Psychology of Marathon Television Viewing: Antecedents and Viewer Involvement'. *Mass Communication and Society*, 21 (3), 275–95

11 Sung, Y.H. et al (2015) *A Bad Habit for Your Health? An Exploration of Psychological Factors for Binge-watching Behaviour.* Puerto Rico: 65th Annual International Communication Association Conference

12 Frey, B.S. et al (2007) 'Does Watching TV Make Us Happy?'. *Journal of Economic Psychology*, 28 (3), 283–313

13 Szabo, A. & Hopkinson, K.L. (2007) 'Negative Psychological Effects of Watching the News on the Television: Relaxation or Another Intervention May Be Needed to Buffer Them!'. *International Journal of Behavioral Medicine*, 14 (2), 57–62

14 Werneck, A.O. et al (2018) 'Associations Between TV Viewing and Depressive Symptoms Among 60,202 Brazilian Adults: The Brazilian National Health Survey'. *Journal of Affective Disorders*, 236, 23–30

15 Scanlan, J.N. et al (2011) 'Promoting Wellbeing in Young Unemployed Adults: The Importance of Identifying Meaningful Patterns of Time Use'. *Australian Occupational Therapy Journal*, 58 (2), 111–19

16 Nguyen, G.T. et al (2008) 'More Than Just a Communication Medium: What Older Adults Say About Television and Depression'. *The Gerontologist*, 48 (3), 300–10

17 Lucas, M. et al (2011) 'Relation Between Clinical Depression Risk and Physical Activity and Time Spent Watching Television in Older Women: A 10-year Prospective Follow-up Study'. *American Journal of Epidemiology*, 174 (9), 1017–27

18 Shiue, I. (2016) 'Modeling Indoor TV/Screen Viewing and Adult Physical and Mental Health: Health Survey for England,

2012'. *Environmental Science and Pollution Research*, 23 (12), 11708–15

19 Fancourt, D. & Steptoe, A. (2019) 'Television Viewing and Cognitive Decline in Older Age: Findings from the English Longitudinal Study of Ageing'. *Scientific Reports*, 9 (2851)

20 Mesquita, G. & Rubens, R. (2010) 'Quality of Sleep Among University Students: Effects of Night-time Computer Television Use'. *Arquivos de Neuro-Psiquiatria*, 68 (5), 720–5

21 Custers, K. & Van den Bulck, J. (2012) 'Television Viewing, Internet Use, and Self-Reported Bedtime and Rise Time in Adults: Implications for Sleep Hygiene Recommendations from an Exploratory Cross-Sectional Study'. *Behavioral Sleep Medicine*, 10, 96–105

22 Mitesh, K. & Tobias, R. (2011) 'A Note on the Relationship Between Television Viewing and Individual Happiness'. *The Journal of Socio-Economics*, 40 (1), 53–8

23 Kubey, R.W. & Csikszentmihalyi, M. (1990) 'Television as Escape: Subjective Experience Before an Evening of Heavy Viewing'. *Communication Reports*, 3 (2), 92–100

24 Hammermeister, J. et al (2005) 'Life Without TV? Cultivation Theory and Psychosocial Health Characteristics of Television-free Individuals and their Television-viewing Counterparts'. *Health Communication*, 17 (3), 253–64

25 Reinecke, L. et al (2014) 'The Guilty Couch Potato: The Role of Ego Depletion in Reducing Recovery through Media Use'. *Journal of Communication*, 64 (4), 569–89

8 Daydreaming

1 Bowie had died earlier that month, aged sixty-nine. I can tell you where I was when I heard the news: you guessed it, I was in bed.

2 Fernyhough, C. & Alderson-Day, B. (2016) 'Descriptive Experience Sampling as a Psychological Method'. In Callard, F. et al (Eds) *The Restless Compendium*. London: Palgrave Pivot

3 Of course, as some cognitive psychologists have pointed out, just because a person is lying in a brain scanner we can't be certain that they are alone in their thoughts, introspecting. They could be wondering how much longer they have to be there or looking at their curious surroundings. See Gilbert, S.J. et al (2007) 'Comment on "Wandering minds"'. *Science*, 317, 43b

4 Biswal, B. et al (1995) 'Functional Connectivity in the Motor Cortex of the Resting Human Brain Using Echo-planar MRI'. *Magnetic Resonance in Medicine*, 34 (4), 537–41

5 Shulman, G.L. (1997) 'Searching for Activations that Generalize Over Tasks'. *Human Brain Mapping*, 5 (4), 317–22

6 Raichle, M.E. (2010) 'The Brain's Dark Energy'. *Scientific American*, 302, 44–9

7 For more on mind wandering and the Rest Test listen to *The Anatomy of Rest*, Episode 2: 'Does the Mind Rest?'. BBC Radio 4, 20 10 2016. https://www.bbc.co.uk/programmes/b07vq2by

8 Raichle, M.E. et al (2001) 'A Default Mode of Brain Function'. *Proceedings of the National Academy of Science*, 98 (2), 676–82

9 Gilbert, S.J. et al (2007) 'Comment on "Wandering Minds"'. *Science*, 317, 43b

10 Fox, M.D. & Raichle, M.E. (2007) 'Spontaneous Fluctuations in Brain Activity Observed with Functional Magnetic Resonance Imaging'. *Nature Reviews Neuroscience*, 8, 700–11

11 Raichle, M.E. (2015) 'The Restless Brain: How Intrinsic Activity Organizes Brain Function'. *Philosophical Transactions of the Royal Society B*, 370 (1668). https://doi.org/10.1098/rstb.2014.0172

12 Smith, K. (2012) 'Neuroscience: Idle Minds'. *Nature*, 489 (7416), 356–8

13 Karlsson M.P. & Frank, L.M. (2009) 'Awake Replay of Remote Experiences in the Hippocampus'. *Nature Neuroscience*, 12 (7), 913–18

14 Bar, M. (2009) 'The Proactive Brain: Memory for Predictions'. *Philosophical Transactions of the Royal Society B*, 364, 1235–43

15 Powell, H. (2016) 'The Quest for Quies Mentis'. In Callard, F. et al (Eds) *The Restless Compendium*. London: Palgrave Pivot

16 Killingsworth, M.A. & Gilbert, D.T. (2010) 'A Wandering Mind is an Unhappy Mind'. *Science*, 330, 932

17 Smallwood, J. & Andrews-Hanna, J. (2013) 'Not All Minds that Wander Are Lost: The Importance of a Balanced Perspective on the Mind-wandering State'. *Frontiers in Psychology*, 4, 441

18 Leger, K.A. et al (2018) 'Let It Go: Lingering Negative Affect in Response to Daily Stressors Is Associated with Physical Health Years Later'. *Psychological Science*, 1283–90

19 Clancy, F. et al (2016) 'Perseverative Cognition and Health Behaviors: A Systematic Review and Meta-Analysis'. *Frontiers of Human Neuroscience*, 10, 534

20 Smallwood, J. & Andrews-Hanna, J. (2013) 'Not All Minds that Wander Are Lost: The Importance of a Balanced Perspective on the Mind-wandering State'. *Frontiers in Psychology*, 4, 441

21 Interview with Michael Scullin, *All in the Mind*. BBC Radio 4, 16 05 2018. https://www.bbc.co.uk/programmes/b0b2jh7g

22 Kerkhof, A. (2010) *Stop Worrying*. Milton Keynes: Open University Press

23 Scullin, M.K. et al (2018). 'The Effects of Bedtime Writing on Difficulty Falling Asleep: A Polysomnographic Study Comparing To-do Lists and Completed Activity Lists'. *Journal of Experimental Psychology: General*, 147 (1), 139–46

7 A Nice Hot Bath

1 An excellent paper summarising bathing practices from Ancient Greece to the twentieth century is Tubergen, A.C. & Linden, S.V.D. (2002) 'A Brief History of Spa Therapy'. *Annals of the Rheumatic Diseases*, 61 (3), 273–5

2 Frosch, W.A. (2007) 'Taking the Waters – Springs, Wells and Spas'. *The FASEB Journal*, 21 (9), 1948–50

3 Antonelli, M. & Donelli, D. (2018) 'Effects of Balneotherapy and Spa Therapy on Levels of Cortisol as a Stress Biomarker: A Systematic Review'. *International Journal of Biometeorology*, 62 (6), 913–24

4 Matzer F. et al (2014) 'Stress-Relieving Effects of Short-Term Balneotherapy – A Randomized Controlled Pilot Study in Healthy Adults'. *Forsch Komplementmed*, 21, 105–10

5 Rapoliene, L. (2014) 'The Balneotherapy Links with Seafarers' Health in Randomized Clinical Trials'. *Sveikatos Mokslai Health Sciences*, 24 (6), 119–27

6 Naumann, J. (2018) 'Effects and Feasibility of Hyperthermic Baths for Patients with Depressive Disorder: A Randomized Controlled Clinical Pilot Trial'. bioRxiv 409276. https://doi.org/10.1101/409276

7 Walker, M. (2017) *Why We Sleep*. London: Allen Lane

8 Horne, J.A. & Reid, A.J. (1985) 'Night-time Sleep EEG Changes Following Body Heating in a Warm Bath'. *Electroencephalography & Clinical Neurophysiology*, 60 (2), 154–7

9 Van den Heuvel, C. (2006) 'Attenuated Thermoregulatory Response to Mild Thermal Challenge in Subjects with Sleep-onset Insomnia'. *Journal of Sleep and Sleep Disorders Research*, 29 (9), 1174–80

10 Raymann, R.J.E.M. et al (2007) 'Skin Temperature and Sleep-onset Latency: Changes with Age and Insomnia'. *Physiology & Behavior*, 90 (2–3), 257–66

11 Whitworth-Turner, C. et al (2017) 'A Shower Before Bedtime May Improve the Sleep Onset Latency of Youth Soccer Players: This Is Interesting'. *European Journal of Sport Science*, 17 (9), 1119–28

12 Faulkner, S.H. et al (2017) 'The Effect of Passive Heating on Heat Shock Protein 70 and Interleukin-6: A Possible Treatment Tool for Metabolic Diseases?'. *Temperature*, 4 (3), 292–304

13 Monk, R. (1991) *Ludwig Wittgenstein: The Duty of Genius*. London: Vintage

14 Suzuki, H. (2015) 'Characteristics of Sudden Bath-related Death Investigated by Medical Examiners in Tokyo, Japan'. *Journal of Epidemiology*, 25 (2), 126–32

15 Kim, S.Y. (2006) 'A Case of Multiple Organ Failure Due to Heat Stroke Following a Warm Bath'. *Korean Journal of Internal Medicine*, 21 (3), 210–12

16 Lee, C.W. (2010) 'Multiple Organ Failure Caused by Non-exertional Heat Stroke After Bathing in a Hot Spring'. *Journal of the Chinese Medical Association*, 73 (4), 212–15

17 Kosatcky, T. & Kleeman, J. (1985) 'Superficial and Systemic Illness Related to a Hot Tub'. *American Journal of Medicine*, 79 (1), 10–12

18 Peake, J.M. (2017) 'The Effects of Cold Water Immersion and Active Recovery on Inflammation and Cell Stress Responses in Human Skeletal Muscle After Resistance Exercise'. *Journal of Physiology*, 595 (3), 695–711

19 Robiner, W.N. (1990) 'Psychological and Physical Reactions to Whirlpool Baths'. *Journal of Behavioral Medicine*, 13 (2), 157–73

6   A Good Walk

1   Thoreau, H.D. (1851) *Walking*. Project Gutenberg. https://www.gutenberg.org/ebooks/1022

2   Solnit, R. (2000) *Wanderlust: A History of Walking*. London: Penguin

3   Oppezzo, M. & Schwartz, D.L. (2014) 'Give Your Ideas Some Legs: The Positive Effect of Walking on Creative Thinking'. *Journal of Experimental Psychology: Learning, Memory, and Cognition*, 40 (4), 1142–52

4   Webb, C.E. et al (2017) 'Stepping Forward Together: Could Walking Facilitate Interpersonal Conflict Resolution?'. *American Psychologist*, 72 (4), 374–85

5   Gros, F. (2014) *A Philosophy of Walking*. London: Verso

6   Samson, A. (2017) 'Think Aloud: An Examination of Distance Runners' Thought Processes'. *International Journal of Sport and Exercise Psychology*, 15 (2), 176–89

7   Sianoja, M. et al (2018) 'Enhancing Daily Well-being at Work through Lunch Time Park Walks and Relaxation Exercises: Recovery Experiences as Mediators'. *Journal of Occupational Health Psychology*, 23 (3), 428–42

8   Chekroud, S.R. (2018) 'Association Between Physical Exercise and Mental Health in 12 Million Individuals in the USA Between 2011 and 2015: A Cross-sectional Study'. *Lancet Psychiatry*, 5 (9) 739–46

9   Public Health England data published in 2018 on brisk walking and physical inactivity in forty- to sixty-year-olds. Public Health England, 04 06 2018. https://www.gov.uk/government/publications/brisk-walking-and-physical-inactivity-in-40-to-60-year-olds

10 Jakicic, J.M. et al (2016) 'Effect of Wearable Technology

Combined With a Lifestyle Intervention on Long-term Weight Loss: The IDEA Randomized Clinical Trial'. *Journal of the American Medical Association,* 316 (11), 1161–71

11 Kerner, C. & Goodyear, V.A. (2017) 'The Motivational Impact of Wearable Healthy Lifestyle Technologies: A Self-determination Perspective on Fitbits with Adolescents'. *American Journal of Health Education,* 48 (5), 287–97

12 Lee, I. et al (2019) 'Association of Step Volume and Intensity with All-Cause Mortality in Older Women'. *JAMA Internal Medicine,* 29 05 2019. doi:10.1001/jamainternmed.2019.0899

13 Etkin, J. (2016) 'The Hidden Cost of Personal Quantification'. *Journal of Consumer Research,* 42 (6), 967–84

5   Doing Nothing in Particular

1 Greaney, M. (2016) 'Laziness: A Literary-historical Perspective'. In Callard, F. et al (Eds) *The Restless Compendium.* London: Palgrave Pivot

2 Traon, A.P.L. et al (2007) 'From Space to Earth: Advances in Human Physiology from 20 Years of Bed Rest Studies'. *European Journal of Applied Physiology,* 101, 143–94

3 Baines, E. & Blatchford, P. (2019) *School Break and Lunch Times and Young People's Social Lives: A Follow-up National Study, Final Report.* London: UCL Institute of Education

4 Bellezza, S. et al (2017) 'Conspicuous Consumption of Time: When Busyness and Lack of Leisure Time Become a Status Symbol'. *Journal of Consumer Research,* 44 (1), 118–38

5 Greaney, M. (2016) 'Laziness: A Literary-historical Perspective'. In Callard, F. et al. (Eds) *The Restless Compendium.* London: Palgrave Pivot

6   US Bureau of Labor Statistics, *Selected Paid Leave Benefits, Table 6*. United States Department of Labor, 07 03 2017. https://www. bls.gov/news.release/ebs2.to6.htm

7   Kasperkevic, J. (2017) 'Why is America so Afraid to Take a Vacation?'. *The Guardian*, 07 09 2015. https://www.theguardian. com/money/2015/sep/07/america-vacation-workaholic-culture-labor-day

8   Strandberg, T.E. et al (2018) 'Increased Mortality Despite Successful Multifactorial Cardiovascular Risk Reduction in Healthy Men: 40-year Follow-up of the Helsinki Businessmen Study Intervention Trial'. *The Journal of Nutrition, Health and Aging*, 22 (8), 885–91

9   Brooks, B. et al (2000) 'Are Vacations Good for Your Health? The 9-year Mortality Experience After the Multiple Risk Factor Intervention Trial'. *Psychosomatic Medicine*, 62, 608–12

10   Kim, S. et al (2017) 'Micro-break Activities at Work to Recover from Daily Work Demands'. *Journal of Organizational Behavior*, 38 (1), 28–44

11   Danziger, S. et al (2011) 'Extraneous Factors in Judicial Decisions'. *Proceedings of the National Academy of Sciences*, 108 (17), 6889–92

12   Glockner, A. (2016) 'The Irrational Hungry Judge Effect Revisited: Simulations Reveal that the Magnitude of the Effect is Overestimated'. *Judgment and Decision Making*, 11 (6), 601–10

13   Sievertsen, H.H. (2016) 'Cognitive Fatigue in School'. *Proceedings of the National Academy of Sciences*, March 2016, 113 (10) 2621–4

14   Bosch, C. & Sonnentag, S. (2018) 'Should I Take a Break? A Daily Reconstruction Study on Predicting Micro-Breaks at Work'. *International Journal of Stress Management*. http://dx.doi.org/10.1037/stroooo117

15   Bönstrup, M. (2019) 'A Rapid Form of Offline Consolidation in Skill Learning'. *Current Biology*, 29 (8), 1346–51

16 Sonnentag, S. & Zijlstra, F.R.H. (2006) 'Job Characteristics and Off-job Activities as Predictors of Need for Recovery, Well-being, and Fatigue'. *Journal of Applied Psychology*, 91, 330–50

17 Jacobson, E. (1979) 'Some Highlights of My Life'. *Journal of Behavior Therapy & Experimental Psychiatry*, 10, 5–9

18 Jacobson, E. (1977) 'The Origins and Development of Progressive Relaxation'. *Journal of Behavior Therapy & Experimental Psychiatry*, 119–23

19 Nathoo, A. (2016) 'From Therapeutic Relaxation to Mindfulness in the Twentieth Century'. In Callard, F. et al (Eds) *The Restless Compendium*. London: Palgrave Pivot

20 Wilson, T. et al (2014) 'Just Think: The Challenges of the Disengaged Mind'. *Science*, 345, 75–7

21 Stiles, A. (2012) 'The Rest Cure, 1873–1925'. Branch, 10. http://www.branchcollective.org/?ps_articles=anne-stiles-the-rest-cure-1873-1925

22 Chin, A. et al (2017) 'Bored in the USA – Experience Sampling and Boredom in Everyday Life'. *Emotion*, 17 (2), 359–68

23 Mann, S. (2016) *The Upside of Downtime: Why Boredom Is Good*. London: Robinson

24 Cowan, N. et al (2004) 'Verbal Recall in Amnesiacs Under Conditions of Diminished Retroactive Interference'. *Brain*, 127, 825–34

25 And if you think Dewar might have been had by participants who spent the break running through the words in their heads, she had a cunning way of preventing that. What she did was to make people memorise words in a foreign language and ensure the words were hard to pronounce. This went some way to stopping people being able to say the words out loud as an aid to memorising them. This demonstrated that the recall of words was genuinely enhanced by doing nothing.

26 The solutions are: all's well that ends well, and a bird in the hand is worth two in the bush.

27 Crivelli, F. et al (2016) 'Somnomat: A Novel Actuated Bed to Investigate the Effect of Vestibular Stimulation'. *Medical & Biological Engineering & Computing,* 54 (6), 877–89

28 Smith, R.P. (1958) *How to Do Nothing with Nobody All Alone by Yourself.* New York: Tin House Books. There's also a lovely summary on Brainpickings, 24 10 2014. https://www.brainpickings.org/2014/10/24/how-to-do-nothing-with-nobody-all-alone-by-yourself/

4 Listening to Music

1 Rhodes, J. (2015) *Instrumental,* Edinburgh: Canongate, 2014

2 Sack, K. (1998) 'Georgia's Governor Seeks Musical Start for Babies'. *New York Times,* 15 01 1998

3 Rauscher, F.H. et al (1993) 'Music and Spatial Task Performance'. *Nature,* 365, 611

4 Chabris, C.F. (1999) 'Prelude or Requiem for the "Mozart Effect"?'. *Nature,* 400, 826–7

5 Schellenberg, E. et al (2006) 'Music Listening and Cognitive Abilities in 10 and 11 Year-olds: The Blur Effect'. *Annals of the New York Academy of Sciences,* 1060, 202–9

6 Pietchnig, J. et al (2010) 'Mozart Effect–Schmozart Effect: A Meta-analysis'. *Intelligence,* 38, 314–23

7 Nantais, K.M. & Schellenberg, E.G. (1999) 'The Mozart Effect: An Artefact of Preference'. Psychological Science, 10 (4), 370–3

8 Trahan, T. et al (2018) 'The Music that Helps People Sleep and the Reasons They Believe it Works'. *PLOS One,* 13 (11) e0206531. doi:10.1371/journal.pone.0206531

9   Saarikallio, S. & Erkkila, J. (2007) 'The Role of Music in Adolescents' Mood Regulation'. *Psychology of Music*, 35 (1), 88–109

10 Konečni, V. et al (1976) 'Anger and Expression of Aggression: Effects on Aesthetic Preferences'. *Scientific Aesthetics*, 1, 47–55

11 North, A.C. & Hargreaves, D.J. (2000) 'Musical Preferences During and After Relaxation and Exercise'. *American Journal of Psychology*, 113, 43–67

12 Bruner, G.C. (1990) 'Music, Mood and Marketing'. *Journal of Marketing*, 54 (4) 94–104

13 Juslin, P. et al (2008) 'An Experience Sampling Study of Emotional Reactions to Music: Listener, Music and Situation'. *Emotion*, 8 (5), 668–83

14 Linneman, A. et al (2015) 'Music Listening as a Means of Stress Reduction in Daily Life'. *Psychoneuroendocrinology*, 60, 82–90

15 Summers, P. (2018) *The Spirit of This Place: How Music Illuminates the Human Spirit*. Chicago: University of Chicago Press, 70

16 Garrido, S. et al (2017) 'Group Rumination: Social Interactions Around Music in People with Depression'. *Frontiers in Psychology*, 8, 490

17 Summers, P. (2018) *The Spirit of This Place: How Music Illuminates the Human Spirit*. Chicago: University of Chicago Press, 150

18 Byrne, D. (2012) *How Music Works*. Edinburgh: Canongate, 137 & 332

3   I Want to Be Alone

1   Wilkinson, R. & Pickett, K. (2018) *The Inner Level*. London: Allen Lane, 117

2   Hawkley, L.C. & Cacioppo, J.T. (2010) 'Loneliness Matters: A Theoretical and Empirical Review of Consequences and Mechanisms'. *Annals of Behavioral Medicine*, 40 (2), 218–27

3   Colette (1974) *Earthly Paradise*. London: Penguin.

4   Larson R.W. et al (1982) 'Time Alone in Daily Experience: Loneliness or Renewal?'. In Peplau, L.A. & Perlman, D. (Eds) *Loneliness: A Sourcebook of Current Theory, Research and Therapy.* New York: Wiley

5   Matias, G.P. et al (2011) 'Solitude and Cortisol: Associations with State and Trait Affect in Daily Life'. *Biological Psychology*, 86, 314–19

6   Long, C.R. & Averill, J.R. (2003) 'Solitude: An Exploration of the Benefits of Being Alone'. *Journal for the Theory of Social Behavior*, 33 (1), 21–44

7   Russell, D.W. et al (2012) 'Is Loneliness the Same as Being Alone?'. *The Journal of Psychology*, 146 (1–2), 7–22

8   This is from an interview I conducted for *The Truth about Mental Health: Four Walls*, BBC World Service, 16 06 2013

9   Markson, D. (1988) *Wittgenstein's Mistress*. Illinois: Dalkey Archive Press

10 Bowker, J. (2017) 'How BIS/BA and Psycho-behavioral Variables Distinguish Between Social Withdrawal Subtypes during Emerging Adulthood'. *Personality and Individual Differences*, 119, 283–8

11 Akrivou, K. et al (2011) 'The Sound of Silence – A Space for Morality? The Role of Solitude for Ethical Decision Making'. *Journal of Business Ethics*, 102, 119–33

12 The BBC Loneliness Experiment was devised by Pamela Qualter, Manuela Barreto and Christina Victor. The results can be found here: Hammond, C. (2018) 'Who Feels Lonely? The Results of the World's Largest Loneliness Study'. *The Anatomy of Loneliness*, BBC Radio 4, 01 10 2018. https://www.bbc.co.uk/programmes/articles/2yzhfv4DvqVp5nZyxBD8G23/who-feels-lonely-the-results-of-the-world-s-largest-loneliness-study

13 The Campaign to End Loneliness. 'Is Loneliness a Growing Problem?'. https://www.campaigntoendloneliness.org/ frequently-asked-questions/is-loneliness-increasing/

14 Valtorta, N.K. et al (2016) 'Loneliness and Social Isolation as Risk Factors for Coronary Heart Disease and Stroke: Systematic Review and Meta-analysis of Longitudinal Observational Studies'. *Heart*, 102 (13), 1009–16

15 Hawkley, L.C. et al (2010) 'Loneliness Predicts Increased Blood Pressure: 5 Year Cross-lagged Analyses in Middle-aged and Older Adults'. *Psychology and Aging*, 25 (1), 132–41

16 Holt-Lunstad, J. et al (2015) 'Loneliness and Social Isolation as Risk Factors for Mortality: A Meta-analytic Review'. *Perspectives on Psychological Science*, 10 (2), 227–37

17 Heinrich, L.M. & Gullone, E. (2006) 'The Clinical Significance of Loneliness: A Literature Review'. *Clinical Psychology Review*, 26 (6), 695–718

18 Cacioppo, J.T. et al (2010) 'Perceived Social Isolation Makes Me Sad'. *Psychology and Aging*, 25 (2), 453–63

19 The interview I did with Barbara Taylor is in *The Anatomy of Loneliness*. BBC Radio 4, 02 10 2019. https://www.bbc.co.uk/ programmes/m0000mj8

20 Mann, T. (1912) *Death in Venice and Other Tales*. London: Vintage Classic Europeans

21 Detrixhe, J. et al (2014) 'A Lonely Idea: Solitude's Separation from Psychological Research and Theory'. *Contemporary Psychoanalysis*, 50 (3), 310–31

22 Trevor, W. (2010) *Felicia's Journey*. London: Penguin

23 Maes, M. et al (2016) 'Loneliness and Attitudes toward Aloneness in Adolescence: A Person-centred Approach'. *Journal of Youth Adolescence*, 45, 547–67

24 Galanki, E.P. (2004) 'Are Children Able to Distinguish Among

the Concepts of Aloneness, Loneliness and Solitude?' *International Journal of Behavioral Development*, 28, 435–43

25 Larson, R.W. (1997) 'The Emergence of Solitude as a Constructive Domain of Experience in Early Adolescence'. *Child Development*, 68 (1), 80–93

26 Danneel, S. et al (2018) 'Developmental Change in Loneliness and Attitudes toward Aloneness in Adolescence'. *Journal of Youth Adolescence*, 47, 148–61

27 Larson, R.W. (1997) 'The Emergence of Solitude as a Constructive Domain of Experience in Early Adolescence'. *Child Development*, 68 (1), 80–93

28 Detrixhe, J. et al (2014) 'A Lonely Idea: Solitude's Separation from Psychological Research and Theory'. *Contemporary Psychoanalysis*, 50 (3), 310–31

29 Larson, R.W. (2014) 'A Comparison of Positive and Negative Episodes of Solitude'. Master's Thesis, Amherst: University of Massachusetts

2 Spending Time in Nature

1 Morris, C. (Ed.) (1949) *The Journeys of Celia Fiennes*. London: The Cresset Press, 67

2 Korpela, K.M. (2003) 'Negative Mood and Adult Place Preference'. *Environment and Behavior*, 35 (3), 331–46

3 Jonson, S.A.K. (2011) 'The Use of Nature for Emotional Regulation: Towards a Conceptual Framework'. *Ecopsychology*, 3 (3), 175–85

4 You can hear the interview I did with Richard Mabey in *All in the Mind*. BBC Radio 4, 26 06 2012. https://www.bbc.co.uk/sounds/play/b01k1nl3

5 Ulrich, R.S. (1984) 'View Through a Window May Influence Recovery from Surgery'. *Science*, 224, 420–1

6 Ulrich, R. et al (1993) 'Exposure to Nature and Abstract Pictures on Patients Recovering from Open Heart Surgery'. *Psychophysiology: Journal of the Society for Psychophysiological Research*, 30, S7

7 For an excellent review of the small number of studies in this area, see Thompson, C.J. (2011) 'Does Participating in Physical Activity in Outdoor Natural Environments Have a Greater Effect on Physical and Mental Well-being than Physical Activity Indoors? A Systematic Review'. *Environmental Science & Technology*, 45 (5), 1761–72

8 Lee, K.E. (2015) '40-second Green Roof Views Sustain Attention: The Role of Micro-breaks in Attention Restoration'. *Journal of Environmental Psychology*, 42 (2015) 182–9

9 Ulrich, R.S. (2008) 'Biophilic Theory and Research for Healthcare Design'. In Kellert, S.R. et al (Eds) *Biophilic Design: The Theory, Science and Practice of Bringing Buildings to Life*. New Jersey: John Wiley

10 Lohr, V.L. & Pearson-Mims, C.H. (2006) 'Responses to Scenes with Spreading, Rounded and Conical Tree Forms'. *Environment and Behavior*, 38, 667–88

11 Joye, Y. & Van den Berg, A. (2011) 'Is Love for Green in our Genes? A Critical Analysis of Evolutionary Assumptions in Restorative Environments Research'. *Urban Forestry & Urban Greening*, 10 (4), 261–8

12 Martens, D. et al (2011) 'Walking in "Wild" and "Tended" Urban Forests: The Impact on Psychological Well-being'. *Journal of Environmental Psychology*, 31, 36–44

13 Parsons, R. (1991) 'The Potential Influences of Environmental Perception on Human Health'. *Journal of Environmental Psychology*, 11, 1–23

14 Gatersleben, B. & Andrews, M. (2013) 'When Walking in Nature Is Not Restorative – The Role of Prospect and Refuge'. *Health & Place*, 20, 91–101

15 Hagerhall, S.M. (2004) 'Fractal Dimensions of Landscape Silhouette Outlines as a Predictor of Landscape Preference'. *Journal of Environmental Psychology*, 24, 247–55

16 Bratman, G.N. et al (2015) 'Nature Experience Reduces Rumination and Subgenual Prefrontal Cortex Activation'. *PNAS*, 112 (28), 8567–72

17 Korpela, K. et al (2017) 'Enhancing Wellbeing with Psychological Tasks Along Forest Trails'. *Urban Forestry & Urban Greening*, 26, 25–30

18 Richardson, M. & Sheffield, D. (2015) 'Reflective Self-attention: A More Stable Predictor of Connection to Nature than Mindful Attention'. *Ecopsychology*, 7 (3), 166–75

19 Jamie, K. (2012) *Sightlines*. London: Sort of Books

20 Earth Science & Remote Sensing Unit High Definition Earth Viewing System. NASA, 30 04 2014. https://eol.jsc.nasa.gov/ESRS/HDEV/

21 Kaplan, R. & Kaplan, S. (1989) *The Experience of Nature: A Psychological Perspective*. Cambridge: Cambridge University Press

22 Ratcliffe, E. & Korpela, K. (2017). 'Time- and Self-related Memories Predict Restorative Perceptions of Favorite Places Via Place Identity'. *Environment and Behavior*, 50 (6), 690–720

23 Wyles, K.J. et al (2017) 'Are Some Natural Environments More Psychologically Beneficial than Others? The Importance of Type and Quality on Connectedness to Nature and Psychological Restoration'. *Environment and Behavior*, 51 (2), 111–43

24 Van den Berg, A. et al (1998) 'Group Differences in the Aesthetic Evaluation of Nature Development Plans: A Multilevel Approach'. *Journal of Environmental Psychology*, 18, 141–57

1 Reading

1 Diener, E. et al (2009) 'New Well-being Measures: Short Scales to Assess Flourishing and Positive and Negative Feelings'. *Social Indicators Research*, 97, (2), 143–56

2 Nell, V. (1988) 'The Psychology of Reading for Pleasure: Needs and Gratifications'. *Reading Research Quarterly*, 23 (1), 6–50

3 There are four red sides and eight white sides.

4 The Sleep Council (2013) *The Great British Bedtime Report*. Published by the consumer education arm of the trading body for bed manufacturers.

5 Rizzolo, D. et al (2009) 'Stress Management Strategies for Students: The Immediate Effects of Yoga, Humor, and Reading on Stress'. *Journal of College Teaching and Learning*, 6 (8), 79–88

6 Jin, P. (1992) 'Efficacy of Tai Chi, Brisk Walking, Meditation, and Reading in Reducing Mental and Emotional Stress'. *Journal of Psychosomatic Research*, 36 (4) 361–70

7 Smith, C.E. (2000) 'The Real-world Reading Practices of Adults'. *Journal of Literacy Research*, 32 (1), 25–52

8 Vogrinčič, A. (2008) *The Novel-Reading Panic in 18th-Century England: An Outline of an Early Moral Media Panic*. Ljubljana: University of Ljubljana

9 Mar, R.A. et al (2011) 'Emotion and Narrative Fiction: Interactive Influences Before, During, and After Reading'. *Cognition and Emotion*, 25 (5), 813–33

10 Huestegge, L. (2010) 'Effects of Vowel Length on Gaze Durations in Silent and Oral Reading'. *Journal of Eye Movement Research*, 3 (5) 1–18

11 Hsu, C.T. et al (2014) 'Fiction Feelings in Harry Potter: Haemodynamic Response in the Mid-cingulate Cortex Correlates

with Immersive Reading Experience'. *Neuroreport*, 25 (17), 1356–61

12 Pullman, P. (2006) 'The War on Words'. *The Guardian*, 06 11 2006

13 Woolf, V. (1932) 'How One Should Read a Book'. In *The Common Reader*. Second Series. London: Vintage

14 Alexander, J. & Jarman, R. (2018) 'The Pleasures of Reading Non-fiction'. *Literacy*, 52 (2), 78–85

15 Baden, D. (2015) 'Shock! Horror! Behind the Ethics and Evolution of the Bad News Business. *The Conversation*, 27 03 2015. http://theconversation.com/shock-horror-behind-the-ethics-and-evolution-of-the-bad-news-business-39211

16 *Guardian Review*, 07 04 2018

17 Billington, J. et al (2016) 'A Literature-based Intervention for People with Chronic Pain'. *Arts & Health*, 8 (1), 13–31

18 Dehghani, M. et al (2017) 'Decoding the Neural Representation of Story Meanings Across Languages'. *Human Brain Mapping*, 38, 6096–106

19 Tamir, D.I. et al (2016) 'Reading Fiction and Reading Minds: The Role of Simulation in the Default Network'. *Social, Cognitive and Affective Neuroscience*, 11 (2), 215–24

20 Feng, S. et al (2013) 'Mind Wandering While Reading Easy and Difficult Texts'. *Psychonomic Bulletin & Review*, 20 (3), 586–92

21 Franklin, M.S. et al (2011) 'Catching the Mind in Flight: Using Behavioral Indices to Detect Mindless Reading in Real Time'. *Psychonomic Bulletin Review*, 18 (5), 992–7

22 Steinbeck, J. (1930) 'In Awe of Words', *The Exonian*, 75th Anniversary Edition, Exeter: Exeter University

23 Rane-Szostak, D. & Herth, K.A. (1995) 'Pleasure Reading, Other Activities, and Loneliness in Later Life'. *Journal of Adolescent & Adult Literacy*, 39 (2), 100–08

24 Massimini, F. et al (1988). 'Flow and Biocultural Evolution'. In M. Csikszentmihalyi & I.S. Csikszentmihalyi (Eds) *Optimal Experience: Studies of Flow in Consciousness*. Cambridge: Cambridge University Press

25 Šimleša, M. et al (2018) 'The Flow Engine Framework: A Cognitive Model of Optimal Human Experience'. *Europe's Journal of Psychology*, 14 (1), 232–53

26 Mar, R.A. et al (2011) 'Emotion and Narrative Fiction: Interactive Influences Before, During and After Reading'. *Cognition and Emotion*, 25 (5), 818–33

27 Rosenbaum, J.E. & Johnson, B.K. (2016) 'Who's Afraid of Spoilers? Need for Cognition, Need for Affect, and Narrative Selection and Enjoyment'. *Psychology of Popular Media Culture*, 5 (30), 273–89

28 Evangelou, M. et al (2005) *Birth to School Study: A Longitudinal Evaluation of the Peers Early Education Partnerhip*. Oxford: Oxford University Research Reports SSU/2005/FR/017

29 Bavishi, M.D. et al (2016) 'A Chapter a Day: Association of Book Reading with Longevity'. *Social Science & Medicine*, 164, 44–8

The Perfect Prescription for Rest

1 Office of National Statistics, *Leisure Time in the UK*. ONS, 24 10 2017. https://www.ons.gov.uk/economy/nationalaccounts/satelliteaccounts/articles/leisuretimeintheuk/2015

2 Office of National Statistics, *Leisure Time in the UK*. ONS, 24 10 2017. https://www.ons.gov.uk/economy/nationalaccounts/satelliteaccounts/articles/leisuretimeintheuk/2015#those-employed-full-time-took-the-least-leisure-time-but-enjoyed-it-most

3   Gershuny, J. (2011) *Time-Use Surveys and the Measurement of National Well-being*. Oxford: Centre for Time-use Research, Department of Sociology, University of Oxford

4   Ragsdale, J.M. et al (2011) 'An Integrated Model of Weekday Stress and Weekend Recovery of Students'. *International Journal of Stress Management*, 18 (2), 153–80

CLAUDIA HAMMOND is an award-winning writer and broadcaster and lectures in psychology at Boston University's base in London. As the presenter of *All in the Mind* she is BBC Radio 4's voice of psychology and mental health. She has been awarded the President's Medal from the British Academy, the British Psychological Society's Public Engagement and Media Award, Mind's Making a Difference Award and the British Neuroscience Award. She is the author of *Emotional Rollercoaster*, *Mind over Money* and *Time Warped*, winner of the British Psychological Society's Best Popular Science Book Award and the Aeon Transmission Award.

@claudiahammond | claudiahammond.com

Cover design by Valeri Rangelov